Micheline Lavallée.

COLLECTION BESCHERELLE

# Les verbes anglais

*Formes et emplois*

**Gilbert Quénelle**
**Didier Hourquin**

HMH

**Catalogage avant publication de la Bibliothèque nationale du Canada**

Quénelle, Gilbert

Bescherelle : les verbes anglais

(Collection Bescherelle)
Comprend des index.

ISBN 2-89428-462-4

1. Anglais (Langue) — Verbe. 2. Anglais (Langue) — Conjugaison. I. Hourquin, Didier. II. Winer, Lise. III. Titre. IV. Titre : Les verbes anglais. V. Collection.

PE1273.Q46 2003          425          C2003-941309-8


Adaptation pour l'Amérique du Nord : Lise Winer, Université McGill
Chargée du projet d'adaptation : Sharnee Chait
Conception maquette : Yvette Heller
Adaptation maquette et mise en pages : Le Groupe Pénéga, pour la version canadienne
Conception et réalisation de couverture : Marc Roberge
Dessins : Corédoc

Éditions Hurtubise HMH ltée
1815, avenue De Lorimier
Montréal (Québec)
H2K 3W6
Téléphone :        (514) 523-1523
Télécopieur :      (514) 523-9969
www.hurtubisehmh.com

Les Éditions Hurtubise HMH bénéficient du soutien du Gouvernement du Canada par l'entremise du Programme d'aide au développement de l'industrie de l'édition (PADIÉ).

ISBN 2-89428-462-4
Dépôt légal - 1ᵉ trimestre  2004
Bibliothèque nationale du Québec
Bibliothèque nationale du Canada

Toute langue a des règles qui posent problème, autant à tous ceux et celles dont c'est la langue maternelle qu'aux apprenants. Mis à part l'orthographe anglaise, dont la complexité est notoire, la grammaire de base de l'anglais et l'emploi des verbes ont de quoi décourager. Faut-il dire *I never went* ou bien *I've never gone* ? Sans parler aussi des verbes irréguliers, réputés si difficiles : est-ce *it sank* ou *it sunk* ? Les verbes anglais ont beau avoir une morphologie relativement pauvre par rapport aux verbes français, leur fonctionnement n'est pas toujours facile à comprendre.

Aujourd'hui, en enseignement des langues, on met plutôt l'accent sur la communication. La forme, cependant, demeure d'une grande importance. Non seulement un usage approprié donne-t-il une meilleure impression, mais une certaine attention portée à la forme pourrait aider l'apprenant à éviter des malentendus, et à exprimer sa pensée avec plus de justesse et de précision. Un anglophone comprendra normalement ce qu'on lui dit, en passant par-dessus les erreurs éventuelles. Mais à partir du moment où l'on exige une communication efficace – et tout particulièrement à l'écrit, où l'on ne peut pas avoir recours à la gestuelle pour signaler la compréhension ou la confusion –, il faut des supports linguistiques sûrs et rapides.

Le Bescherelle des verbes français, *L'Art de conjuguer*, constitue un outil privilégié, apprécié d'un grand public. Ce Bescherelle des verbes anglais est d'une utilisation tout aussi facile et agréable, autant par son format bien connu que par la rigueur de son contenu.

Cet ouvrage comporte de nombreuses aides à l'apprentissage :
• des tableaux qui servent de référence rapide et pratique ;
• des explications complètes appuyées d'exemples ;
• des exemples de verbes de base et de particules qui peuvent les accompagner ;
• des schémas qui fournissent des représentations visuelles claires ;
• des éléments d'usage grammatical divers pour aider, par exemple, le lecteur à décider rapidement s'il faut choisir un infinitif ou bien un participe.

Lise Winer
Professeure, Department of Integrated Studies in Education
Université McGill, Montréal

# SOMMAIRE

**GRAMMAIRE DU VERBE** )      9

**Temps et aspects** .......................... **10**
À savoir ...................................... 10
Présent – avenir – present perfect – prétérit – pluperfect .... 12
Tableau récapitulatif ........................... 22

**Auxiliaires ordinaires : be, have, do, let** ..... **24**
À savoir ...................................... 24
Be – have – do – let ........................... 26

**Auxiliaires modaux** ....................... **34**
À savoir ...................................... 34
Shall / should – will / would – can / could, may / might –
ought to / must / need / dare ....................... 36
Tableau récapitulatif ........................... 44

**Verbes à particule : les verbes** ............. **46**
À savoir ...................................... 46
Be – stand – go – come – run – fall – take – get –
put – set ..................................... 48

**Verbes à particule : les particules** ......... **58**
À savoir ...................................... 58
À la recherche du sens .......................... 60
Up – out – in – down – on – over – with – to – from –
about – around / round – vingt autres particules ......... 62

**Formation des verbes** ..................... **74**

**Compléments du verbe** ................... **76**
À savoir ...................................... 76
Forme en *-ing* – infinitif – style indirect ................. 78

**Le passif** ................................. **84**

## Tableaux de conjugaison)     87

**Tableaux des temps** . . . . . . . . . . . . . . . . . . . . . . **88**
Présent – prétérit – present perfect – pluperfect – futur –
futur antérieur – conditionnel présent – conditionnel passé . . . 88
Prononciation . . . . . . . . . . . . . . . . . . . . . . . . . . . . . 96
Modifications orthographiques . . . . . . . . . . . . . . . . . . . 97

**Tableau des contractions** . . . . . . . . . . . . . . . . . **98**
Comment poser une question . . . . . . . . . . . . . . . . . . . 100
Les *tags* . . . . . . . . . . . . . . . . . . . . . . . . . . . . . . . . 102

**Tableau des verbes irréguliers** . . . . . . . . . . . . **104**


## Index )     115

**Index général** . . . . . . . . . . . . . . . . . . . . . . . . . . **115**

**Verbes à complémentation** . . . . . . . . . . . . . . . **167**

**Verbes à particule** . . . . . . . . . . . . . . . . . . . . . . . **175**

**Verbes irréguliers** . . . . . . . . . . . . . . . . . . . . . . . **209**

**Appendice** . . . . . . . . . . . . . . . . . . . . . . . . . . . . . **220**

# COMMENT UTILISER CE LIVRE

Le **Bescherelle** n'est ni un livre de grammaire classique, ni un dictionnaire : c'est un outil de travail complémentaire qui vise à susciter une réflexion. Son utilisation permet de mieux comprendre la grammaire du verbe anglais comme le produit d'un système de pensée différent du système de pensée français.

En anglais, un petit nombre de formes verbales permet d'exprimer un grand nombre de sens. En effet, la personne qui parle (le locuteur) peut nuancer une même forme selon la durée relative de l'action (aspect) et selon son état d'esprit du moment (modalité). De plus, grâce à l'emploi de particules, l'anglais peut multiplier à l'infini les formes et les sens à partir des formes de base.

À partir de ces constats, trois types d'outils sont proposés aux lecteurs.

## 1 La grammaire du verbe

Elle permet d'analyser avec une précision suffisante la valeur des temps et des aspects du verbe en anglais en général, et de ses auxiliaires ordinaires et modaux.

Elle explique aussi la formation et le sens des verbes à particule, la place et le sens des principaux types de compléments du verbe ainsi que l'importance de la forme passive.

Le texte est construit en doubles pages articulées en paragraphes courts auxquels il est facile de se reporter. Deux synthèses donnent une vue d'ensemble sur les temps et sur la modalité.

## 2 Les tableaux

Ils présentent de manière synthétique toutes les formes usuelles de la conjugaison, les contractions et les différents types de verbes irréguliers.

## 3 Les index

L'index général comprend tous les verbes (6 000 environ), réguliers et irréguliers, simples ou à particule, anciens ou nouvellement entrés dans la langue d'aujourd'hui. Ceux-ci comprennent presque tous les mots d'usage courant et beaucoup de mots d'usage restreint aux spécialistes qu'on emploie en Amérique du Nord.

*Litt.* indique des mots d'usage surtout littéraire.

*Arch.* indique des mots appartenant à des champs sémantiques spécialisés (religieux, juridique, etc.).

*Fam.* indique des mots appartenant au registre oral ou familier.

Une telle richesse exclut la possibilité d'introduire toute traduction des verbes.

Cependant, dans les cas où des sens multiples deviennent importants, une note explicative est fournie.

L'index général est complété par des index spécifiques : un index des verbes à complémentation, un index des verbes à particule et un index des verbes irréguliers.

Pour chaque catégorie, un renvoi est prévu aux pages correspondantes de la grammaire du verbe et des tableaux.

# LISTE ALPHABÉTIQUE DES POINTS DE GRAMMAIRE ABORDÉS

About . . . . . . . . . . . . . . . . . . . . . 71
Ago . . . . . . . . . . . . . . . . . . . . . 18, 82
Always + forme en -ing . . . . . . . 13
Around . . . . . . . . . . . . . . . . . . . . 71
Aspects . . . . . . . . . . . . . . . . . 10-11,
22-23
Auxiliaires modaux . . . . . . . . . . . 34-35,
44-45
Auxiliaires ordinaires . . . . . . . . . 24-33
Avenir . . . . . . . . . . . . . . . . . . . 14-15
Be able to . . . . . . . . . . . . . . . 40
Be allowed to . . . . . . . . . . . . . 41
Be going to . . . . . . . . . . . . . . . 14
Be to . . . . . . . . . . . . . . . . . . . 15, 42
Be . . . . . . . . . . . . . . . . . . . . . 24, 26-27,
48
Been / gone . . . . . . . . . . . . . . . 26
Can . . . . . . . . . . . . . . . . . . . . 40-41, 44-45
Capacité . . . . . . . . . . . . . . . . . 40-41, 44-45
Come . . . . . . . . . . . . . . . . . . . 51
Compléments du verbe . . . . . . . 76-83
Conditionnel . . . . . . . . . . . . . . . 37, 39
Conjugaisons . . . . . . . . . . . . . . 87-95
Conseil . . . . . . . . . . . . . . . . . . 32, 37,
44-45
Contractions . . . . . . . . . . . . . . . 98-99
Could . . . . . . . . . . . . . . . . . . . 40-41, 44-45
Dare . . . . . . . . . . . . . . . . . . . . 43
Devoir / obligation . . . . . . . . . . . 35, 37,
42, 44-45
Do . . . . . . . . . . . . . . . . . . . . . 30-31
Down . . . . . . . . . . . . . . . . . . . 65
Faire . . . . . . . . . . . . . . . . . . . . 29
Faire faire . . . . . . . . . . . . . . . . 28
Fall . . . . . . . . . . . . . . . . . . . . . 53
For . . . . . . . . . . . . . . . . . . . . . 16, 73
Forme d'insistance . . . . . . . . . . 25, 30
Forme fréquentative . . . . . . . . . 39
Forme simple ou en -ing ? . . . . . 13
From . . . . . . . . . . . . . . . . . . . . 70
Get . . . . . . . . . . . . . . . . . . . . . 55, 85
Give . . . . . . . . . . . . . . . . . . . . 85

Had better . . . . . . . . . . . . . . . . 25
Have . . . . . . . . . . . . . . . . . . . . 28-29
Have to . . . . . . . . . . . . . . . . . . 15, 42
If . . . . . . . . . . . . . . . . . . . . . . 37, 39
Il y a . . . . . . . . . . . . . . . . . . . . 18, 27
In . . . . . . . . . . . . . . . . . . . . . . 64
Infinitif ou -ing ? . . . . . . . . . . . . 78-81
Interdiction . . . . . . . . . . . . . . . . 36, 44-45
Let . . . . . . . . . . . . . . . . . . . . . 32-33
Make / have . . . . . . . . . . . . . . . 24, 28
Make / do . . . . . . . . . . . . . . . . 25
May / might . . . . . . . . . . . . . . . 40-41,
44-45
Modalités . . . . . . . . . . . . . . . . . 34
Modifications orthographiques . . . 97
Must . . . . . . . . . . . . . . . . . . . . 42, 44-45
Nécessité . . . . . . . . . . . . . . . . . 42, 44-45
Need . . . . . . . . . . . . . . . . . . . . 43
Obligation . . . . . . . . . . . . . . . . 42, 44-45
On . . . . . . . . . . . . . . . . . . . . . 66
« On » (traduction du français « on ») . . 84
Ought to . . . . . . . . . . . . . . . . . 42, 44-45
Out . . . . . . . . . . . . . . . . . . . . . 63
Over . . . . . . . . . . . . . . . . . . . . 67
Particules . . . . . . . . . . . . . . . . . 46-47,
58-73
Passé . . . . . . . . . . . . . . . . . . . 16-21
Passif . . . . . . . . . . . . . . . . . . . 84-85
Permission . . . . . . . . . . . . . . . . 40-41,
44-45
Place des particules . . . . . . . . . . 59
Pluperfect . . . . . . . . . . . . . . . . . 20-21
Préfixes . . . . . . . . . . . . . . . . . . 75
Prépositions . . . . . . . . . . . . . . . 58
Présent . . . . . . . . . . . . . . . . . . 12-13
Present perfect . . . . . . . . . . . . . 16-17
Prétérit . . . . . . . . . . . . . . . . . . 18-19
Prétérit modal . . . . . . . . . . . . . . 19
Probabilité . . . . . . . . . . . . . . . . 41, 42,
44-45
Prononciation . . . . . . . . . . . . . . 96
Put . . . . . . . . . . . . . . . . . . . . . 56

# LISTE ALPHABÉTIQUE DES POINTS DE GRAMMAIRE ABORDÉS

| | | | |
|---|---|---|---|
| *Question tags* | 102-103 | Style indirect | 82-83 |
| Questionnement | 100-101 | Suffixes | 74-75 |
| *Rather* | 29, 101 | Suggestion | 40-41, |
| Redoublement consonne finale | 97 | | 44-45 |
| Réponses courtes | 102 | *Tags* | 102-103 |
| Reprises interrogatives : | 102-103 | *Take* | 54 |
| n'est-ce pas, étonnement, | | Temps | 10-11 |
| constatation, aussi, non plus ; | | *There is* | 27 |
| contradiction | | *To* | 69 |
| *Round* | 71 | Transitif / intransitif | 76-77 |
| *Run* | 52 | *Up* | 62 |
| *Set* | 57 | *Used to* | 18 |
| *Shall / should* | 36, 37, | Verbes irréguliers | 104-113 |
| | 44-45 | *Will / would* | 38-39, |
| *Since* | 16 | | 44-45 |
| *Stand* | 49 | *With* | 68 |

## SYMBOLES DE PRONONCIATION

Cet ouvrage donne la prononciation selon l'alphabet phonétique international (API). Voici les symboles utilisés, accompagnés d'exemples.

### LES CONSONNES

Les symboles b, d, f, h, k, l, m, n, p, r, s, t, v, w et z se prononcent comme la lettre-consonne correspondante. Les autres symboles sont :

| | | | | | | | |
|---|---|---|---|---|---|---|---|
| g | get, go | ʒ | vision, pleasure | ŋ | thing, sing | dʒ | jar, giant |
| j | yes, yawn | θ | thin, think | x | loch | | |
| ʃ | she, show | ð | this, then | tʃ | chip, check | | |

### LES VOYELLES

| | | | | | |
|---|---|---|---|---|---|
| æ | cat, cast, have | ɒ | hot, cost, saw | ʌu | house, out |
| ɑr | alarm, barn | r | pore, born, wore | ei | day, awake, break |
| e | bed, meadow | ʌ | run, flung, done | o: | no, mow, sold |
| ə | ago, about | ʊ | put, stood | ɔi | boy, spoil |
| ɜr | her, burst | u: | too, lose, slew | au | how, found |
| ɪ | sit, pick | ai | my, thrive, strike | | |
| i: | see, beat | əi | pipe, tight | | |

# GRAMMAIRE DU VERBE

# TEMPS ET ASPECTS

## À SAVOIR

### IL Y A TEMPS (*TIME*) ET TEMPS (*TENSE*)

Pour évoquer le temps qui passe, qui s'écoule du passé au présent et du présent à l'avenir, c'est-à-dire le **temps chronologique** (en anglais : *time*), les langues se servent de formes appelées **temps grammaticaux** (en anglais : *tenses*).

Par exemple, pour le temps chronologique du passé, le français a le choix entre les quatre temps grammaticaux que sont l'imparfait, le passé simple, le passé composé et le plus-que-parfait. L'anglais, lui, dispose de trois temps grammaticaux : le *present perfect*, le *preterite* (en français : prétérit) et le *pluperfect*.

### Deux pièges à éviter

- D'une part, il n'y a pas de correspondance parfaite, à l'intérieur de chacun des deux systèmes, entre temps chronologique et temps grammatical.
  On peut utiliser, par exemple, en anglais comme en français, un temps grammatical du présent pour parler de l'avenir.
  *What are you doing tomorrow?*
  Que faites-vous demain ?

- D'autre part, il n'y a pas de parallélisme entre les deux systèmes de temps grammaticaux français et anglais pour la même tranche de temps. Par exemple, pour traduire le verbe dans la situation suivante du passé :
  *When she saw him in Montreal...*

on peut se servir :

– soit du passé composé *(quand elle l'a vu)*, si le moment de la rencontre n'est pas précisé par le contexte ;

– soit du passé simple *(quand elle le vit)*, si les circonstances sont par ailleurs précisément indiquées ;

– soit de l'imparfait *(quand elle le voyait)*, si cette rencontre est habituelle.

## LA DURÉE ET L'ASPECT

Le verbe anglais n'exprime pas le temps qui passe comme le fait le verbe français. En anglais, on a l'impression que les temps chronologiques (le passé, le présent et l'avenir) sont liés les uns aux autres dans une même durée, alors qu'en français, on a tendance à les séparer plus nettement entre eux.

C'est pourquoi, quand nous cherchons à comprendre un verbe anglais, il nous faut tenir compte de ce qu'on appelle son **aspect** : la **durée** de l'événement (action ou état) qu'il exprime, le fait qu'il vient de commencer, qu'il se répète ou pas. Cette notion, le verbe français ne peut l'exprimer tout seul ; il faut lui adjoindre une expression appropriée.

Par exemple, pour reprendre la situation précédente :

*When Margaret saw him in Montreal, he was speaking to a police officer.*

Quand Margaret le vit à Montréal, il parlait avec un agent de police.

la forme *was speaking* donne à penser que cette conversation avait commencé avant que Margaret ne le voie et qu'elle a sans doute continué après. Ce que le français pourra rendre en adjoignant au verbe une expression comme « être en train de » : *Quand elle le vit, il était en train de parler à un agent de police.*

Mais regardons les choses de plus près pour chacun de ces temps qui se succèdent dans le temps chronologique *(time)*.

# 1. LE PRÉSENT

Le temps chronologique du présent s'étend en anglais bien avant et bien après ce qu'en français on nomme le moment présent ; c'est pourquoi les formes pouvant exprimer ce *present time* sont nombreuses.

## LA FORME EN -ING

- La forme en -ing (ou *continuous*) montre **concrètement, dans sa durée, une action en cours relativement longue**, dont on ne précise ni quand elle a commencé, ni quand elle s'achèvera.
    *I'm reading a book by Stephen King.*
    Je suis en train de lire un livre de Stephen King.
    Plusieurs adverbes ou expressions adverbiales peuvent préciser le temps chronologique : *now, today, this week, for the time being*, etc.

- À cet aspect peut s'ajouter l'expression d'une **modalité** (cf. p. 34), par exemple, une supposition dans :
    *She must be reading it too.*
    Elle doit (être en train de) le lire aussi.

En résumé, **la forme en -ing me permet de « m'impliquer » dans la description de l'action**.

## LA FORME SIMPLE

En employant cette forme, l'anglais quitte le concret du moment présent, comme si l'action était « vue d'en haut », pour parler :

- d'un trait caractéristique d'un personnage ;
    *He reads slowly.* Il lit lentement.

- d'une habitude (le présent simple est alors accompagné d'un adverbe comme *often, never, generally, usually, always*, ou autres expressions appropriées) ;
    *On Sundays she usually reads in bed.*
    Le dimanche, elle lit au lit.

- d'une référence à une autorité (*the dictionary / Shakespeare says...*) ;
    *Some grammar books call this the simple present.*
    Certaines grammaires appellent ceci le présent simple.

- d'un règlement, d'un usage ;
    *The law forbids photocopying books.*
    La loi interdit de photocopier les livres.
    *The British send their greeting cards in the beginning of December.*
    Les Britanniques envoient leurs cartes de vœux début décembre.

- d'une « vérité éternelle », en dehors de ma responsabilité.
    *Birds of a feather flock together.* Qui se ressemble s'assemble.

En résumé, **la forme simple me permet de parler de l'action avec détachement, comme si je n'y étais pas directement impliqué.**

## FORME SIMPLE OU EN *-ING* ?

Des verbes comme *know, love, believe, remember, think*, etc. ne résultent pas d'une action volontaire, mais expriment des **processus mentaux, indépendants de la volonté.** Dans ce sens, ils **ne peuvent pas être employés à la forme en *-ing*.**
    *I think I love you.*
    Je pense que je t'aime. (*think* = « avoir l'impression de »)
    *I feel you're right.*
    J'ai le sentiment que tu as raison.

Mais quand le verbe prend la valeur d'une action, la forme en *-ing* redevient possible.
    *What are you doing? I'm thinking about you.*
    Que fais-tu ? Je pense à toi. (ici, *think* = « évoquer », « réfléchir », et résulte d'une démarche volontaire)

## YES, BUT...

Pour exprimer sa manière de voir à un moment donné, on peut se donner le droit d'inverser les rôles convenus et habituels des formes simple et en *-ing*.

- On trouvera un présent en *-ing* pour décrire, avec une nuance de regret, de reproche, ou d'irritation, une action habituelle.
    *He's always borrowing my books!*
    Il faut toujours qu'il m'emprunte mes livres !

- On trouvera un présent simple pour décrire une action en cours dans le présent, au lieu de la forme en *-ing*, à condition que cette action soit brève, et pour ne pas donner l'impression d'une sorte de « ralenti ».
    *I put my pen down and get up: someone is knocking at the door.*
    Je pose mon stylo et je me lève : on sonne à la porte.

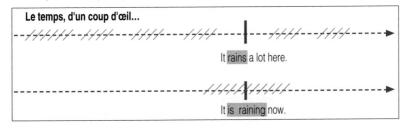

**Le temps, d'un coup d'œil...**

It rains a lot here.

It is raining now.

# 2. L'AVENIR

L'anglais n'a pas de forme spécialisée pour exprimer l'avenir, mais emprunte **différentes formes verbales**, accompagnées d'adverbes ou de compléments de temps comme *soon, tomorrow, shortly...*

## FORMES EN *-ING*

> *Next week I'm visiting the National Gallery.*
> La semaine prochaine, je visite / je visiterai le Musée des Beaux-Arts.
> *I'm going to write a book about English painting.*
> Je vais écrire un livre sur la peinture anglaise.

Avec le présent en *-ing* et la formule *be going to*, **l'avenir est considéré comme presque réalisé**, tant l'intention d'agir est forte, ou la probabilité ou l'imminence de l'action marquée. La forme en *-ing*, une fois encore, actualise le sens, rend plus concrète l'action envisagée. C'est « comme si c'était fait ».

## FORME SIMPLE

> *OK... so this is the plan for tomorrow: I get up early and meet you at the entrance at 7:00 a.m.*
> Bon, voici le programme pour demain : je me lève tôt et je te retrouve à l'entrée à sept heures.

Ici, comme toujours, la forme simple me montre plus en recul. L'action est envisagée comme **imminente** puisqu'elle paraît fermement décidée, mais **d'une manière plus abstraite**, comme si quelqu'un d'autre avait pris la décision. C'est « comme ça que cela doit se passer ».

## L'AUXILIAIRE *WILL*

> *We'll write / We'll be writing to you.* On vous écrira.

*Will* est ici un simple **auxiliaire du futur**. La forme simple et la forme en *-ing* sont à peu près équivalentes, la forme en *-ing* étant plus concrètement imaginable, la forme simple mentionnant seulement l'action comme devant se réaliser.

## LES NUANCES MODALES

> *We will write to you soon.*

- Si *will* est mentionné en toutes lettres et non sous sa forme contractée, il prend une valeur modale et induit ici une nuance du type : « Vous pouvez compter sur moi. » À l'expression du futur, *will* ajoute une notion de **volonté** : « Soyez assuré que nous vous écrirons bientôt. »

- D'autres modaux comme *can, may, might*, etc. (cf. p. 40-41) placés dans un contexte de futur avec des adverbes appropriés (*tomorrow, next month*, etc.) permettent eux aussi d'exprimer l'avenir.

  *I may write a report tonight.*
  Il se peut que j'écrive un rapport ce soir.
  *I might write a report tonight.*
  Il se pourrait que j'écrive un rapport ce soir.

Dans ce même cadre, on peut placer :
- *be to* et la forme infinitive, qui exprime une obligation inéluctable, provenant, par exemple, d'un emploi du temps « imposé » ;

  *I am to write the first part of the report next week.*
  Il est prévu que j'écrive la première partie du rapport la semaine prochaine.
- *have to* et la forme infinitive, qui suggère une obligation moins impérative.

  *I have to write soon.*
  Il faut que j'écrive bientôt.

## *Yes, but...*

- En français, nous employons deux futurs dans une même phrase.
  Je partirai quand il viendra.

- En anglais, le verbe de la **subordonnée de temps** est dans ce cas au présent.
  *I will go when he comes.*

- Mais, dans une interrogative indirecte, il n'est pas surprenant de trouver, en anglais comme en français, le futur dans les deux propositions.
  *I'll ask him when he will come.*
  Je lui demanderai à quelle heure il arrivera.

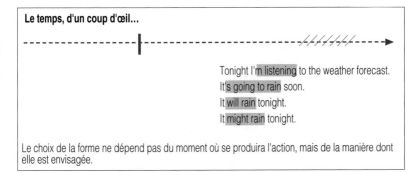

**Le temps, d'un coup d'œil...**

Tonight I'm listening to the weather forecast.
It's going to rain soon.
It will rain tonight.
It might rain tonight.

Le choix de la forme ne dépend pas du moment où se produira l'action, mais de la manière dont elle est envisagée.

# 3. LE *PRESENT PERFECT*

C'est le temps grammatical du passé le mieux lié au présent chronologique : son nom ne contient-il pas le mot *present* ? Quand je l'emploie, je dispose même d'une gradation de moyens pour exprimer comment son influence est ressentie au présent, ou reportée au temps présent. Attention ! Le *present perfect* ressemble au passé composé français, mais il n'en est pas l'équivalent : il peut se traduire aussi par le présent de l'indicatif.

## UN PASSÉ « VU D'EN HAUT »

Quand je demande à un ami :
> *Have you (ever) played tennis with my sister?*
> As-tu (jamais) joué au tennis avec ma sœur ?

**je ne m'intéresse pas aux circonstances** – quand ?, comment ?, où ?, pourquoi ?. Je veux simplement savoir si cette action a eu lieu ou non. De même, dans les exemples suivants :
> *We have visited San Francisco.*
> Nous avons visité San Francisco.
> *They have bought a new car.*
> Ils ont acheté une voiture neuve.
> *It's the first time I have met him.*
> C'est la première fois que je le rencontre.

En employant le *present perfect* dans sa forme simple, je suis comme « détaché » par rapport au fait en question.

## UN PASSÉ VU DE PLUS PRÈS

Si, à la question : *Have you (ever) played tennis with my sister?*, mon interlocuteur se contente de répondre : *Yes, I have*, il n'est guère explicite. Mais il peut dire :
> *Yes, I have played with her since last spring.*
> Oui, je joue avec elle depuis le printemps dernier.

ou encore :
> *Yes, I have played with her for months.*
> Oui, cela fait des mois que je joue avec elle.

Grâce à l'emploi de *since*, de *for*, ou avec des mots ou expressions comme *lately, recently, up to now*, etc., **l'action semble se rapprocher** au point de presque « englober » le présent. On s'attend à ce que l'action ait de nouveau lieu, parce qu'elle n'a pas encore été accomplie.

## UN PASSÉ « À PORTÉE DE LA MAIN »

Si maintenant on me répond :
> *Oh! I have just played with her.* Oh ! Je viens de faire une partie avec elle.

**le passé est si proche qu'il touche le présent**, le joueur est, pour ainsi dire, encore essoufflé. De même dans, par exemple : *It has just rained* ou *I have just poured your tea*.

## UN PASSÉ... PRÉSENT

La **forme en -*ing*** permet d'exprimer une opinion plus concrètement qu'avec la forme simple. Ainsi, pour traduire : « J'ai joué au tennis », *I have been playing tennis* exprime plus d'effort que *I have played*.

> *I have been playing a good match.*
> J'ai joué une excellente partie.

ne peut être dit qu'avec chaleur, alors que *I have played a good match* est bien moins vraisemblable. De même dans :

> *You have been smoking again!*
> Tu as encore fumé !

ou :

> *I have been working for ten hours.*
> Sous-entendu : C'est long ! Il n'est même pas nécessaire d'ajouter *hard*.

L'emploi de cette forme indique que l'action continue toujours, jusqu'au moment où l'on en parle, et qu'elle n'a pas encore été accomplie (*I have been playing a good match*), ou que l'on s'attend à ce qu'elle ait de nouveau lieu (*You have been smoking*).

## YES, BUT...

Au lieu de dire : *Have you played tennis with him?*, on aurait pu aussi poser la question : *Did you play tennis with him?*
Dans ce cas, mon interlocuteur a en tête une date qu'il peut donner. Il se sert du *preterite*, autre temps grammatical du passé, qui introduit une valeur différente.

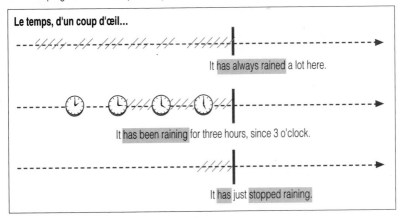

**Le temps, d'un coup d'œil...**

It has always rained a lot here.

It has been raining for three hours, since 3 o'clock.

It has just stopped raining.

# 4. LE PRÉTÉRIT

À la différence du *present perfect*, le prétérit (en anglais : *preterite* ou *past*) établit une **coupure nette avec le présent** chronologique.

## LE TEMPS DU RÉCIT

- Le prétérit peut être traduit par l'imparfait, par le passé composé ou par le passé simple, mais dans tous les cas **les faits sont bien séparés du présent**.
    *I lived in San Francisco then. I moved to Montreal three years ago.*
    Je vivais alors à San Francisco. J'ai déménagé à Montréal il y a trois ans.
  La période concernée peut être relativement longue (*lived*) ou courte (*moved*).

- *Used to*, qui insiste encore plus sur l'aspect révolu de l'action ou de l'événement, peut teinter le passé d'une coloration affective. *Used to have* indique que cela a déjà été vrai auparavant, mais que ce n'est plus vrai maintenant, au moment où l'on parle.
    *I used to have lots of friends there.*
    J'y avais beaucoup d'amis. (sous-entendu : c'était le bon temps)

## UN PASSÉ « À LA LOUPE »

Contrairement au *present perfect*, **le prétérit incite à s'intéresser aux circonstances**.
C'est ainsi que l'on peut préciser, entre autres :

- le temps, par une expression qui date bien l'action ;
    *He bought his car last October / three months ago.*
    Il a acheté sa voiture en octobre dernier / il y a trois mois.
  Remarquons au passage que *ago* exprime bien que le temps s'en est allé : dans *ago*, il y a *go*.

- la manière ;
    *She called me on her cell phone.*
    Elle m'a appelé de son téléphone cellulaire.

- le lieu ;
    *I met him in Vancouver.*
    Je l'ai rencontré à Vancouver.

## « ACTIONS-POINTS » ET « ACTIONS-TRAITS »

- Le **prétérit simple** peut aussi évoquer dans leur simplicité une **succession d'actions rapides** (actions-points) qui ponctuent la narration.
    *I knocked at the door, someone opened, I saw Louise.*
    J'ai frappé à la porte, on a ouvert, c'était Louise.
  On traduit par le passé simple, par le passé composé, ou par l'imparfait.

- **La forme en -ing**, au contraire, décrit une **action qui s'inscrit dans une durée** (action-trait).
    *"What were you doing, at ten p.m., when I tried to call you?" "I was working."*
    « Que faisais-tu hier soir, à dix heures, quand j'ai essayé de t'appeler ? » « Je travaillais. »

  La forme en -ing avec le prétérit exprime une action qui continue dans le passé par rapport à une action qui a eu lieu à un moment précis dans le passé.

- On peut utiliser la forme en -ing pour l'expression du futur dans le style indirect avec le *simple past* d'un verbe comme *tell*, par exemple..
    *She told me she was going on vacation in the following week.*
    Elle m'a dit qu'elle partait en vacances la semaine suivante.

- On peut introduire une modalité quand, au lieu de dire simplement :
    *The house stood on the hill.*
    La maison se dressait sur la colline.
  on ajoute une nuance affective.
    *My parents' house was standing on the hill, you know.*
    Tu sais, c'est la maison de mes parents qui était sur la colline.

## LE PRÉTÉRIT MODAL )

Les emplois de la forme simple et de la forme en -ing ne surprennent plus quand on en a bien compris le fonctionnement, mais ils sont plus subtils quand il s'agit d'exprimer une modalité particulière. Par exemple, le prétérit, appelé prétérit modal, est d'usage après *as if, as though*, ou encore dans *It's time...* ou *I wish...*

| | |
|---|---|
| *It's time we left.* | *I wish he visited us more often.* |
| Il est temps que nous partions. | Je voudrais qu'il nous rende visite plus souvent. |

C'est le subjonctif français qui correspond à ces attitudes subjectives.

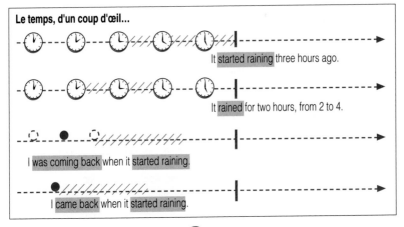

Le temps, d'un coup d'œil...

It started raining three hours ago.

It rained for two hours, from 2 to 4.

I was coming back when it started raining.

I came back when it started raining.

# 5. LE *PLUPERFECT*

Ce temps grammatical, appelé aussi *past perfect*, indique une action qui s'est accomplie avant qu'une autre action s'achève dans sa totalité, alors que le *present perfect* a un aspect progressif dans le temps présent.

## Un passé dans le passé )

- Quand on l'emploie, on dispose donc d'une même gradation de moyens pour exprimer comment le passé est ressenti. Ce temps est très comparable au plus-que-parfait et au passé antérieur français. Il peut aussi se traduire par l'imparfait.

Suivons cette gradation, mais cette fois en partant du plus proche. Comparez :

*I have just read a sci-fi book.*
Je viens de lire un livre de science-fiction.
*I had just read that book when the sequel was published.*
Je venais de lire ce livre quand la suite a été / fut publiée.

L'événement : *I had just read that book* est seulement mentionné. Il est positionné par rapport à un autre événement : *the sequel was published*, qui sert de point de référence, évoqué par le prétérit.

*I had been reading the first chapter when the light went out.*
Je lisais le premier chapitre quand la lumière s'éteignit.

Ici, *I had been reading the first chapter...* évoque une durée plus évidente, plus concrète. Soit parce qu'elle apparaît encore « chaude » à celui qui parle, soit parce que l'action durait encore au moment de l'autre événement, *when the light went out*, qui sert de point de référence.

- On retrouve tout naturellement ce système au style indirect.
  - Style direct : He said: *"I have read it."*
  - Style indirect : He said that he *had read it.*

C'est le moment passé où les paroles sont prononcées qui sert de point de référence.

## Une durée plus précise )

Comme avec le *present perfect*, la durée de l'action est souvent précisée par un complément de temps (*for two weeks, since three o'clock*, etc.) ou une référence à un événement, un état de fait passé.

*She had known him since they went on a hiking trip three years ago.*
Elle le connaissait depuis qu'ils sont allés faire de la randonnée pédestre, il y a trois ans.

> *It was after the Flood, but the Earth had not dried yet.*
> Le Déluge avait cessé, mais la Terre n'avait pas encore séché.

## LE *PLUPERFECT* MODAL

Comme le prétérit, le *pluperfect* peut avoir une valeur modale (cf. p. 19).
> *I wish he had visited us more often.*
> J'aurais aimé qu'il nous rende visite plus souvent.

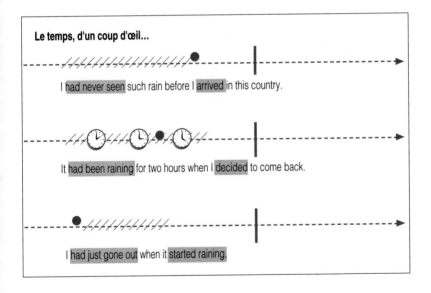

**Le temps, d'un coup d'œil...**

I had never seen such rain before I arrived in this country.

It had been raining for two hours when I decided to come back.

I had just gone out when it started raining.

# TEMPS ET ASPECTS

| Temps et aspects en anglais traduits par... | | Plus-que-parfait | Passé antérieur |
|---|---|---|---|
| **Pluperfect** | | | |
| | I had seen him before. | Je l'avais vu auparavant. | |
| Il peut être rendu plus concret par la forme en -ing.<br>**Valeur modale :** I wish I had. | I had just parked the car... /<br>I had been parking the car when she arrived. | | Quand j'eus garé la voiture, elle arriva. |
| **Preterite** | | | |
| Tantôt « action-trait » :<br>forme en -ing.<br>Tantôt « action-point » :<br>forme simple.<br>**Valeur modale :** It's time we left. | I was parking the car when he arrived.<br>When I came in I saw her immediately. | | |
| **Present perfect** | | | |
| Très lié au présent. Il en est encore rapproché par have just et par la forme en -ing.<br>**Valeur modale :** You've been smoking again! | I have known him for years, since 1990, in fact.<br>We have met often. | | |
| **Present** | | | |
| S'étend souvent bien avant et bien après le moment où on parle. Encore prolongé par la forme en -ing mais ce n'est pas toujours possible.<br>**Valeur modale :** He's always borrowing money. | I often write to her.<br>I'm meeting him tomorrow.<br>I am writing her a letter but I write slowly. | | |
| **Future** | | | |
| Pas de forme spécialisée. Forme simple moins concrète que la forme en -ing.<br>La contraction 'll a un sens moins fort que will.<br>**Valeur modale :** tous les degrés de probabilité (cf. p. 44-45). | I'll write to her some time.<br>I'll be writing to her sometime.<br>I will always write.<br>I will have seen him by then. | | |

| Passé composé | Passé simple | Imparfait | Présent | Futur antérieur | Futur simple |
|---|---|---|---|---|---|
| | | Je venais de garer la voiture quand elle arriva. | | | |
| Je garais la voiture quand il est arrivé. | | Je garais la voiture quand il arriva. | | | |
| Quand je suis arrivé, je l'ai vue tout de suite. | Quand j'arrivai, je la vis tout de suite. | | | | |
| | | | Je le connais depuis des années, en fait depuis 1990. | | |
| Nous nous sommes vus souvent. | | | | | |
| | | | Je lui écris souvent. | | |
| | | | Je vais le rencontrer demain. | | Je le rencontrerai demain. |
| | | | Je suis en train de lui écrire mais j'écris lentement. | | |
| | | | | | Je lui écrirai un jour. |
| | | | | | J'écrirai toujours, c'est certain. |
| | | | | Je l'aurai vu d'ici là. | |

# AUXILIAIRES ORDINAIRES
## be, have, do, let

## À SAVOIR

Certains **auxiliaires** – *be, have, do* et *let* – sont employés pour former la conjugaison des autres verbes. D'autres, dits auxiliaires modaux, donnent au verbe une « couleur » qui permet à celui qui parle de traduire ses intentions.

### EMPLOIS EN TANT QU'AUXILIAIRES

- **Be** permet de construire toutes les formes en *-ing*.
  *What are you doing tomorrow?*
  *We'll be writing to you.* (cf. p. 14)
  Il sert le passif (cf. p. 84).
  *I was born before you.* Je suis né avant toi.
  *I'll be laughed at.* On se moquera de moi.

- **Have** contribue à la formation de tous les temps composés (cf. p. 16-17 et 20-21).
  - Le *present perfect*.
    *Have you ever visited Mexico?* Avez-vous jamais visité le Mexique ?
  - Le *pluperfect*.
    *She had known him since they went hiking three years ago.*
    Elle le connaissait depuis qu'ils sont allés faire de la randonnée pédestre, il y a trois ans.

  Quand l'action est en cours, qu'elle n'a pas encore été accomplie, il faut aussi employer *be*.
    *What have you been doing?* Qu'est-ce que tu fabriquais encore ?

- **Do** est de règle pour toutes les formes interrogatives et négatives d'un verbe ordinaire à la forme simple (cf. tableaux, p. 88-89).

- **Let** est au service de l'impératif.
    *Let us go! / Let's go!* Allons !      *Let him go!* Qu'il parte !

### EMPLOIS EN TANT QUE « SUPPLÉANTS »

- **Be** s'associe de plus à *here* et *there* : il permet de constater un état de fait.
    *There are no clouds in the sky today.* Il n'y a pas de nuages dans le ciel aujourd'hui.

- **Have** remplace *make* pour exprimer la cause.
    *I had my watch repaired.* J'ai fait réparer ma montre.

*Have* donne ici à la phrase un sens passif, mais il peut aussi lui donner un sens actif.

*I had (ou I made) Sophie apologize to her teacher.*
J'ai obligé Sophie à s'excuser auprès de son enseignante.

- *Let* peut, comme *have*, prendre une valeur de cause.

*They let the children play with the dog.*
Ils ont laissé les enfants jouer avec le chien.

*The police arrested someone, but they let him go.*
Les policiers ont arrêté quelqu'un, mais ils l'ont relâché.

## EMPLOIS À PART ENTIÈRE

- Chacun de ces auxiliaires ordinaires peut aussi se comporter comme un verbe à part entière.

*Be* est le verbe d'état par excellence, capable d'exprimer l'âge (*She is 13.* Elle <u>a</u> treize ans.) ou l'état physique ou mental (*I am fine.* Je <u>vais</u> bien.).

*Have* est l'égal de *take* quand on dit : *Have a cup of coffee* (Prenez une tasse de café) ou *I had a good time* (J'ai passé un bon moment).

*Do* est aussi le rival de *make* et s'en distingue en plusieurs circonstances (cf. p.31). On dit *to do business* (faire des affaires) et *to make a deal* (faire une affaire).

*I'm making a cake which you can eat tomorrow.*
Je fais un gâteau que vous pouvez manger demain.

*Let* a aussi le sens de « louer » en Grande-Bretagne (en Amérique du Nord, on utilise plutôt *rent*).
*My house is to let.*

- Par voie de conséquence, certains auxiliaires peuvent être... auxiliaires d'eux-mêmes.

*Don't do that!* Ne faites pas ça !
*He has had his day.* Il a eu son heure de gloire.

- Comme de nombreux autres verbes, ils peuvent aussi s'adjoindre diverses particules (cf. p. 46).

*Be* : *Are you up?* Tu es levé ?
*Have* : *Can I have my book back?* Puis-je récupérer mon livre ?
*Do* : *They did away with the witnesses.* Ils se sont débarrassés des témoins.
*Let* : *Don't let me down.* Ne me laisse pas tomber.

## EMPLOIS COMME AUXILIAIRES MODAUX

- *Be, have* et *do* permettent même d'exprimer la modalité.

*I am to write the first part of the report next week.* (cf. p. 15)
Il est prévu que j'écrive la première partie du rapport la semaine prochaine.

*You had better write to thank them.*      *I do like grammar.* (do = forte insistance)
Tu ferais mieux de leur écrire pour les remercier.      La grammaire me passionne.

# 1. BE

*Be* joue un rôle très important pour les verbes anglais : il participe à leur fonctionnement et il est riche de valeurs propres. D'où la place qu'il tient dans les dictionnaires.

## VERBE AUXILIAIRE

- Grâce à ses huit formes différentes, pleines (*I am, he / she is, they are,* etc.) et contractées (*I'm, he's / she's, they're,* etc.), et avec l'aide de *have, has, had,* ce verbe intervient presque partout dans la conjugaison, simple et en *-ing* (cf. tableaux, p. 88-95).

- Il est à la base de la voix passive (cf. p. 84), comme équivalent du français « on », par exemple.
  *I have been fired.* On m'a renvoyé.

## VERBE SUPPLÉANT

- Employé avec *go, be* fait concurrence à *have*. Comparez :
  - *He's gone / He is gone: the door is locked.*
    Il est parti : la porte est fermée à clé.
  - *He's just gone / He has just gone.*
    Il vient de partir.

  Dans la première phrase, *is gone* exprime un état résultant d'une action, d'un événement. Dans la seconde, *has gone* est un simple *present perfect.*

- Attention : les deux formes contractées sont identiques. Ainsi la phrase : *She's gone to Calgary* se comprend-elle :
  - *She is gone to Calgary.* (sous-entendu : elle y est partie définitivement, elle n'en reviendra pas)
  - *She has gone to Calgary.* (sous-entendu : elle y est partie, mais elle en reviendra)
  Seul le contexte peut nous renseigner.

- Ne confondez pas non plus *has been* avec *has gone.*
  *She's been to Calgary / She has been to Calgary.*
  Elle est allée à Calgary. (sous-entendu : elle en est revenue)

- Emploi avec *here* et *there*.
  *Here they are.* Les voilà.
  *There are ten people.* Il y a dix personnes.
  Ces emplois (constatation d'un état de fait) peuvent parfois surprendre un Francophone, mais ils sont néanmoins cohérents en anglais : *be* se conjugue « normalement » sans être perturbé par la présence de *here* ou *there*.
  *There being nobody else...*
  Comme il n'y avait personne d'autre...

*Shouldn't there be a police officer here?*
Ne devrait-il pas y avoir un policier ici ?
*Rocky, come here! There's a good dog!*
Rocky, viens ici ! Toi, tu es un bon chien !

- *It is* est proche de *there is*, pour exprimer :
  - La distance : *How far is it to Toronto?* À quelle distance d'ici se trouve Toronto ?
  - Le temps qu'il fait : *It is foggy.* Il y a du brouillard.
  - La durée : *It is five years since he left.* (Surtout pas *there is*.) Cela fait cinq ans qu'il est parti.

## VERBE À PART ENTIÈRE

- *Be* désigne ici un état, au sens plein du terme. Pensez au fameux : *To be, or not to be* de Shakespeare. C'est ainsi qu'il peut exprimer :
  - L'âge.
    *How old are you?*
  - La condition physique.
    *How are you? I am fine, thanks.*
  - Le fait d'exister.
    *Shakespeare is the best English playwright that ever was.*
    Shakespeare est le meilleur dramaturge anglais de tous les temps.

- Quand la phrase est sans ambiguïté, avec *when, if, though, unless, until,* on peut omettre verbe et sujet.
    *When a boy, he used to be quite mischievous.*
    Quand il était jeune, il était très espiègle.

- On voit donc que dans cet emploi, *be* peut être classé avec d'autres « verbes d'état » comme *appear, become, feel, get, go, grow, make, seem, smell, sound, taste,* etc.

## YES, BUT...

- Attention, on dira :
    *There was* (et non *there were*) *ten minutes to wait.*
    Il y avait dix minutes d'attente. (sous-entendu une période de dix minutes, que l'on ne compte pas précisément)

- Notez par ailleurs que le français « il y a » ne se traduit pas automatiquement par *there is / there are.*
    *What's the matter?*
    Qu'est-ce qu'il y a ? Qu'est-ce qui se passe ?

## 2. HAVE

*Have* n'a que quatre formes pleines : *have*, *has*, *had* et *having*, mais attention aux formes contractées affirmative et négative, qui peuvent être confondues avec celles de *be* : *he's* peut se comprendre *he is* ou *he has* (cf. p. 26).

### VERBE AUXILIAIRE

Il permet de former le *present perfect* et le *pluperfect* de tous les verbes ordinaires (cf. tableaux, p. 90-91).

> *Have you finished your coffee?*
> Tu as fini ton café ?

### VERBE SUPPLÉANT

- *Have* a un emploi « causatif » qui le rapproche de *make*.
  *Make*, cependant, est plus fort que *have*, et implique un certain degré de contrainte :
  > *I had the boy's hair cut.*
  > J'ai fait en sorte que le garçon se fasse couper les cheveux. (On ne connaît pas les sentiments du garçon.)
  > *I made the boy cut his hair.*
  > J'ai obligé le garçon à se faire couper les cheveux. (On comprend que le garçon était plutôt réticent.)

- Mais attention à certaines ambiguïtés. Considérez la phrase :
  > *He had his watch stolen.*

  Détachée de son contexte, elle peut signifier, au sens passif :
  > On lui a volé sa montre.

  et, au sens actif :
  > Il a fait voler la montre de quelqu'un par quelqu'un d'autre.

- Attention aussi à l'ordre des mots. Comparez :
  > *She had her hair cut.*
  > Elle s'est fait couper les cheveux.
  > *She had cut her hair.*
  > Elle s'était coupée les cheveux.

### VERBE À PART ENTIÈRE

- Le premier sens plein de *have* est un sens statique : la possession.
  > *She has a cell phone. Do you have one?*
  > Elle a un téléphone cellulaire. Et vous ?

- Le deuxième sens plein est dynamique et exprime plusieurs notions équivalentes de :
  - **prendre**

    *He is having a bath.*
    Il est en train de prendre un bain.

    *I had coffee at Rachel's yesterday.*
    J'ai pris le café chez Rachel hier.

  - **donner**

    *We had a party to celebrate Tom's success.*
    On a donné une soirée pour célébrer le succès de Tom.

  - **faire**

    *I have a walk every morning.*
    Je fais une promenade à pied tous les matins.

    *Do you want to have a ride on my motorcycle?*
    Veux-tu aller faire un tour en moto avec moi ?

  - **recevoir**

    *I had a fax from her.*
    J'ai reçu une télécopie d'elle.

    *Every time it rains, I have trouble with my car.*
    Chaque fois qu'il pleut, j'ai des ennuis avec ma voiture.

  - **accepter**

    *I won't have you out after midnight!*
    Je refuse que tu sois dehors après minuit !

    *Another delay? I won't have it!*
    Un autre retard ? Je ne tolérerai pas ça !

- Il peut, comme quelque trois mille verbes à part entière, être accompagné de diverses particules (cf. liste des verbes à particule, p. 175).

    *I'll have it out with him as soon as I see him.*
    Je mettrai les choses au point avec lui dès que je le verrai.

    *They had it in for me from the very beginning.*
    Dès le tout début, ils en ont eu contre moi.

## AUXILIAIRE MODAL

La « coloration » modale (ferme intention, opinion) est encore plus nette dans des tournures comme :

*You'd better apologize to your boss.*
Tu ferais mieux de t'excuser auprès de ton patron.

*I'd rather do it myself.*
J'aimerais mieux le faire moi-même.

# 3. *DO*

*Do* a cinq formes pleines : *do* pour l'infinitif et le présent (mais *does* à la troisième personne du singulier), *did* au prétérit, *done* au participe passé, *doing* à la forme en *-ing*. Ses formes contractées sont sans ambiguïté : *don't, doesn't, didn't*. Il se partage à peu près également entre son rôle d'auxiliaire et son rôle de verbe à part entière.

## Verbe auxiliaire )

*Do* et *did* ne font que marquer le temps et la troisième personne aux formes simples interrogative et négative (cf. tableaux, p. 88-89).
> *Does / Did John play the piano?*

## Verbe suppléant )

- Dans une question ou une réponse, *do* **évite la répétition** du verbe.
> *You draw better than I do. So does she.*
> Vous dessinez mieux que moi. Elle aussi.
> *They speak German. Oh, do they?*
> Ils parlent allemand. Vraiment ?
> *She plays the piano, doesn't she?*
> Elle joue du piano, n'est-ce pas ?
> *Does she play well? Yes, she does. / No, she doesn't. / No, she does not.*
> Elle joue bien ? Oui. / Non.

Remarquez que la forme pleine *does not* donne plus de force à la négation. On pourrait traduire par : Oh non !

- *Do* peut prendre une **valeur emphatique**, qui exprime un premier degré de modalité.
> *He did say it.*
> Il l'a bien dit.
> *John does play the piano beautifully.*
> John joue du piano vraiment merveilleusement. (on insiste sur le sens – l'excellence du jeu du pianiste)
> *He owns or did own a piano.*
> Il possède, ou du moins possédait autrefois, un piano. (on insiste sur le temps – le passé)

De même avec l'impératif.
> *Do tell her that she'll be welcome.* Dis-lui bien qu'elle sera la bienvenue.

Comme vous avez pu le constater dans les exemples, on peut, à l'écrit, souligner *do* et *did* pour bien indiquer qu'il s'agit d'une forme d'insistance. À l'oral, c'est une inflexion de la voix qui les met en valeur.

## VERBE À PART ENTIÈRE )

- *Do* a de nombreux emplois d'usage courant avec le premier sens de « **faire** » en général.
  *What are you doing?*

  Ces emplois, très variés, peuvent être :
  • Transitifs :
  *Do the meat* (couper la viande), *do one's best* (faire de son mieux), *do one's hair* (se coiffer), *do one's shoes* (cirer ses chaussures), etc.
  • Intransitifs :
  *I can't do without you.* Je ne peux vivre sans toi.
  *Do as you would be done by.* Ne faites pas aux autres ce que vous ne voudriez pas qu'on vous fasse.

  Parmi ces emplois, plusieurs appartiennent à la langue familière : *He's done for!* (Il est fichu !) *I'm all done in!* (Je suis épuisé !)

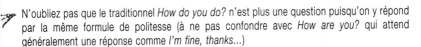

N'oubliez pas que le traditionnel *How do you do?* n'est plus une question puisqu'on y répond par la même formule de politesse (à ne pas confondre avec *How are you?* qui attend généralement une réponse comme *I'm fine, thanks...*)

- *Do* et *make*
  On dit *do business* mais *make a deal*, comme nous l'avons observé plus haut. *Do* et *make* sont souvent proches mais non interchangeables. *Make* exprime plutôt l'activité elle-même, d'une manière concrète, avec le sens original de « fabriquer ». *Do* exprime plutôt le résultat de cette activité.

  Comparez :
  • *To make money* (gagner de l'argent), *to make mistakes* (faire des fautes), *to make the best of it* (en tirer le meilleur parti), etc.
  • *To do one's duty* (faire son devoir), *to do one's best* (faire de son mieux).

## AUTRES EMPLOIS )

Bien qu'il ne puisse pas être employé comme auxiliaire modal, *do* peut être, comme *be* ou *have*, très prolifique comme verbe à particule (cf. liste, p. 175) et, à ce titre, exprimer une certaine modalité. Voyez par exemple :
*I could do with a cup of coffee.*
Je prendrais bien une tasse de café.
*Well done, Catherine!*
Bravo, Catherine !
*It isn't done.*
Cela ne se fait pas.

# 4. LET

Avec *let*, nous nous rapprochons du domaine des verbes ordinaires : son rôle d'auxiliaire est en effet mineur par rapport à ses emplois à part entière et ses possibilités d'association avec des particules pour former de nombreux composés.

Il n'a que trois formes : *let*, *lets* et *letting*.

## VERBE AUXILIAIRE

● *Let* auxiliaire ne sert qu'à former le mode **impératif**.

> *Let him stay here!*
> Qu'il reste ici !
> *Don't let the cat get out!*
> Que le chat ne sorte pas !
> *Let's go to a movie.*
> Allons au cinéma.
> *Let them think that!*
> Qu'ils le pensent !

Il s'agit moins, on le voit, d'un ordre que d'un **conseil**, d'une **suggestion**, d'une **invitation**.

● Très employé à la première personne du pluriel, qui implique celui qui parle dans l'action proposée, *let* est beaucoup plus rare à la première personne du singulier, pour exprimer comme un encouragement qu'on se donnerait à soi-même.

> *Let me think....*
> Réfléchissons... Voyons...

La troisième personne du singulier et du pluriel exprime une sorte de vœu ou parfois un acquiescement, une résignation.

En somme, on trouve dans toutes ces formes **une valeur modale**, parfois un souhait, plutôt qu'un ordre.

> *Let them be happy! May they be happy!*
> Qu'ils soient heureux !

● À la **forme négative**, *let* existe dans un registre littéraire :

> *Let us not waste our time.*
> Ne perdons pas notre temps.

et dans un registre familier avec *do* et *you* :

> *Don't let me catch you again!*
> Que je ne t'y reprenne pas !

- Le sens de base de ce **verbe irrégulier** (*let – let – let*) est « laisser, permettre ».
    > *Who let you into the house?*
    > Qui vous a fait entrer dans la maison ?

- De ce sens, on passe à celui de « louer », surtout en Grande-Bretagne (en Amérique du Nord, on utilise plutôt *rent*).
    > *My house is now to let.*
    > Ma maison est à louer, maintenant.

    Un emploi intransitif est alors possible.
    > *A house that would let easily...*
    > Une maison qui se louerait facilement...

- *Let* garde un peu de son sens impératif, dans par exemple :

    | | |
    |---|---|
    | *Let me help you.* | *Don't let the child go out!* |
    | Permettez que je vous aide. | Ne laissez pas sortir l'enfant ! |
    | *Let me tell you this...* | *Let the cat in!* |
    | Laissez-moi vous dire ceci... | Faites entrer le chat ! |

## Locutions verbales )

*Let* est riche d'emplois avec :

- Des adjectifs.
    > *Let him alone.* Laisse-le tranquille.
    > *Let the dog loose / free.* Libérez le chien.

- Des particules (cf. p. 58-73).
    > *She let the cat out of the bag.*
    > Elle a vendu la mèche.
    > *The engine let out a cloud of smoke.*
    > La locomotive cracha un nuage de fumée.
    > *Don't let me down.*
    > Ne me laisse pas tomber.
    > *Don't let on about the surprise party!*
    > Ne dites rien sur la surprise-partie !
    > *You don't know what you're letting yourself in for.*
    > Vous ne savez pas dans quoi vous vous engagez.

# Auxiliaires modaux

## À SAVOIR

### Définition

Il s'agit d'une dizaine d'auxiliaires qui, associés aux verbes simples ou composés, réguliers ou irréguliers, expriment la modalité, c'est-à-dire l'**attitude d'esprit de celui qui parle**, autrement dit son humeur (*mood* en anglais).

Comparez :
> *Do you want some coffee?*

qui n'est qu'une sèche demande de renseignement, et :
> *Would you like some coffee?*

qui exprime plus de chaleur et de sollicitude.

### Caractères communs

À la différence de *be, have, do* et *let*, les modaux ne peuvent pas être utilisés seuls comme verbes à part entière.

À ce titre :
- ils ne sont jamais précédés de *to* ;
- ils ne sont suivis que d'une forme infinitive sans *to* ;
- leur forme interrogative se fait par simple inversion du sujet ;
- ils ne prennent pas de *s* à la troisième personne du singulier ;
- ils ne sont jamais précédés d'un auxiliaire ordinaire.

### Peu de formes mais beaucoup de sens

*Shall* et *should*, *will* et *would*, *can* et *could*, *may* et *might*, *must* et *ought to* : les formes sont relativement peu nombreuses.

Mais les sens et les emplois sont très diversifiés – il y a par exemple deux emplois de *should* – et se recouvrent partiellement d'une forme à l'autre. On n'étudiera que les principaux modaux, en les séparant en trois groupes selon l'attitude de celui qui parle (le « locuteur »).

## SHALL / SHOULD, WILL / WOULD )

Avec ces auxiliaires, on imagine l'action comme si elle était réalisée. Il faudra pourtant distinguer *shall / should*, qui impliquent davantage l'idée d'un devoir à accomplir, et *will / would* qui ont plutôt le sens de « vouloir ». Dans les deux cas, on observera des modalités plus ou moins fortes.

Par exemple, *will* est plus fort dans :
    *I will see him today.* Je le verrai aujourd'hui. (sous-entendu : j'en ai la ferme intention)
que dans :
    *Will you come for a drink?* Voulez-vous prendre un verre avec moi ?


## CAN / COULD, MAY / MIGHT )

L'action paraît alors beaucoup plus libre : tout semble possible. Sa réalisation va dépendre des capacités du sujet, personne ou chose, de l'existence d'une opposition ou d'une autorisation extérieure, ou des circonstances.

Par exemple, si on dit :
    *I may go to Nova Scotia next year.*
    Il se peut que j'aille en Nouvelle-Écosse l'an prochain.
on est encore incertain, mais moins incertain que si l'on dit :
    *I might go to Nova Scotia next year.*
    Il se pourrait que j'aille en Nouvelle-Écosse l'an prochain.


## MUST, OUGHT TO, SHOULD, HAVE TO, BE TO )

Ici, l'action est placée sous le signe de l'obligation dont la source peut être intérieure ou extérieure au sujet. Nous avons déjà rencontré *have to* et *be to*, p. 15.

Par exemple, quand je dis :
    *I have to read this book.*
c'est parce qu'on me l'a demandé, alors que :
    *I must read this book.*
supposerait que c'est un acte que je m'impose à moi-même.


## YES, BUT... )

- Attention aux formes négative et interrogative : par exemple, la forme négative de *I have to go to Toronto for a business meeting* n'est pas *I have not to go* mais *I don't have to go*...

- En français aussi, bien sûr, nous disposons de moyens d'exprimer la modalité. Mais ce sont plus souvent des expressions que de simples auxiliaires. D'où, en anglais, toujours plus de rapidité, mais aussi parfois plus d'ambiguïté.

# 1. SHALL

*Shall* ne se rencontre plus qu'assez rarement dans la langue quotidienne actuelle en Amérique du Nord. *Will* ou *'ll* sont d'usage courant, sauf dans des situations très formelles, dans le cas d'un ordre impérieux ou d'une interdiction formelle, par exemple, où l'on emploierait plutôt *shall*. Les trois emplois principaux de *shall* peuvent être classés d'après la modalité qu'ils expriment, dans un ordre croissant.

## SIMPLE AUXILIAIRE DU FUTUR )

> *Tomorrow I shall be 25.*
> Demain j'aurai 25 ans.

Cet emploi, où *shall* est contracté en *'ll*, est réservé à la première personne du singulier et du pluriel. Il se confond aussi avec *will*, à la forme simple et à la forme continue : *We'll be writing to you.* (cf. p. 14)

À la forme négative, il devient *shall not* ou plus souvent *shan't*. En Amérique du Nord, *won't (will not)* remplace *shan't*.

> *We shan't be there before lunch.*
> Nous n'y serons pas avant le déjeuner.

## PROPOSITION POLIE )

> *Shall we dance?* Vous dansez ?

Réservé à la forme interrogative, *shall* traduit, sur un ton poli, une proposition ou une offre d'aide.

> *Shall I open the window?*
> Voulez-vous que j'ouvre la fenêtre ?

## ORDRE IMPÉRIEUX OU INTERDICTION FORMELLE )

> *They shall not pass!*
> Ils ne passeront pas !

Cet emploi, un peu archaïque, aux deuxième et troisième personnes du singulier et du pluriel, se rencontre souvent dans la Bible.

> *Thou (= You) shalt (=shall) not kill.*
> Tu ne tueras point.

On le trouve encore aujourd'hui dans des textes de loi.

> *The fine shall not exceed $100.*
> L'amende ne devra en aucun cas dépasser 100 $.

Il permet aussi d'exprimer une ferme détermination.

> *You shall obey him!* (sous-entendu : pas question de ne pas lui obéir !)

# 2. SHOULD

*Should* est plus courant et plus complexe. Il peut s'employer à toutes les personnes. Il se contracte en *'d*, qu'il ne faut pas confondre avec la contraction de *had*.

## FUTUR DANS LE PASSÉ

On l'emploie surtout dans les interrogatives indirectes. Cet usage est presque exclusivement britannique. *Will* et *would* sont les formes courantes en Amérique du Nord. Comparez :
> *I don't know when we shall (will) meet again.* Je ne sais pas quand on se reverra.
> *I didn't know when we should (would) meet again.* Je ne savais pas quand on se reverrait.

## SOUHAIT, CONSEIL, OBLIGATION

> *I should be on holiday by now!* Je devrais déjà être en vacances !
> *I should write to thank them.* Je devrais leur écrire pour les remercier.
> *Shouldn't you go and see her?* Est-ce que vous ne devriez pas aller la voir ?

À ces emplois peut s'ajouter l'expression du regret ou du reproche.
> *I should have written to him.* J'aurais dû lui écrire.
> *They should have told you, shouldn't they?* Ils auraient pu te prévenir, non ?

## PROBABILITÉ (MOYENNE)

> *She is the better runner, so she should win the race.*
> Elle est la meilleure coureuse, elle devrait donc gagner la course.
> *The car shouldn't be making that noise.* La voiture ne devrait pas faire ce bruit.

## CONDITIONNEL

> *If you should see him, please give him this message.*
> Si jamais tu devais le voir, fais-lui ce message, s'il te plaît.

Dans la langue châtiée, en début de phrase, *should* renforce le caractère hypothétique de la situation : *Should she change her mind...* Au cas (peu probable) où elle changerait d'avis...

## SUBJONCTIF

> *It is surprising that he should be so ignorant.* C'est étonnant qu'il soit si ignorant.
> *Let's go now, lest she should / for fear that she should change her mind.*
> Allons-y maintenant, de peur qu'elle change d'avis.

# 3. WILL / WOULD

*Will* et *would* ont plus de caractères communs que *shall* et *should* et seront étudiés parallèlement.
On se rappellera que *will* et *would* sont les formes courantes en Amérique du Nord. *Will*, dans son sens actuel, contient **l'idée de volonté, de désir**.
C'est ainsi qu'on dira de quelqu'un : *He has a strong will.* (Il a une forte volonté.)
Cela se retrouve dans le proverbe : *Where there is a will there is a way*. (Vouloir, c'est pouvoir.)
Ce qui conduit à commencer l'étude par le sens le plus fort.

## VOLONTÉ, ORDRE, FERME INTENTION

> *I will see him today.*
> Je le verrai aujourd'hui. (sous-entendu : j'y suis décidé)

On insiste en utilisant la forme pleine, que l'on prononce fermement. (Comparez avec : *I'll see him*, qui n'est qu'une forme neutre et indique un simple futur.)

De même pour exprimer un refus :
> *Little Claire won't go to bed before nine o'clock.*
> La petite Claire refuse de se coucher avant neuf heures.
> *My car won't start.*
> Ma voiture refuse de démarrer.

Il existe d'ailleurs un verbe à sens plein, d'un emploi relativement rare : *will* (vouloir) pour dire par exemple : *It is as God wills* (Comme Dieu le veut) ou *to will somebody's happiness* (vouloir le bien de quelqu'un).

Au passé, on peut dire :
> *I called her but she wouldn't answer.*
> Je l'ai appelée mais elle n'a pas voulu répondre.

## INVITATION, REQUÊTE

> *Will you please sit down?*
> Voulez-vous vous asseoir ?
> *Won't you come with us?*
> Et si vous veniez avec nous ?

L'emploi de *would* permettra de se montrer plus poli, plus prévenant.
> *Would you mind closing the window?*
> Puis-je vous demander de fermer la fenêtre, s'il vous plaît ?
> *Would you please sit down?*
> Veuillez vous asseoir...

> *She'd be about 70.* Elle doit avoir 70 ans.
> *Oh good — that will/that'll be the mailman.*
> C'est bien, ce doit être le facteur.
> *It would have been about 10 p.m. when she came in.*
> Elle a dû venir vers 22 heures.

## RÉPÉTITION, HABITUDE )

- C'est ce qu'on appelle la « forme fréquentative », employée généralement dans des expressions figées ou idiomatiques et parfois difficile à rendre correctement en français.
  > *Boys will be boys.*
  > Un garçon, c'est toujours un garçon.

☞ N'employez dans ce sens que la forme pleine, pour ne pas confondre avec le simple futur.

- Au passé, faites la différence entre *would* et *used to*.
  > *When he was stressed at work, he would smoke a lot.*
  > Il fumait beaucoup quand le stress le gagnait au travail.

  *Would* laisse supposer qu'il recommencera peut-être à fumer, alors que *He used to* impliquerait qu'il a sans doute définitivement cessé de fumer.
  > *He used to smoke, but he stopped two years ago.*
  > Il fumait, mais il a arrêté il y a deux ans.

## LES VALEURS PROPRES DE *WOULD* )

- Futur dans le passé
  Comparez :
  > *She says that she'll come back.*
  > Elle dit qu'elle reviendra.

  > *She said that she'd come back.*
  > Elle a dit qu'elle reviendrait.

- Auxiliaire du conditionnel
  - Présent
    > *He would go with you if you asked him.*
    > Il irait avec toi si tu le lui demandais.

  - Passé
    > *He would have gone with you if you'd asked him.*
    > Il serait allé avec toi si tu le lui avais demandé.

- Pour *would* comme pour *should*, la forme pleine n'est obligatoire que dans les questions et les réponses du type : *Yes, I should... Yes, I would...*

# 4. CAN / COULD, MAY / MIGHT

*Can/could* et *may/might* introduisent l'idée que la réalisation de l'acte envisagé va dépendre soit des **capacités** de la personne ou de la chose, soit des autres à qui on demande une **permission**, à qui on fera une **suggestion**, soit des circonstances, ce qui déterminera une échelle de **probabilités**.

## CAPACITÉ : *CAN / COULD*

● Au présent et au passé.
> *I could drive all night before the accident, but now I can't.*
> Je pouvais conduire toute la nuit avant l'accident, mais maintenant je ne peux plus.

● Aux autres temps, on utilise *be able to*.
> *I'll never be able to read all this!* Je ne pourrai jamais lire tout ça !

Au passé, *could* et *be able to* peuvent avoir un sens légèrement différent. Comparez :
> *When I was young, I could drive all night...*
> Quand j'étais jeune, je pouvais conduire toute la nuit...
>
> *... but yesterday I wasn't able to drive for more than a few hours.*
> ... mais hier j'ai réussi à conduire seulement pendant quelques heures.

Dans la première phrase, *could* exprime plutôt une capacité permanente, tandis que dans la deuxième, il s'agit d'une circonstance particulière, à un moment donné.

● Ces auxiliaires sont particulièrement employés :
  ● Avec les verbes de perception.
> *Can you hear me?* se traduit simplement par : Vous m'entendez ?

  ● Pour exprimer un savoir-faire.
> *She can speak Italian.* Elle parle l'italien.

● Retenons enfin que la forme négative peut exprimer une impossibilité ou un fait hautement improbable.
> *It can't be true!* Ce n'est pas vrai !

## PERMISSION : *CAN / COULD / MAY / MIGHT*

● Au présent, ils s'emploient pour demander une permission, selon la progression suivante : *can < could < may < might*. Comparez :
> *Can I/Could I/May I/Might I borrow your book?* Je peux / Pourrais-je / Puis-je t'emprunter ton livre ?

*Might*, lui, s'emploie avec le sens de permission seulement :
  ● Au style indirect pour rappeler des paroles passées.
> *She said you could/might borrow her book.* Elle a dit que tu pouvais emprunter son livre.

• Pour exprimer un excès de politesse teinté d'ironie.

> *Might I borrow your book?* Pourrais-tu me faire l'honneur de me prêter ton livre ?

● Au passé et au présent, on pourra utiliser l'équivalent *be allowed to*, avec encore une fois une nuance.

> *When I was younger I could stay up until midnight.*
> Quand j'étais plus jeune, j'avais le droit de veiller jusqu'à minuit.
> *Yesterday I was allowed to stay up until midnight.*
> Hier soir, j'ai eu le droit de veiller jusqu'à minuit.

Ici encore, l'équivalent *be allowed to* insiste plus sur le caractère circonstanciel, momentané, de la modalité.

● Dans les autres cas, seul un équivalent est possible.

> *I don't know if she'll be allowed to / if she'll have the right to come.*
> Je ne sais pas si elle aura le droit de venir.

Attention : si la forme négative *can't* peut exprimer un refus, la forme négative de *may* ou *could* serait *mustn't*.

> *You can't / mustn't come.*
> Je t'interdis de venir.

## SUGGESTION : *CAN / COULD / MIGHT*

> *We can / could go to a movie.*
> Nous pouvons / pourrions aller au cinéma.

Les deux formulations sont à peu près équivalentes, mais *could* est plus courant.

*Can* et *could* peuvent s'accompagner d'une vraie hypothèse.

> *We can go to a movie, if you feel like going out.*
> Nous pouvons aller au cinéma, si tu as envie de sortir.

*Might* peut laisser planer un léger doute.

> *We might go to a movie...* (Peut-être pourrait-on...)

## PROBABILITÉ : *CAN / COULD / MAY / MIGHT*

● *Can, could, may* et *might* permettent une gradation du plus au moins probable selon l'appréciation de celui qui parle.

> *He can win the game* : il a toutes les chances de gagner la partie.
> *He could win the game* : pourquoi pas, mais cela va dépendre.
> *He may win the game* : ce n'est pas exclu.
> *He might win the game* : il y a vraiment peu de chances.

● Si l'appréciation porte sur une action en cours, ils sont suivis de la forme en *-ing*.

> *She can / could / may / might be working.*

● Au passé : *She can / could / may / might have missed her bus.*

# 5. *OUGHT TO / MUST / NEED / DARE*

Avec ces modaux, la réalisation de l'acte paraît obligée. Cette **obligation** peut venir du sujet lui-même, ou des autres, ou encore d'une loi morale supérieure. Il n'est donc pas étonnant que ces auxiliaires expriment aussi des degrés de probabilité plus élevés.

## OBLIGATION : *OUGHT TO / MUST* )

*I ought to write to my father.*
Je devrais écrire à mon père.

Le sens est proche de : *I should write*. (cf. p. 37)

* Pour exprimer une nécessité plus forte, on aura recours à *must*, **au présent**, si elle est **d'origine interne**.
  *I must read this book.*
  Il faut que je lise ce livre.
  (sous-entendu : c'est un acte que je m'impose à moi-même, j'en ai décidé ainsi)

* Si cette nécessité **vient de l'extérieur**, on utilisera un équivalent comme *have to*.
  *I have to read this book.* (sous-entendu : parce qu'on me l'a demandé)

* *Have (got) to, be to, be obliged to* sont des formules presque équivalentes qui peuvent servir à d'autres temps que le présent.
  *I have to finish this report today. I've got to finish this report today.*
  Il faut que je termine ce rapport aujourd'hui.

Attention ! Il y a deux réponses possibles à la question : *Do you think I must / have to wait for her?*
*No, you don't have to (wait).*
Non, ce n'est pas nécessaire.
*No, you mustn't.*
Non, je te l'interdis.

## PROBABILITÉ )

* Pour exprimer une probabilité moyenne, il existe un deuxième emploi de *ought to*.
  *They ought to be here soon.*
  Ils devraient bientôt arriver.

* Si l'on emploie *must*, il s'agit même d'une quasi-certitude.
  *It must be very cold outside.*
  Il fait certainement très froid dehors.

La forme négative serait : *It can't be cold outside* (c'est impossible qu'il fasse froid...).

- Au passé :
    *He must have borrowed this book from Jane.*
    Il a certainement emprunté ce livre à Jane.

- Il existe un nom correspondant à ce sens.
    *This book is a must.*
    Il faut absolument lire ce livre.

## *NEED* ET *DARE*

Ils ont tous les deux un emploi modal et un emploi à part entière.

- L'emploi de *need* modal est limité en anglais moderne aux seules formes négative et interrogative. *Have to* et *should* sont des formes équivalentes, et plus courantes dans la langue de tous les jours.
    *You needn't wait for me. / You don't have to wait for me.*
    Inutile de m'attendre.
    *Need I wait for you? / Should I wait for you?*
    Faut-il que je t'attende ?

- *Need*, verbe ordinaire, régulier, a le sens de « avoir besoin ».
    *I don't need to read this.*
    Je n'ai pas besoin de lire ceci.
    *This car needs to be repaired / needs repairing.*
    Cette voiture a besoin d'une réparation.
    *When I needed some advice, I always called her.*
    Quand j'avais besoin d'un conseil, je l'appelais toujours.

- *Dare* modal obéit aux mêmes usages, avec le sens de « oser ».
    *How dare you say such things?*
    Comment osez-vous dire des choses pareilles ?
    *How dare you!*
    Vous avez du culot !
    *I don't dare speak to her.*
    Je n'ose lui adresser la parole.

- Comme verbe ordinaire, régulier, *dare* peut être suivi de la forme infinitive avec ou sans *to*.
    *I don't dare (to) go alone.*
    Je n'ose pas y aller seul.

# AUXILIAIRES MODAUX

| Modalités | *Shall* | *Should* | *Will* | *Would* |
|---|---|---|---|---|
| **Suggestion, invitation** | Shall we dance? | | Will you please sit down? | Would you please sit down? |
| **Interdiction** | They shall not pass! | | You will speak to nobody! | |
| **Conseil, souhait, obligation** | | I should write to them. | | |
| **Probabilité plus ou moins grande** | | She should win the game. | | |
| **Impossibilité, fait très improbable** | | | | |
| **Volonté, ferme intention** | | | I will see him today. | She wouldn't answer. |
| **Supposition, conjecture** | | | That <u>will</u> be the newspaper. | It would have been about 10 p.m. |
| **Répétition, habitude, forme fréquentative** | | | Boys will be boys. | He would smoke a lot. |
| **Capacité** | | | | |
| **Permission** | | | | |

Ce tableau ne reprend que les principaux exemples d'emplois des dix principales modalités analysées.

# TABLEAU RÉCAPITULATIF

| Can | Could | May | Might | Ought to | Must |
|-----|-------|-----|-------|----------|------|
| We can go to a movie. | We could go to a movie. | | We might go to a movie. | | |
| | | | | | You mustn't smoke here. |
| | | | | I ought to write to them. | I must read this book. (ou have to) |
| He can win the game. | She could be working. | He may win the game. | He might win the game. | They ought to be here soon. | She must be reading your book. |
| It can't be true! | | | | | |
| | | | | | |
| | | | | | |
| | | | | | |
| I can drive. (ou am able to) | I could drive all night. | | | | |
| Can I borrow your book? (ou Am I allowed to) | Could I borrow your book? | May I borrow your book? | She said you might borrow it. | | |

Observez les modalités les plus nuancées et les auxiliaires les plus sollicités. Une richesse qui ne va pas sans ambiguïté.

# VERBES À PARTICULE
## Les verbes

## À SAVOIR

La moitié des verbes anglais sont beaucoup plus riches de sens qu'il ne le paraissent. Comment en profiter ?

- Prenons, un verbe très courant, comme *go*. Il peut signifier :
  - se déplacer
    *We've gone five kilometres from the station.*
    Nous avons fait cinq kilomètres depuis la gare.
  - évoluer
    *How are things going at your new school?*
    Comment ça va à ta nouvelle école ?
  - convenir
    *These colours don't go with your new shoes.*
    Ces couleurs jurent avec tes nouvelles chaussures.

Observons-le maintenant au centre d'un « carrefour » de phrases possibles et cherchons-en le sens, en commençant par *when*.

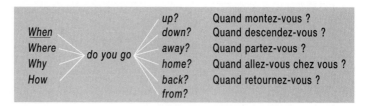

| When | | *up?* | Quand montez-vous ? |
| Where | | *down?* | Quand descendez-vous ? |
| Why | *do you go* | *away?* | Quand partez-vous ? |
| How | | *home?* | Quand allez-vous chez vous ? |
| | | *back?* | Quand retournez-vous ? |
| | | *from?* | |

- Même si toutes les combinaisons ne sont pas possibles (on ne peut poser la question ~~When do you go from?~~), les sens du verbe se multiplient grâce à l'association de petits mots invariables.
  À l'origine, ce sont le plus souvent des adverbes comme *out*, ou des prépositions comme *from*, mais parfois aussi des noms comme *home*, ou des adjectifs. Par souci de simplification, nous les appellerons ici **particules**.

Certains verbes, très « prolifiques », peuvent s'associer ainsi à dix, vingt particules différentes pour former des *phrasal verbs* ou « verbes à particule ». Richesse d'autant plus grande que chaque association peut avoir parfois plusieurs acceptions !

## RICHESSE DE TROIS MILLE VERBES

À côté de *go*, existent de nombreux verbes de mouvement comparables, comme *walk* (marcher), *move* (se mouvoir), *glide* (glisser), *flow* (couler), etc. Ils sont prêts à s'associer avec à peu près les mêmes particules.

> *He shuffled back to his bed.*
> Il regagna son lit en traînant les pieds.

Sur plus de six mille verbes que compte la langue anglaise, environ trois mille, particulièrement productifs, peuvent s'associer chacun à cinq, dix, vingt, voire plus de trente particules différentes, si bien que l'ensemble des « verbes à particule » ainsi formés atteint un total d'une douzaine de mille.

## COMMENT LES UTILISER ?

Devant un tel foisonnement de sens, il ne faut ni se « jeter à l'eau » en espérant deviner le sens juste, ni recourir systématiquement au dictionnaire.

Nous proposons plutôt l'approche suivante :
– apprendre à reconnaître les verbes « de base » (cf. la liste, page 115) ;
– étudier de plus près une dizaine de verbes parmi les plus utiles et les plus « prolifiques » : leur sens de base, les particules avec lesquelles ils s'associent le plus souvent, et quelques expressions idiomatiques courantes mais pas toujours prévisibles ;
– étudier particulièrement une dizaine de particules parmi les plus usuelles : classe, fonction, place, ainsi que quelques expressions idiomatiques.

L'immense terrain occupé par ces verbes ne saurait être entièrement couvert, mais au moins ces indications vous aideront-elles à ne pas vous perdre. Vous trouverez également, en appendice, d'autres exemples de verbes à particule employés dans des phrases.

# 1. *BE*

Nous avons étudié *be* comme « auxiliaire » et « suppléant » (cf. p. 26-27). Nous avons observé qu'il est aussi un verbe à part entière. Dans cet emploi, c'est le verbe d'état par excellence, qu'on peut rapprocher de verbes comme *appear, become, feel, look*, etc.

## LES PARTICULES

● *Be* compte donc parmi les verbes pouvant s'associer à un grand nombre de particules qui lui donnent son dynamisme. Les dictionnaires spécialisés dénombrent un très grand nombre de cas. Les autres classent plus souvent les expressions avec chaque particule, puisqu'elles conservent avec *be* leur sens propre. L'ordre de fréquence est à peu près le suivant.

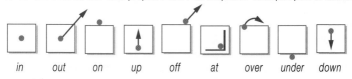

in   out   on   up   off   at   over   under   down

● La particule a parfois une valeur adverbiale.

| | |
|---|---|
| *Is the nail in?* | *The tide is out.* |
| Le clou est-il enfoncé ? | C'est marée basse. |

● Elle a parfois aussi une valeur prépositionnelle.

*Is she on a diet? On the pill?*
Est-ce qu'elle suit un régime ? Est-ce qu'elle prend la pilule ?

● Parfois adverbe et préposition s'associent.

| | |
|---|---|
| *It's up to me.* | *Be off with you!* |
| Cela dépend de moi. | Allez-vous-en ! |

## EXPRESSIONS IDIOMATIQUES

*That's him all over.*
C'est tout à fait lui.
*It's all over for him.*
Il est fichu.
*He's always at her.*
Il la harcèle sans cesse.
*She felt that winning the contest was the be-all and end-all.*
Gagner le concours, croyait-elle, était plus important que tout.

*Why are you down on action movies?*
Pourquoi n'aimes-tu pas les films d'action ?
*She is under the weather.*
Elle n'est pas très bien en ce moment.

# 2. STAND

## LE VERBE DE BASE

*Stand* est aussi un verbe de position. Il exprime l'idée d'« être » mais la prolonge : c'est « être debout », « s'élever », « se dresser », « se maintenir » pour les êtres vivants et pour les choses, au propre et au figuré, aux emplois transitif et intransitif.

*He stood the child on the chair.*      *The child has learned to stand now.*
Il a mis l'enfant debout sur la chaise.     L'enfant sait se tenir debout maintenant.

## LES PARTICULES

Comme pour *be*, chacune d'elles greffe sur le verbe son sens propre pour préciser la position ou suggérer un mouvement.

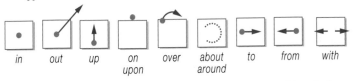

   *in*       *out*      *up*      *on*      *over*     *about*    *to*     *from*     *with*
                             *upon*           *around*

*To, from* et *with* servent souvent à préciser un mouvement par rapport à quelqu'un ou quelque chose d'autre. Toutes les autres particules – auxquelles on peut ajouter *by, off* et *for* – sont utilisables à peu près à égalité d'emploi.

*They stood up when the principal came in.*    *She stands up for human rights.*
Ils se sont levés quand le directeur est entré.   Elle défend les droits de l'homme.

*They stood around, waiting for the lecture*    *He won't do anything good if I don't*
*to begin.*                                 *stand over him.*
Ils se tenaient là, debout, à attendre que    Il ne fera rien de bon si je ne suis pas
le cours commence.                       sur son dos.

*The silhouette of the house stood out*     *We're standing by for further news.*
*against the sky.*                         Nous nous tenons prêts, en attendant
La silhouette de la maison se détachait    d'autres nouvelles.
à l'horizon.

## EXPRESSIONS IDIOMATIQUES

*If she criticizes you again, stand up to her!*   *This lottery ticket doesn't stand a chance*
Si elle te critique encore, fais-lui face !     *of winning.*
*I waited for her but she stood me up.*       Ce billet de loterie n'a aucune chance
Je l'ai attendue, mais elle m'a posé un lapin.   d'être gagnant.

Notons au passage des noms composés comme *a stand-in* (un remplaçant, une doublure), ou *a standby* (une chose sûre ou fiable).

# 3. GO

Go a deux familles de sens plutôt dynamiques.

- L'une est de valeur concrète : « aller », « se rendre à », « fonctionner ».

  *We've gone five kilometres.*
  Nous avons fait cinq kilomètres.

  *How are things going? / How's it going?*
  Comment ça va ?

- L'autre est de valeur abstraite, figurée : « convenir », « devenir ».

  *These colours don't go together.*
  Ces couleurs jurent.

  *He's going bald.*
  Il devient chauve.

## LES PARTICULES

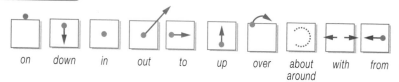

on   down   in   out   to   up   over   about around   with   from

Les emplois les plus nombreux se font avec *on* et *down* qui soulignent la continuité, l'inflexion ou l'arrêt d'un mouvement, au propre et au figuré.

*What's going on here?*
Qu'est-ce qui se passe ici ?

*The price of vegetables goes down in the summer.*
L'été, le prix des légumes baisse.

*Work goes with success.*
Le travail va de pair avec le succès.

*She goes around with a tough crowd.*
Elle fréquente une bande de durs.

On trouve aussi, associés à *go*, d'assez nombreux adjectifs ou noms qui jouent ainsi le rôle de particules.

*go bad* : mal finir
*go slow* : y aller lentement

*go easy* : y aller doucement
*go halves* : partager

## EXPRESSIONS IDIOMATIQUES

*That won't go down with the committee.*
Ça ne prendra pas avec le comité.

*He's going in for karate.*
Il va faire du karaté.

*She's going all out in her studies.*
Elle se donne à fond dans ses études.

*Go for it!*
Fonce !

*She's a real go-getter!*
C'est une vraie battante !

*She never goes back on her word.*
Elle ne revient jamais sur sa parole.

# 4. COME

Come a essentiellement un sens dynamique, propre (venir, arriver) et figuré (devenir).

Come (and) have a drink! Come to think of it, you're right.
Viens prendre un verre ! Tout bien pesé, tu as raison.

To come and go. Come what may.
Aller et venir. Advienne que pourra.

## LES PARTICULES

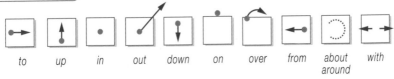

| to | up | in | out | down | on | over | from | about around | with |

- Très nombreuses sont les associations avec quatre particules de mouvement : *to, up, out* et *down*, aux sens propre et figuré, avec des particules adverbiales ou prépositionnelles, et assez souvent les deux successivement.

  She comes up to Montreal from time to time. He often comes up with good ideas.
  Elle monte à Montréal de temps en temps. Il sort souvent de bonnes idées.

- Il y a peu d'emplois avec les autres particules. Citons cependant :
  Tell me how it all came about. Explique-moi comment tout ça s'est produit.

- À noter ici encore l'usage assez fréquent de noms ou d'adjectifs jouant le rôle de particules adverbiales.

  come alive : s'animer       come clean : « tout avouer »
  come good : bien finir malgré tout   come full circle : changer complètement
  come true : se réaliser           d'avis

## EXPRESSIONS IDIOMATIQUES

She came down with the flu. Come off it!
Elle a attrapé la grippe. À d'autres ! Mon œil !

The extra money came in handy. Come on!
L'argent supplémentaire s'est avéré utile. Tu plaisantes !

À noter un nom composé : *a comeback* (un retour sur scène) qui est passé dans l'usage en français.

# 5. RUN

## LE VERBE DE BASE

*Run* a une dizaine de sens différents, tous dynamiques, aussi bien comme intransitif que comme transitif. À côté du sens premier de « courir », on trouve ceux de « fonctionner » et « faire fonctionner ».

*She left the engine running.*
Elle a laissé tourner le moteur.

*They're running a new bus line.*
Ils ont ouvert une nouvelle ligne d'autobus.

Dans un contexte politique, on trouvera :

*They plan to run two candidates.*
Ils ont l'intention de présenter deux candidats.

*He's running for president.*
Il se présente à la présidence.

## LES PARTICULES

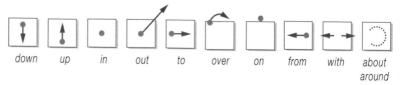

down | up | in | out | to | over | on | from | with | about around

Elles n'ont pas beaucoup à apporter sauf dans les sens figurés.

*There's no need to run all my ideas down.*
Ce n'est pas la peine de dénigrer toutes mes idées.

*This job is running him down.*
Ce travail l'épuise.

*That's a good idea — let's run with it!*
C'est une bonne idée. Allons-y !

*You're run up quite a bill.*
Tu as vraiment laissé monter la facture.

*Time is running out.*
Il nous reste peu de temps.

*That kind of dog often runs to fat.*
Cette race de chien se laisse souvent grossir.

*I need to run off a few copies before the meeting.*
Je dois tirer quelques copies en vitesse avant la réunion.

## EXPRESSIONS IDIOMATIQUES

*Her imagination runs away with her.*
Elle se laisse emporter par son imagination.

*Last time I saw her she ran on at great length about herself.*
La dernière fois que je l'ai vue, elle n'en finissait pas de parler d'elle.

*Curly hair runs in the family.*
C'est de famille, les cheveux bouclés.

*I was fine this morning, but I suddenly ran out of gas.*
J'allais bien ce matin, mais tout à coup, je n'avais plus d'énergie.

# 6. *FALL*

*Fall* exprime évidemment, au sens propre, un mouvement vers le bas, une chute. Au sens figuré, il évoque une sorte de commencement soudain.

*I'm going to fall asleep.*
Je vais m'endormir.

*He fell silent.*
Il se tut.

## Les particules

| in | out off | on | from | to | down | over | back |

On peut ajouter à ces particules, à la place de *up*, des mots comme *away, back* ou *behind*.

- *In* peut avoir une valeur adverbiale aussi bien que prépositionnelle, au sens propre et au sens figuré.

  *The roof has fallen in.*
  Le toit s'est effondré.

  *She fell in love with him immediately.*
  Elle est immédiatement tombée amoureuse de lui.

  *She fell in with his plans immediately.*
  Elle est tout de suite tombée d'accord
  avec ses projets.

- *Fall out* n'exprime pas seulement une sorte de chute, de retombée. Il rend aussi l'idée d'arriver, de devenir ou de se disputer.

  *Everything fell out as we had hoped.*
  Tout s'est passé comme nous l'espérions.

  *They fell out over the inheritance.*
  Ils se sont brouillés au sujet
  de l'héritage.

- Les emplois avec *on* sont multiples, selon le lieu de la « chute ».

  *He always seems to fall on his feet.*
  Il semble toujours retomber sur ses pieds.

  *My birthday falls on a Sunday this year.*
  Mon anniversaire tombe un dimanche
  cette année.

## Expressions idiomatiques

*The comedian's jokes fell flat.*
Les blagues de l'humoriste sont
tombées à plat.
*We almost fell over laughing.*
Nous étions morts de rire.

*During the Depression, many people fell
on hard times.*
Beaucoup de gens ont connu des jours
difficiles pendant la Dépression.

# 7. TAKE

## LE VERBE DE BASE

Les sens issus de *take* (prendre) sont nombreux. Citons :
- mener
    *He'll take you to the station.* Il vous conduira à la gare.
- consommer
    *Do you take sugar in your coffee?* Vous mettez du sucre dans votre café ?
- utiliser
    *It takes two people to do this job.* Il faut deux personnes pour faire ce travail.
- occuper
    *Take a seat, please.* Asseyez-vous, s'il vous plaît.
- choisir
    *What are you taking next year, chemistry or physics?*
    Tu choisis quoi, l'an prochain, la chimie ou la physique ?
- durer
    *The train trip from Toronto to Montreal takes five hours.*
    Le voyage en train de Toronto à Montréal dure cinq heures.

## LES PARTICULES

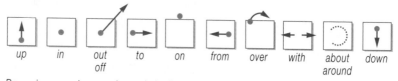

up    in    out off    to    on    from    over    with    about around    down

Pour mieux prendre conscience de la diversité des sens, regardons de plus près *take up*.

*Who will take breakfast up to your mother?*    *The table takes up too much room.*
Qui montera le petit-déjeuner à ta mère ?    La table prend trop d'espace.
*When did you first take up golf?*    *I'll take you up on that.*
Quand t'es-tu mis au golf ?    Je vous prends au mot.

## EXPRESSIONS IDIOMATIQUES

*Do you want to take in a movie?*    *He took to tennis like a duck to water.*
Veux-tu aller au cinéma ?    Il est devenu un mordu du tennis.
*Don't take it out on me!*    *Take it easy!*
Ne t'en prends pas à moi !    Doucement !

Noms composés : *take-out* (mets à emporter), *the take-home pay* (le salaire net), *a give-and-take* (des concessions mutuelles).

# 8. GET

## LE VERBE DE BASE

- Verbe transitif, *get* a de nombreux sens issus du premier : « obtenir ».
  *Did you get the bread?* Tu as acheté le pain ?

- Le plus remarquable est dit « causatif ».
  *I must get my hair cut.* Je dois me faire couper les cheveux.

- Comme intransitif, il a souvent un sens « résultatif ».
  *She's getting old.* Elle vieillit.

## LES PARTICULES

Elles sont nombreuses à s'accrocher à ce verbe, exprimant des mouvements divers et abstraits.

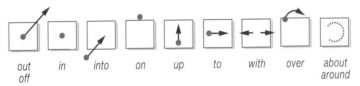

| out off | in | into | on | up | to | with | over | about around |

*The scandal has got out.*
Le scandale a éclaté.

*He got off with a fine.*
Il s'en est tiré avec une amende.

*I couldn't get a word in.*
Je n'ai pas pu placer un mot.

*They got into trouble with the law.*
Ils se sont attiré des ennuis avec la justice.

*I can't get over the fact that he got through his exams.*
Je n'en reviens pas qu'il ait réussi ses examens.

*Let's get down to work.*
Mettons-nous au travail.

*He knows how to get around people.*
Il sait s'y prendre avec les gens.

## EXPRESSIONS IDIOMATIQUES

*She must have got up on the wrong side of the bed.*
Elle a dû se lever du pied gauche.

*Get your act together and start working!*
Fais un effort et commence à travailler !

*He doesn't get out much anymore.*
Il ne sort plus beaucoup.

*Let's get down to brass tacks. Can you afford this?*
Venons-en aux faits. Peux-tu te payer cela ?

*We must have gotten our wires crossed.*
Il a dû y avoir malentendu entre nous.

Encore quelques noms composés : *the getaway* (la fuite), *a get-together* (une petite fête).

# 9. PUT

Put n'a le plus souvent que le sens de « poser », « mettre ».
>He put a lot of money in real estate.
>Il a placé beaucoup d'argent dans l'immobilier.

Le sens peut aussi être figuré.
>How shall I put it?
>Comment dire ?

>I put it to you that she is innocent.
>Mettons qu'elle soit innocente.

## LES PARTICULES

Out, que l'on peut associer à off, de même que in et up sont de loin les plus fréquentes. From, over, about sont quasi absentes, remplacées par away, back et through.

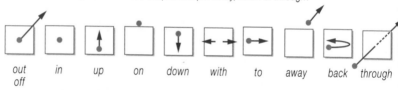

| out off | in | up | on | down | with | to | away | back | through |

>Don't forget to put out the fire.
>N'oublie pas d'éteindre le feu.

>She's always putting herself out for them.
>Elle se met toujours en quatre pour eux.

>Put it off till tomorrow.
>Remets ça à demain.

>My accident put me off swimming.
>Mon accident m'a dégoûté de la natation.

>"He's loyal," she put in.
>« Il est loyal, » fit-elle remarquer.

>Posters have been put up all over the town.
>On a collé des affiches dans toute la ville.

>The argument she put up is not valid.
>L'argument qu'elle a avancé ne tient pas.

>Can you put on the light?
>Peux-tu allumer ?

>Don't put on an English accent.
>Ne fais pas semblant d'avoir l'accent anglais.

>I put down my name for the mixed doubles.
>Je me suis inscrit pour le double mixte.

>He put his mistake down to overwork.
>Il a attribué sa faute au surmenage.

## EXPRESSIONS IDIOMATIQUES

>I won't put up with this!
>Je ne le tolérerai pas !

>Don't put me down in front of the boss!
>Ne me rabaissez pas devant le patron !

# 10. *SET*

## LE VERBE DE BASE

*Set* peut être considéré comme terminant une série d'actes. Comparez : *get* (obtenir une chose), *take* (la prendre), *put* (la mettre quelque part) et enfin *set* (l'installer).

Au sens propre :
*My village is set on the top of the hill.*
Mon village est situé au sommet de la colline.

*She had her hair set.*
Elle s'est fait faire une mise en plis.

Au sens figuré, *set* a parfois une valeur causative.
*It set me thinking.* Cela m'a donné à réfléchir.

## LES PARTICULES

Elles ne modifient pas beaucoup le sens premier, déjà « fixé » (*set*), mais elles le précisent ou l'infléchissent.

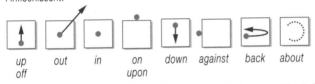

up
off

out

in

on
upon

down

against

back

about

*He set up a business in Montreal.*
Il a monté une affaire à Montréal.
*They set up house together.*
Ils se sont mis en ménage.
*This dress does not set off her eyes.*
Cette robe ne met pas ses yeux en valeur.

*This law has set back the cause of justice.*
Cette loi a fait régresser la cause
de la justice.
*They are set against moving to Ottawa.*
Ils sont contre le fait de déménager
à Ottawa.

*Set* accepte aussi les particules *apart* et *aside*.

*We set apart some clothes
for the baby.*
On a mis de côté des vêtements
pour le bébé.

*Let's set aside our differences.*
Mettons de côté nos différends.

## EXPRESSIONS IDIOMATIQUES

*She has set her sights on becoming a doctor.*
Elle veut absolument devenir médecin.
*He'll never set the world on fire.* Il n'a pas inventé la poudre.

# VERBES À PARTICULE
## Les particules

## À SAVOIR

Ces petits mots (ou groupes de mots), associés à un grand nombre de verbes, forment de multiples expressions verbales (*phrasal verbs*), de sens très variés.

### NATURE DE LA PARTICULE

- Elle peut être un adverbe.
  *I can't put the lid on, the box is too full.*
  Je ne peux pas mettre le couvercle, la boîte est trop pleine.

- Ce peut être une préposition, qui donc introduit un complément.
  *Put the plates on the table gently, please.*
  Mettez les assiettes doucement sur la table, je vous prie.

- Le même verbe peut être suivi d'un adverbe, puis d'une préposition.
  *I know who put him up to cheating.* Je sais qui l'a poussé à tricher.
  *I put up new curtains.*
  J'ai installé des nouveaux rideaux.

- La particule peut être aussi, mais plus rarement, un pronom comme *it*, qui devient donc ainsi une sorte d'adverbe.
  *She took it out on John.*       *He lords it over everybody.*
  Elle s'est défoulée sur John.    Il agit en maître.

- Ce peut être encore un adjectif, ou un nom.
  *I hope my dreams will come true.* J'espère que mes rêves se réaliseront.
  *When will you phone home?* Quand téléphoneras-tu chez toi ?

- Le verbe, enfin, peut être suivi de plusieurs mots, traditionnellement associés, et former des « idiotismes ».
  *She has a tendency to get above herself.*
  Elle a tendance à avoir une trop bonne opinion d'elle-même.
  *Silence fell when the teasing got beyond a joke.*
  Le silence se fit quand les plaisanteries devinrent trop sérieuses.

## FONCTION

La fonction la plus apparente et la plus commune de la particule est de **dynamiser** le verbe de base.

- Elle le dynamise d'autant plus nettement que le sens de ce verbe est plus vague. C'est le cas, par exemple, de *get*, avec lequel elle prend son sens plein.

    *He got up at ten o'clock.*          *She got up on the chair and jumped.*
    Il se leva à dix heures.              Elle monta sur la chaise et sauta.

    *I'll get off at the next stop.*
    Je descendrai (du train, du métro, de l'autobus, etc.) au prochain arrêt.

- Lorsque le verbe est déjà porteur d'une idée de mouvement, celui-ci est précisé par la particule. C'est le cas, par exemple, de *drive*, de *walk* ou de *jump*.

    *He first drove to the station, then (drove) away, then (drove) back and finally decided to drive home.*
    D'abord, il roula vers la gare, s'en éloigna, revint en arrière et, enfin, décida de revenir chez lui.

- Elle peut même transformer un verbe de position en verbe de mouvement.

    *I'll lie down for a while.* Je vais m'allonger un moment.

- Quelques verbes formés à partir du nom d'un objet n'existent pas sans particule.

    *The boat keeled over.* Le bateau chavira. (*a keel* = une quille)


## PLACE

- Avec un verbe intransitif, la particule se place presque toujours immédiatement après le verbe.

    *Come in and sit down.* Entrez et asseyez-vous.

    Parfois, elle se place en tête de phrase, pour insister sur la rapidité du mouvement.

    *Off we go.* Et nous voilà partis.

- Avec un verbe transitif, il convient de faire la différence entre particule adverbiale et particule prépositionnelle.

  ### • Particule adverbiale.
  Si le complément est un groupe nominal court, on la trouve soit avant, soit après.

    *Bring up the chairs. Bring the chairs up.* Remonte les chaises.

    Si le complément est un pronom, elle est toujours placée après.

    *Bring them up from the basement.* Remonte-les du sous-sol.

    Elle ne peut se trouver séparée du verbe par un complément long.

    *Bring in the chairs that you put outside yesterday.*
    Rentre les chaises que tu as sorties hier.

  ### • Particule prépositionnelle.
  Elle se place évidemment avant le complément, sauf dans une proposition relative et à la forme interrogative.

    *This is the person (whom) I brought the chairs for.*      *Who(m) shall I give the chairs to?*
    Voici la personne pour qui j'ai apporté les chaises.       À qui vais-je donner les chaises ?

# À LA RECHERCHE DU SENS

## COMPLEXITÉ )

Ce qui rend la recherche du sens plus difficile, c'est que les particules peuvent non seulement caractériser un mouvement ou un état, mais se rapporter à des êtres animés aussi bien qu'à des objets, et donner au verbe un sens concret, propre, ou un sens abstrait, figuré. Il faut donc essayer de repérer, d'après le contexte, dans quelle direction fonctionne la particule.

## LE FONCTIONNEMENT LE PLUS SIMPLE )

Ce n'est pas tant le verbe que le rôle de la particule qui pose problème. On donnera donc la priorité à celle-ci, en traduisant d'abord le résultat de l'action exprimée par la particule. On traduira ensuite le verbe qui décrit la manière dont l'action est accomplie.

## LES IDIOTISMES )

- Dans l'usage, la fonction dynamisante de la particule n'est pas toujours clairement reconnaissable. Les dictionnaires généraux, selon leur ambition, donnent, à la suite de chaque verbe ordinaire, une liste d'emplois avec telle ou telle particule. Il existe aussi plusieurs dictionnaires spécialisés dans les *phrasal verbs*. Seul le recours à ces ouvrages permettra d'élucider le sens de certains verbes à particule : si le sens de *go up* est évident, auriez-vous pu deviner, par exemple, celui de *make up* ?

    *She makes up her eyes beautifully.*
    Elle se maquille très joliment les yeux.
    *He's made up the whole story.*
    Il a inventé toute l'histoire.
    *We'll have to make up for lost time.*
    Il nous faudra rattraper le temps perdu.
    *Let's kiss and make up!*
    Si on faisait la paix ?
    *Make up your mind.*
    Décide-toi.

• Nous avons retenu dix particules très fréquentes, qui feront l'objet d'une étude détaillée dans les pages suivantes. Les voici dans leur ordre de fréquence : 1. *up*, 2. *out*, 3. *in*, 4. *down*, 5. *on*, 6. *over*, 7. *with*, 8. *to*, 9. *from*, 10. *about / around.*

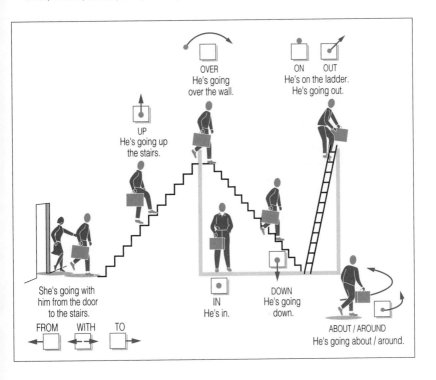

OVER
He's going
over the wall.

ON    OUT
He's on the ladder.
He's going out.

UP
He's going up
the stairs.

She's going with
him from the door
to the stairs.

FROM    WITH    TO

IN
He's in.

DOWN
He's going
down.

ABOUT / AROUND
He's going about / around.

• Pour les vingt autres particules les plus fréquentes, cf. p. 72-73.

# 1. *UP*

*Up* exprime le plus souvent un mouvement, dans le sens concret vers le haut, ou une position « en hauteur », pour les êtres vivants comme pour les choses. Dans les sens abstraits et figurés, il s'agit plutôt de mouvements ou de positions approchant d'un paroxysme, de la perfection, de l'achèvement d'une action.

*She threw the ball up.* Elle a jeté la balle en l'air.
*He drove up the street.* Il remonta la rue en voiture.

LES ASSOCIATIONS )

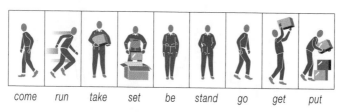

come    run    take    set    be    stand    go    get    put

*I like watching the sun come up.*
J'aime regarder le soleil se lever.
*All my time is taken up with
committee meetings.*
Les réunions de comité me
prennent tout mon temps.

*The ship has run up the red flag.*
Le navire a hissé le drapeau rouge.
*I'll take that up with the new teacher.*
J'en parlerai au nouveau professeur.

EXPRESSIONS IDIOMATIQUES )

*The status of the project is up in the air.*
L'état du projet est incertain.
*What's up (with you)?*
Qu'est-ce que tu as ?

*He's up to no good.*
Il prépare quelque sottise.
*I don't feel up to it.*
Je ne m'en sens pas le courage.

Cette particule est si robuste qu'elle peut même assumer le rôle d'un verbe à elle toute seule.
*She just suddenly upped and left.*
Sans plus attendre, elle est partie brusquement.

Retenez le nom composé *setup*, qui signifie « situation » ou « installation ».
*I don't like that setup at all.*          *Program setup.*
Je n'aime pas du tout l'allure de tout ça.   Installation du logiciel.

# 2. OUT

Au propre comme au figuré, *out* apporte l'idée de « dehors », de « à l'extérieur ».

| | |
|---|---|
| *The ball is out of bounds.* | *Out with it!* |
| La balle est sortie du terrain. | Dis ce que tu as à dire ! |
| *He lives out of town.* | *She feels out of it.* |
| Il ne vit pas en ville. | Elle se sent en marge. |

## LES ASSOCIATIONS )

get   put   set   fall   be   stand   take   come   go   run

- Elles se font surtout avec les verbes rendant compte de positions et de mouvements de personnes ou de choses, en particulier *get*.

  | | |
  |---|---|
  | *The news has just got out.* | *That wasn't what I set out to do.* |
  | La nouvelle vient de paraître. | Ce n'est pas ce que je voulais faire initialement. |

- Les sens sont nombreux avec *be, run, come*.

  | | |
  |---|---|
  | *The secret is out.* | *The tulips are out.* |
  | On a vendu la mèche. | Les tulipes sont en fleurs. |
  | *We've run out of gas.* | *It came out that he was not working.* |
  | On est tombés à court d'essence. | Il s'avéra qu'il ne travaillait pas. |

## EXPRESSIONS IDIOMATIQUES )

| | |
|---|---|
| *Let's hang out at the mall.* | *I'm afraid you're out of luck.* |
| Allons flâner au centre commercial. | Je crains que vous n'ayez pas de chance. |
| *That child is wearing me out.* | *That style is out!* |
| Cet enfant m'épuise. | Ce style est démodé ! |
| *Watch out — they're out for blood!* | *I'm really put out with them.* |
| Fais attention ! Ils cherchent à se venger ! | Je ne suis vraiment pas content d'eux. |

On retrouve ce mot comme préfixe dans de nombreux composés : *outdated* (suranné), *outlive* (survivre), etc. (cf. p. 75).

# 3. *IN*

## Sens de base

- Avec *in*, il s'agit surtout de décrire des positions à l'intérieur d'un lieu, d'une période, de circonstances.

  *Is anybody in?* Il y a quelqu'un ?
  *Come in! / Get in!* Entrez !

- Il y a beaucoup d'emplois au figuré.
  *We're in the money.* Nous sommes riches.

## Les associations

| be | stand | fall | take | get | put | come | go | run | set |

*I wasn't in on it.*
Je n'étais pas dans le coup.

*The train is in.*
Le train est en gare.

*We took in a movie on our way home.*
On est allés au cinéma au retour.

*She couldn't take in the situation.*
Elle n'arrivait pas à bien comprendre la situation.

*He's got in with bad company.*
Il a de mauvaises fréquentations.

*She got in with a scholarship.*
Elle est entrée grâce à une bourse.

*She has come in first.*
Elle a le premier prix.

*They fell in with party-goers at the hotel.*
Ils se sont joints à des fêtards à l'hôtel.

*I put in three hours a day looking after him.*
Je consacre trois heures par jour à m'occuper de lui.

*He doesn't go in for reading very much.*
Il ne s'intéresse pas beaucoup à la lecture.

*The rain has set in for the night.*
Il va pleuvoir toute la nuit.

*Sarah stood in for me at the office while I was on holiday.*
Sarah m'a remplacé au bureau lorsque j'étais en vacances.

## Expressions idiomatiques

*Our candidate is in.*
Notre candidate a été élue.

*The teacher had it in for me.*
Le professeur en avait contre moi.

# 4. DOWN

## SENS DE BASE

- Au sens propre, *down* exprime un mouvement vers le bas jusqu'à un effet d'anéantissement ou d'échec.

  *He fell down.*　　　　　　　　　　*Down with the tyrant!*
  Il est tombé.　　　　　　　　　　　À bas le tyran !

- Au figuré, *down* indique une diminution, une réduction.

  *Please slow down.* Ralentis, s'il te plaît.
  *Prices seldom go down.*
  Les prix vont rarement à la baisse.

## LES ASSOCIATIONS

go　　run　　come　　put　　get　　set　　take　　be　　fall

*She feels a little run down.*　　　　*I took down all that you said.*
Elle se sent à plat / mal fichue.　　　J'ai pris en note toutes vos paroles.
*I put him down as a crook.*　　　　*She came down with the flu.*
Je le prends pour un escroc.　　　　Elle a attrapé la grippe.
*Don't let things get you down.*　　　*She's falling down on the job.*
Ne te laisse pas abattre.　　　　　　Elle ne réussit pas dans son travail.

## EXPRESSIONS IDIOMATIQUES

*He's down and out.*　　　　　　　*I am down on my luck.*
Il est sans le sou.　　　　　　　　Je n'ai pas de chance.
*Let's get down to business!*　　　　*She's always putting you down.*
Mettons-nous au travail !　　　　　Elle est toujours en train de te rabaisser.

Remarquez l'emploi de *down* dans certains mots composés comme a *down-to-earth person* (une personne qui a les pieds sur terre) ou *down-under* (aux antipodes).

Enfin, comme *up*, le mot peut être un verbe en soi.
*The Canadiens downed the Red Wings last night.*
Les Canadiens ont battu les Red Wings hier soir.

# 5. ON

- Au sens propre, *on* évoque un état de contact.
  *Put your hat on. / Put on your hat.*    *Don't throw it on (to) the floor.*
  Mets ton chapeau.                        Ne le jette pas sur le plancher.

- Au sens figuré, on dira :
  *She put a good face on a bad situation.* Elle a fait contre mauvaise fortune bon cœur.

- *On* exprime aussi une progression, une continuité.
  *Read on.* Continuez à lire.             *I'll follow on after you.* J'enchaînerai après vous.

Ne confondez pas les deux sens de *on*. Comparez :
  *Go on!* Continue !
  *The police had no clue to go on.* La police n'avait aucun indice sur quoi s'appuyer.

## LES ASSOCIATIONS )

go    be    get    put    set    take    fall    come    stand    run

*On* est le plus souvent associé aux verbes décrivant plutôt des positions et des mouvements.

*We'll come on the 1st of May.*          *They set the police on the wrong track.*
Nous viendrons le premier mai.           Ils ont mis la police sur une fausse piste.

*"Get on!" the bus driver said.*         *I feel that I am taking on too much.*
« Montez ! » dit le chauffeur d'autobus.  J'ai l'impression d'en prendre trop.

*The Stratford Theatre has put*          *They put me on to a good deal.*
*"Macbeth" on.*                          Ils m'indiquèrent une bonne aubaine.
On joue « Macbeth » à Stratford.

## EXPRESSIONS IDIOMATIQUES )

*We had a drink on the house.*           *She's on the pill.*
Le patron a offert la tournée.           Elle prend la pilule.

*We see them on and off.*                *Are we on for lunch?*
On les voit de temps à autre.            Est-ce qu'on va dîner ensemble ?

Noms composés : *onlooker* (badaud, spectateur), *online* (en réseau), *onshore* (à terre).

# 6. OVER

## SENS DE BASE

- Au sens propre, *over* ajoute l'idée d'un mouvement par dessus ou d'une position au-dessus de quelque chose.

    *The plane was flying over Halifax.* L'avion survolait Halifax.

- Au figuré, *over* décrit souvent une évolution dans le temps ou ce qui reste à la fin d'une période.

    *Over the last ten years he has travelled a lot.*
    Il a beaucoup voyagé ces dix dernières années.
    *Take what is left over.* Prenez ce qui reste.
    *Game over.* Fin de la partie.

## LES ASSOCIATIONS

go  come  run  fall  get  take  put  stand  set

*Let's go / run over the events of that period.*
Révisons les événements de cette période.
*What came over her?*
Qu'est-ce qui lui a pris ?
*The car ran over the bicycle in the driveway.*
La voiture a écrasé une bicyclette dans l'allée.

*The chair fell over.*
La chaise a basculé.
*I can't get over the fact that he got through his exam.*
Je n'en reviens pas qu'il ait réussi son examen.
*He took over the shop from his father.*
Il a repris le magasin de son père.

## EXPRESSIONS IDIOMATIQUES

*They think you're all over the hill if you are 60.*
Ils pensent qu'on est fichu après 60 ans.
*He's gone over the edge.*
Il a dépassé les bornes.

*She's falling over herself to be nice.*
Elle se met en quatre pour être aimable.
*Let's get this over with!*
Finissons-en !

Notons enfin que *over* entre dans la composition de nombreux mots, dont beaucoup de verbes : *overwork* (surmener), *overcook* (trop cuire), *overlook* (laisser échapper), etc.

# 7. WITH

- *With* ne peut être qu'une particule prépositionnelle. Elle est très utilisée, à cause de la diversité de ses sens.

- Initialement, elle indique l'accompagnement, la relation, et jusqu'à l'harmonie entre personnes et choses.

*Who(m) do you work with?*
Avec qui travaillez-vous ?

*She lives with two roommates.*
Elle habite avec deux colocataires.

*Fill all the glasses with water.*
Remplissez tous les verres d'eau.

- Mais le sens peut s'étendre jusqu'à exprimer, entre autres :
  - La manière : *Please handle this package with care* (avec grand soin).
  - Le moyen : *I saw it with my own eyes* (de mes propres yeux).
  - La cause : *She's shivering with cold* (de froid).
  - Le temps : *With time, he's gaining wisdom* (le temps passant)

## LES ASSOCIATIONS )

*With* est employée avec pratiquement tous les verbes les plus prolifiques, et très souvent à la suite d'une autre particule.

*Come on, don't be old-fashioned, get with it.*
Allons, ne sois pas vieux jeu, sois dans le coup.

*Try to get on well with him.*
Essaie de te mettre bien avec lui.

*He is in with some very well-known people.*
Il fréquente des gens très connus.

*How are things with you?*
Et vous, comment ça va ?

## EXPRESSIONS IDIOMATIQUES )

*Are you with me?*
Vous me suivez ? / Vous me comprenez ?

*Get with it! She's lying to you!*
Ouvre les yeux ! Elle te ment !

*Couldn't you put up with him just a bit longer?*
Ne pourriez-vous pas le supporter un peu plus longtemps ?

Remarquez enfin les verbes *withdraw* (retirer), *withstand* (supporter) et les noms dérivés : *withdrawal* (retrait)...

# 8. *TO*

*To* illustre, au propre comme au figuré, la direction d'un mouvement et éventuellement son aboutissement.

*You should go to their house.*
Vous devriez aller chez eux.

*He's our ambassador to Belgium.*
Il est notre ambassadeur en Belgique.

En anglais, on imagine plus précisément ce mouvement qu'en français. De même dans les exemples suivants.

*It is a quarter to four.*
Il est quatre heures moins le quart.

*One person to a room.*
Une personne par pièce.

Remarquez que *to* est traduit en français par des formulations utilisant des prépositions différentes.

## LES ASSOCIATIONS

go    come    take    get    put    run    set    stand    be

*I have come to the last chapter in the book.*
J'en suis au dernier chapitre du livre.

*She has taken to jogging.*
Elle s'est mise à faire du jogging.

*How can I get the package to him?*
Comment lui faire parvenir le colis ?

*I'll put / set him to work right away.*
Je vais le mettre au travail tout de suite.

*Trains to Moncton have been delayed.*
Les trains à destination de Moncton ont du retard.

*Have you been to Paris?*
Êtes-vous allé à Paris ?

## EXPRESSIONS IDIOMATIQUES

*What would you say to a beer?*
Que diriez-vous d'une bière ?

*Here's to you!*
À la vôtre !

*There's nothing to it.*
Rien de plus facile.

*That actor has gone to the dogs.*
Ce comédien est ruiné.

*It stands to reason that she got the promotion.*
On comprend qu'elle ait eu la promotion.

*I don't think she's equal to the task.*
Je ne crois pas qu'elle soit à la hauteur de la tâche.

*He's just come to.*
Il vient de reprendre connaissance.

# 9. FROM

- *From* ne peut être que préposition.

- Au sens propre, il marque un point de départ, souvent associé à *to*, qui peut désigner un point d'arrivée. Il est alors souvent traduit par « de », « depuis ».

| | |
|---|---|
| *From next week on...* | *Where are you from?* |
| À compter de la semaine prochaine... | D'où êtes-vous ? |
| *Judging from appearances...* | *From what I have heard...* |
| Apparemment... | D'après ce que j'ai entendu dire... |
| *A portrait painted from life.* | *Breakfast is served from 6 a.m. to 10 a.m.* |
| Un portrait d'après nature. | On sert le petit déjeuner de 6 h à 10 h. |

Il précède d'autres prépositions comme *behind, above, over there.*

## Les associations )

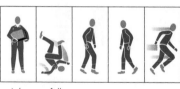

take    fall    go    come    run

*The teacher took the exam text from the newspaper.*
Le professeur a puisé le texte de l'examen dans le journal.

*He has stolen a lot of money from his clients.*
Il a volé beaucoup d'argent à ses clients.

*Keep him from talking to her.*
Empêchez-le de lui parler.

*Let's go inside and take shelter from the rain.*
Rentrons nous abriter de la pluie.

*She comes from Vancouver.*
Elle vient de Vancouver.

*He is running from the law.*
Il fuit la justice.

*I haven't heard from them in years.*
Cela fait des années que je n'ai pas eu de leurs nouvelles.

## Expressions idiomatiques )

*They are living from hand to mouth.*
Ils vivent au jour le jour.

*She did it herself from start to finish.*
Elle l'a fait elle-même, du début à la fin.

# 10. *AROUND / ABOUT / ROUND*

Ces particules apportent à peu près le même sens à la majorité des verbes de notre liste :
« non loin », « autour », « aux alentours ». *Around* est d'usage courant en Amérique du Nord.
*About* n'est presque jamais employé dans le sens de déplacement ou d'emplacement. On
emploie aussi *round*, mais moins souvent que *around*. On se référera à l'appendice, page
220, pour des exemples précis de *about*, *around* et *round*.

> *She is around somewhere.*        *He walked around the lake.*
> Elle n'est pas loin.        Il a fait le tour du lac.

**LES ASSOCIATIONS**

   go     come    get     run     take     be     stand    set

*I always go around by bus.*
Je circule toujours en bus.

*Your birthday will come around soon.*
Ce sera bientôt ton anniversaire.

*Stories have been going round about him.*
Des rumeurs ont couru à son sujet.

*How do you go about getting permission?*
Comment s'y prend-on pour avoir
l'autorisation ?

*She was about to call the police.*
Elle était sur le point d'appeler la police.

*What about me?*
Et moi, alors ?

*No, it's the other way around.*
Non, c'est dans l'autre sens.

*She is always out and about somewhere.*
Elle est toujours sortie quelque part.

*This singer has been around for years.*
Ça fait des années que ce chanteur se
produit sur scène.

**EXPRESSIONS IDIOMATIQUES**

*What goes around comes around.*
On récolte ce que l'on sème.

*Their wedding anniversary is just
around the corner.*
C'est bientôt leur anniversaire
de mariage.

Un mot composé intéressant : *I don't know his whereabouts.* (Je ne sais où il est exactement.)

# 11. VINGT AUTRES PARTICULES

Elles peuvent être adverbe ou préposition. Elles sont ici données dans l'ordre alphabétique, accompagnées de leur sens de base, d'un exemple et d'une expression idiomatique.

- *Above* : au-dessus, en haut (plus haut qu'avec *over*).

  *It's thirty degrees above zero outside.*
  Dehors, il fait trente degrés au-dessus de zéro.

  *This is above me.*
  C'est trop compliqué pour moi.

- *Across* : de l'autre côté d'une ligne ou d'une surface.

  *She lived across the street.*
  Elle vivait de l'autre côté de la rue.

  *He couldn't get it across to me.*
  Il n'a pas pu me le faire comprendre.

- *Against* : contre ; contraire de *with*.

  *He was leaning against the fence.*
  Il s'appuyait contre la clôture.

  *She put money aside against her retirement.*
  Elle a mis de l'argent de côté en prévision de la retraite.

- *Along* : mouvement le long d'une ligne.

  *There were trees along the road.*
  Des arbres longeaient la route.

  *Come along, children!*
  Venez, les enfants !

- *Apart* : à côté, à l'écart.

  *It came apart in my hands.*
  Ça s'est démonté tout seul.

  *You can't tell them apart.*
  On ne peut pas les distinguer l'un de l'autre.

- *At* : indique une position et une direction.

  *He aimed at the target.*
  Il visa la cible.

  *She feels at home here.*
  Elle se sent chez elle ici.

- *Away* : éloignement, absence.

  *Did you take my book away?*
  As-tu emporté mon livre ?

  *Right away.*
  Immédiatement, tout de suite.

- *Back* : en arrière (*back* indique un retour en arrière, ou à une position antérieure).

  *He ran without looking back.*
  Il courait sans se retourner.

  *Don't go back on your word!*
  Ne reviens pas sur ta parole !

- *Before* : en avant dans le temps, dans le lieu, dans l'ordre ; contraire de *after*.

  *You should have told me before.*
  Tu aurais dû me le dire avant.

  *I never put business before pleasure.*
  Je ne mets jamais le travail avant le plaisir.

- *By* : position ou mouvement à côté d'un repère.

  *She rushed by me.*
  Elle est passée à côté de moi en courant.

  *It's difficult but we'll get by.*
  C'est difficile mais nous y arriverons.

- *For* : vers une destination, un but, un désir, une certitude.
    *I took something for the flu.*         *We're in for it!*
    J'ai pris quelque chose contre la grippe.   Ça va barder !

- *Forth* : mouvement vers l'avant (proche de *forward*).
    *She was walking back and forth.*     *He brought forth many ideas.*
    Elle marchait de long en large.       Il a proposé des idées intéressantes.

- *Into* : mouvement vers l'intérieur, changement d'état.
    *The car crashed into a wall.*       *I'm not into it.*
    La voiture s'est écrasée contre un mur.   Ça n'est pas mon truc.

- *Like* : comparaison entre deux états ou mouvements.
    *It smells like gas.*             *What's she like?*
    Ça sent l'essence.             De quoi a-t-elle l'air ?

- *Of* : marque des rapports comme l'origine, la possession, la cause.
    *This bracelet is made of gold.*     *What do you think of this?*
    Ce bracelet est en or.          Qu'en dis-tu ?

- *Off* : interruption, éloignement, contraste avec *on*.
    *The farm is about 500 metres off the road.*  *Good bye, I'm off.*
    La ferme se situe à environ 500 mètres   Au revoir, je m'en vais.
    de la route.

- *Past* : mouvement près de ou au-delà.
    *He ran past me.*             *She is past caring.*
    Il est passé près de moi en courant.   Elle n'en a plus rien à faire.

- *Through* : traversée par l'intérieur, à travers.
    *I saw her through the window.*     *He got through all his exams.*
    Je l'ai vue par la fenêtre.         Il a été reçu à tous ses examens.

- *Under* : sous, au-dessous.
    *The dog is under the table.*      *Look in the phone book under "plumbers".*
    Le chien est sous la table.       Cherche dans l'annuaire sous la rubrique
                                  « plombiers ».

- *Within / Without* : à l'intérieur / à l'extérieur.
    *The fire truck arrived within minutes.*  *I can't do without this book.*
    La voiture à incendie est arrivée en    Je ne peux me passer de ce livre.
    l'espace de quelques minutes.

# FORMATION DES VERBES

Comme les noms ou les adjectifs, les verbes sont souvent des « hybrides ». Tantôt ils se sont formés à partir de mots appartenant à une autre catégorie par simple **conversion** ; tantôt ils sont le résultat de l'addition de deux mots, c'est une **composition** ; tantôt ils sont créés à l'aide d'un préfixe ou d'un suffixe, et l'on parle de **dérivation**.

## PAR CONVERSION

- C'est encore un caractère de l'anglais que d'avoir, par exemple, la possibilité de passer du nom *bottle* au verbe *to bottle* (mettre en bouteille) et même au verbe à particule *to bottle up* qui, au figuré, signifie « contenir », « refouler ».

| | |
|---|---|
| *He tends to bottle up his anger.* | *She headed the transition team.* |
| Il a tendance à ravaler sa colère. | Elle dirigeait l'équipe de transition. |
| *He's coated the cake with sugar.* | *She hammered her point home.* |
| Il a enrobé le gâteau de sucre. | Elle répétait son argument. |

- L'anglais peut passer, de même, de l'adjectif au verbe.

| | |
|---|---|
| *Calm down.* | *They emptied all the bottles.* |
| Calme-toi. | Ils ont vidé toutes les bouteilles. |

Notez qu'il y a parfois cependant un changement d'orthographe comme dans *advice* (des conseils) qui devient *to advise*, ou un déplacement de l'accent, comme dans *a 'present* qui devient *to pre'sent*.

## PAR COMPOSITION

Les exemples en sont plus rares, mais on peut toujours en créer, du moment qu'on se fait comprendre.

| | |
|---|---|
| *The car backfired.* | *He sleepwalks.* |
| Le voiture pétaradait. | Il est somnambule. |
| *The plan backfired.* | *She spends her time daydreaming.* |
| Le projet a échoué. | Elle ne cesse de rêvasser. |

## PAR DÉRIVATION

- **Suffixes**
  Certains sont d'origine française et correspondent parfaitement à la façon de faire en français, comme *-ize / -ise* : *nationalize*, « nationaliser ».

Un grand nombre, en -en, ont un sens réfléchi ou passif, et sont construits à partir d'adjectifs. Ils appartiennent au langage concret des couleurs, des dimensions et des formes.

*Her parents' praise softened*
*her disappointment.*
Les éloges de ses parents ont
atténué sa déception.

*This new information weakens*
*your argument.*
Cette nouvelle information affaiblit
votre argument.

- **Préfixes**
  - *Dis-*, dont le sens est négatif.
    *I disagree with you: you are distorting the meaning of my words.*
    Je ne suis pas d'accord avec vous, vous dénaturez mes paroles.

  - *Re-*, qui, comme en français, marque la répétition ou le retour.
    *He reappeared in the meetings as soon as he was reappointed.*
    Il a reparu dans les réunions dès qu'il a été réintégré.

  - *Mis-*, qui souligne une erreur.
    *I don't know if I was misled or misunderstood.*
    Je ne sais pas si on m'a envoyé dans la mauvaise direction ou si on m'a mal compris.

  - *Over-*, qui marque un excès.
    *"I am overworked." "Oh, come on! Don't overdo it."*
    « Je suis surmené. » « Oh, ça va ! N'en fais pas trop ! »

  - *Un-* (défaire).
    *They unearthed the body and uncovered the truth about the murder.*
    Ils déterrèrent le corps et découvrirent la vérité sur le meurtre.

  - *Under-* (contraire de *over-*).
    *They had underestimated the opposition and understated its case.*
    Ils ont sous-estimé l'opposition et minimisé les arguments de celle-ci.

  - *In-* (ou *en-*) et *inter-*.
    *We're inquiring about a tutor who interacts well with children.*
    Nous recherchons un tuteur qui communique bien avec les enfants.

  - *Sub-*.
    *The storm subsided.* La tempête se calma.

  - *Trans-*.
    *He was transfixed with fear.* Il fut pétrifié de peur.

  - *For-* a le sens de *away* dans, par exemple, *forbid*.
    *They forbid their children to see certain movies.*
    Ils interdisent à leurs enfants de voir certains films.

  - *Fore-* a le sens de *in front of*, en avant.
    *You should have foreseen it.* Vous auriez dû le prévoir.

  - *Counter-*.
    *They counteracted their increasing costs by raising prices.*
    Ils contrecarraient la hausse de leurs coûts en augmentant les prix.

# COMPLÉMENTS DU VERBE

## À SAVOIR

Qu'ils soient groupe du nom ou groupe du verbe, les compléments du verbe forment un système aussi diversifié et étendu que le système des particules.

VERBES TRANSITIFS ET VERBES INTRANSITIFS )

- **Verbes transitifs**
  > *Tell me, have you read this book ?*
  > Dites-moi, est-ce que vous avez lu ce livre ?

  Est transitif tout verbe qui, comme *read* ici, peut être suivi d'un complément direct.

- **Verbes intransitifs**
  > *Come in and sit down.* Entrez et asseyez-vous.

  Les verbes *come in* et *sit down* sont intransitifs, car ils ne peuvent jamais avoir de complément direct.

- **De nombreux verbes peuvent être transitifs et intransitifs.**
  > *He has adapted his book for the stage.*
  > Il a adapté son livre pour la scène.
  > *She refused to adapt.*
  > Elle a refusé de s'adapter.

VERBES TRANSITIFS AVEC UN COMPLÉMENT )

- **Le complément est un groupe du nom.**
  Très nombreux sont les verbes simples complétés directement par un groupe du nom ou par un pronom. La syntaxe, dans ce cas, ne pose pas de problème.
  > *Have you read all these books? Yes, I have read them all.*
  > Avez-vous lu tous ces livres ? Oui, je les ai tous lus.

  La construction est plus complexe en ce qui concerne la place du complément quand il s'agit de verbes à particule (cf. p. 59).

- **Le complément est un groupe du verbe.**
  Il existe plusieurs types de complémentation, chacune apportant sa nuance particulière.
  - La forme infinitive avec *to*.
    > *I want him to come at once.*
    > Je veux qu'il vienne tout de suite.

- La forme infinitive sans *to*.
    *I heard him open the door.*
    Je l'ai entendu ouvrir la porte.
- Forme en *-ing*.
    *I can't resist asking the question.*
    Je ne résiste pas à l'envie de poser la question.
- Préposition suivie d'une forme en *-ing*.
    *I'm interested in going to Cuba this summer.*
    Ça m'intéresse d'aller à Cuba cet été.
- Complétive introduite par *that*, en particulier au style indirect.
    *She said that she was intrigued by the idea.*
    Elle a dit que l'idée l'intriguait.
- Interrogative indirecte.
    *He wondered why she looked so angry.*
    Il se demanda pourquoi elle avait l'air tellement fâchée.
- Verbe au prétérit modal (cf. p. 19).
    *I wish you were here.*
    Je regrette que tu ne sois pas ici.

## VERBES TRANSITIFS AVEC DEUX COMPLÉMENTS

- **Complément direct + complément indirect.**
    *You gave your friend a strange answer.*
    *You gave a strange answer to your friend.*
    Vous avez donné à votre ami une réponse étrange.

Remarquez la place du complément indirect *your friend* selon que l'on emploie la préposition *to* ou non.

Autres verbes de cette catégorie utilisant :
- **to**: read, sell, send.
- **for**: look, bring, buy, choose, find, get, pay, reach.
- **from**: buy, steal.

- *Attribut du complément direct ou indirect.*
    *Reading makes me happy.*
    La lecture me rend heureux.
    *Love has made him a different man.*
    L'amour a fait de lui un autre homme.

L'attribut du complément peut être un adjectif *(happy)* ou un groupe du nom *(a different man)*.

Trois de ces constructions font l'objet des pages qui suivent : **la forme en -ing**, l'infinitif et **le style indirect**.

# 1. LA FORME EN -*ING*

Avec la forme en -*ing*, l'action est souvent vue de manière **concrète**. Dans beaucoup de cas, cette forme exprime une **attitude personnelle** envers l'action concernée :

• Soit plutôt favorable.
> *I enjoy going to movies...*
> J'aime beaucoup aller au cinéma...

• Soit plutôt défavorable.
> *... but I avoid watching horror films.*
> ... mais j'évite de voir des films d'horreur.

• Soit neutre.
> *Have you ever considered working in Europe?*
> Avez-vous jamais envisagé de travailler en Europe ?

## STRUCTURES )

● **Construction directe**
> *I enjoy walking on the beach.*
> J'aime bien me promener sur la plage.

Cette construction est adoptée par de très nombreux verbes comme *enjoy, appreciate, avoid, detest, dread* (craindre), *consider*, etc.

● **Après une préposition**
> *She would benefit from taking a course in accounting.*
> Cela lui ferait du bien de suivre un cours de comptabilité.

Parmi les verbes de ce type, les plus fréquents sont *consent to* (consentir à), *congratulate on* (féliciter de), *reproach for / with* (reprocher de), *think of* (envisager), *agree about* (être d'accord pour), etc.

● **Avec un complément interposé ou, plus souvent, un génitif**
> *I enjoy John / him coming to talk with me.*
> *I enjoy John's / his coming to talk with me.*
> J'aime quand John / il vient bavarder avec moi.

Notez quelques expressions courantes bâties sur ces structures :
*I don't mind, I can't bear, I can't stand, it's no use, it's no good, it is(n't) worth*, etc.
> *I can't bear his talking all the time.*
> Je ne supporte pas son bavardage permanent.
> *It's no use buying expensive shoes that you'll only wear once.*
> Cela ne sert à rien d'acheter des chaussures coûteuses que tu ne mettras qu'une seule fois.

- **Après des verbes exprimant une perception**

> *I can smell something burning.*
> Je sens qu'il y a quelque chose qui brûle.
> *Can you hear that bird singing in the distance?*
> Entends-tu cet oiseau qui chante au loin ?
> *He felt a spider creeping up his leg.*
> Il sentit qu'une araignée grimpait le long de sa jambe.
> *Look at that horse running in the meadow.*
> Regarde ce cheval qui court dans le pré.
> *I can see something climbing up the tree.*
> Je peux voir quelque chose qui monte dans l'arbre.

Remarquez l'emploi bien particulier de la forme en *-ing* associée aux particules *into* et *out of* après certains verbes exprimant la manière dont on peut influencer quelqu'un (*into* pour persuader et *out of* pour dissuader) :

coax (câliner), pressure (faire pression), shock, badger (importuner), etc.

> *I'll try talk to her into accepting the proposal.*
> Nous allons lui parler pour la persuader d'accepter la proposition.
> *The boss pressured them into working overtime.*
> Le patron a exercé des pressions sur eux afin qu'ils fassent des heures supplémentaires.
> *The bad news shocked me out of going on holiday.*
> La mauvaise nouvelle m'a bouleversé à un point tel que je ne suis pas parti en vacances.
> *She coaxed the cat into coming down the tree.*
> À force de cajoleries, elle a réussi à faire descendre le chat de l'arbre.
> *She badgered her parents into teaching her to drive.*
> Elle a harcelé ses parents pour qu'ils lui apprennent à conduire.

Notez qu'une fois encore le verbe indique le moyen, et la particule le résultat (cf. p. 60).

## 2. L'INFINITIF

Avec l'infinitif, l'action est vue le plus souvent d'une manière plus **abstraite**. L'action est achevée, considérée plutôt dans son résultat. Bon nombre de ces verbes expriment, grâce à l'infinitif, le **désir** de voir l'action achevée, le but atteint.

### Structures )

● **La forme infinitive sans *to***
 • Après des verbes de perception.
   *Did you hear / see him open the door?*
   Vous l'avez entendu / vu ouvrir la porte ?

 • Après *make*, exprimant la notion de « faire faire ».
   *The teacher made her do all her homework.*
   L'enseignant lui a fait faire tous ses devoirs.

● **La forme infinitive avec *to***
 • Construction directe.
   *I can't afford to go to a movie every evening.*
   Je n'ai pas les moyens d'aller au cinéma tous les soirs.
   *I want / wish / hope to buy a new car.*
   Je veux / je souhaite / j'espère m'acheter une voiture neuve.

 • Avec un complément interposé, après des verbes comme *allow, order, beg, want*, etc.
   *I want them to be ready at one o'clock.*
   Je veux qu'ils soient prêts à treize heures.

### Yes, but... )

● **Infinitif ou forme en *-ing* ?**
 Vous avez sans doute remarqué que certains verbes se construisaient tantôt avec une forme en *-ing*, tantôt avec un infinitif. Le choix se fera selon que vous considérez l'action d'une manière concrète, dans sa réalisation (employez alors la forme en *-ing*) ou d'une manière abstraite, en considérant l'action achevée, dans son résultat (avec l'infinitif).

Comparez par exemple :
*Has she really left? I didn't see her go.*
Est-elle vraiment partie ? Je ne l'ai pas vu s'en aller.
*She is about to leave. I can see her putting on her coat.*
Elle est sur le point de partir. Je la vois qui enfile son manteau.

Dans le premier exemple, seul le résultat de l'action, terminée, compte (elle est partie et je ne l'ai pas vu faire), tandis que dans le deuxième, c'est le fait de la voir enfiler son manteau qui me signale son départ imminent.
De même pour d'autres verbes exprimant la perception, comme *listen, see, watch, feel, notice,* etc.

● On peut aussi considérer qu'avec la forme en *-ing*, on se tourne plutôt vers le passé tandis qu'avec l'infinitif on se tourne plutôt vers l'avenir, par exemple dans l'expression d'une intention. Comparez :
*Last time I saw him, I remember asking him about his favourite restaurants.*
La dernière fois que je l'ai vu, je me rappelle l'avoir interrogé au sujet de ses restaurants préférés.
*Next time I meet him I must remember to ask him about a good Indian restaurant.*
La prochaine fois que je le verrai, il faut que je pense à lui parler d'un bon restaurant indien.

Dans le premier cas, je me souviens d'une action passée, tandis que dans le deuxième, je fais référence à une action que je dois accomplir, et qui appartient donc à l'avenir.

Cette remarque concerne aussi :
• Des verbes comme *advise, intend, propose, suggest, recommend,* etc.
*I advise arriving early.*
Je conseille d'arriver tôt. (sous-entendu : j'ai toujours, jusqu'à présent, été de cet avis)
*I advise you to arrive early.*
Je vous conseille d'arriver tôt. (sous-entendu : à la séance où vous comptez aller)

• Des verbes exprimant une opinion.
*I hate missing the beginning of a movie.*
Je déteste rater le début d'un film. (sous-entendu : et il en a toujours été ainsi)
*I would hate to miss the beginning of the movie.*
Je détesterais manquer le début du film. (... que je compte aller voir)

# 3. LE STYLE INDIRECT

Le style indirect permet de rapporter les paroles d'autrui. Deux constructions sont possibles.

## COMPLÉTIVE INTRODUITE PAR *THAT* )

- La construction est simple, similaire au français, si vous rapportez, au présent grammatical, des paroles qui viennent d'être prononcées.
    *He says that he is delighted with your offer.*
    Il dit qu'il est ravi de votre proposition.
    *She admits that she has not finished yet.*
    Elle admet ne pas avoir encore fini.

- Mais si vous introduisez votre phrase par un **verbe au passé**, un certain nombre de **transformations** s'imposent. Observez le passage du style direct au style indirect quand les paroles que l'on rapporte sont :
  - Au présent.
      *"I am delighted with her offer."*
      *He said that he was delighted with her offer.*
      Il a dit qu'il était ravi de sa proposition.
  - Au *present perfect.*
      *"I haven't finished yet."*
      *She added that she hadn't finished yet.*
      Elle ajouta qu'elle n'avait pas encore fini.
  - Au prétérit.
      *"I met him twenty years ago."*
      *She announced that she had met him twenty years before.*
      Elle annonça qu'elle l'avait rencontré vingt ans auparavant.
  - Au *pluperfect.*
      *"I had just finished when the bell rang."*
      *He mentioned that he had just finished when the bell rang.*
      Il signala qu'il venait de finir quand la cloche sonna.
  - Au futur.
      *"I'll phone you as soon as I know the answer."*
      *She said that she'd phone me as soon as she knew the answer.*
      Elle a dit qu'elle me téléphonerait dès qu'elle connaîtrait la réponse.

 Remarquez l'emploi du prétérit après l'expression de temps *as soon as*, « parallèle » à l'emploi du présent après un verbe au futur (cf. p. 15).

- Accompagnées d'un auxiliaire modal.

    *"I may decide to come later," he said.*
    *He said that he might decide to come later.*
    Il a dit qu'il pourrait décider de venir plus tard.

    *"You must follow the instructions," she said.*
    *She reminded me that I had to follow the instructions.*
    Elle me rappela que je devais suivre les directives.

## INTERROGATIVE INDIRECTE

Vous retrouverez là les mêmes règles, tout en faisant attention au passage de la forme interrogative à la forme affirmative.

    *"Why did you decide not to speak to her?"*
    *I asked him why he had decided not to speak to her.*
    Je lui ai demandé pourquoi il avait décidé de ne pas lui parler.

    *"Will you bring the cake (that) you have made?"*
    *She asked him if he would bring the cake (that) he had made.*
    Elle lui demanda s'il apporterait le gâteau qu'il avait préparé.

## YES, BUT...

En anglais courant, vous pourrez utiliser indifféremment :

    *She said that Mario lived in New York.*
    *She said that Mario lives in New York.*

La deuxième phrase, où le présent grammatical n'a pas été transformé en prétérit, insiste plus sur le fait que les paroles que l'on rapporte correspondent toujours à une réalité au moment où l'on parle. Il est implicite que Mario vit encore à New York au moment où on parle. Dans le cas contraire, seule la première phrase est possible.

# LE PASSIF

Cette forme est plus importante et plus fréquente en anglais qu'en français. Elle permet de donner la première place à qui subit l'action chaque fois qu'on le désire. **Le choix entre la voix active et la voix passive est**, ici encore, de **la responsabilité de celui qui parle.**

## STRUCTURE DE BASE

- La structure de base est : **sujet + auxiliaire** *be* **+ participe passé** (+ *by* + complément).
  *I was hired by the company in 1999.* J'ai été embauché par l'entreprise en 1999.

- Cette tournure peut s'utiliser à tous les temps : passé, présent, futur.
  *I will be hired if he is satisfied with my job interview.*
  Je serai embauché s'il est satisfait de mon entretien.

- Elle n'est pas incompatible avec la forme en *-ing*.
  *I am being tested on my skills.* On est en train de vérifier mes compétences.

- Elle peut aussi s'accompagner de modaux.
  *I might be hired as early as Monday.*
  Il se pourrait qu'on m'engage dès lundi.

- Elle peut s'associer aux divers types de complémentation vus précédemment.
  *I couldn't stand waiting any longer.*
  Je ne pouvais pas supporter d'attendre plus longtemps.

- Dans le cas d'un verbe à particule, celle-ci reste accolée à son verbe de base.
  *I think all the purchases will be accounted for.*
  Je pense qu'on tiendra compte de tous les achats.
  *In my previous job, this was always taken care of by someone else.*
  Dans mon emploi précédent, quelqu'un d'autre s'est toujours occupé de cela.

- Dans tous les cas, c'est l'auxiliaire *be* qui prend la marque du temps ou de la modalité.

- Le complément d'agent introduit par *by* n'est utilisé que si l'on tient à identifier l'auteur de l'action.

## SENS : TRADUCTION DU FRANÇAIS « ON »

Le passif permet d'attirer l'attention sur qui subit l'action plutôt que sur son auteur. Il est donc normal de préférer le passif quand la phrase à la voix active aurait pour sujet :
- Un pronom personnel indéterminé : *they* (ils, les gens).
  *He has been fired.*
  Il a été renvoyé. Il s'est fait renvoyer. On l'a renvoyé.

- Un pronom indéfini *(someone, somebody…)*.
  *The company has been taken over.* L'entreprise a été rachetée.
- Un nom avec un sens général.
  *Incompetent employees are not thought much of.*
  On n'apprécie pas beaucoup les employés incompétents.

## AUTRES EMPLOIS

- **Construction de *say* et des verbes de sens voisin** *(think, believe, report, etc.)*
  À la tournure :
    *People say that he has been fired for incompetence.*
  il faudra, à moins de vouloir insister sur *people*, préférer l'une des deux formules suivantes :
    *It is said that the president has fired him for incompetence.*
    On dit que le président l'a renvoyé pour incompétence.
    *The president is said to have fired him for incompetence.*
    On dit du président qu'il l'a renvoyé pour incompétence.
  La première tournure permet de rendre la cause encore plus vague, la seconde met le sujet en pleine lumière. Il y a, dans les deux cas, une nuance d'incertitude que l'on peut traduire en français par un conditionnel :
    Le président l'aurait renvoyé pour incompétence.

- **Le passif avec *get***
  *Get*, avec son sens lexical « devenir », exprime plus fortement le changement d'état que *be*.
    *He got fired when they saw he was not prepared for the job.*
    Il a été renvoyé dès qu'ils ont vu qu'il ne convenait pas pour le poste.

- **Le double passif**
  Comparez :
    *My job has been given to her. / She has been given my job.*
    On lui a donné mon poste.
  Cette seconde tournure est très souvent employée, car c'est la personne qui devient à nouveau le centre de la phrase. Elle est propre à des verbes exprimant un rapport d'un individu à un autre : *give, offer, bring, buy, tell, ask, teach*, etc.

## YES, BUT…

Au passif, les verbes suivis, à la voix active, de l'infinitif sans *to*, récupèrent leur préposition.
Comparez :
  *They made her do too much work. She was made to do too much work.*
  *They saw her leave the building. She was seen to leave the building.*
On pourra dire aussi : *She was seen leaving the building.*

# TABLEAUX
# DE CONJUGAISON

- **Tableaux des temps**[1] . . . . . . . . . . . . . . . 88
  Prononciation . . . . . . . . . . . . . . . . . . . . . . 96
  Modifications orthographiques . . . . . . . . . . 97

- **Tableau des contractions** . . . . . . . . . . . . . 98
  Comment poser une question . . . . . . . . . . . 100
  Les *tags* . . . . . . . . . . . . . . . . . . . . . . . . . 102

- **Tableaux des verbes irréguliers** . . . . . . . . 104

---

1. Remarques :

Les formes interro-négatives s'utilisent de préférence contractées. Les formes non contractées sont généralement employées à l'écrit, ou bien pour marquer l'emphase, à l'oral. Une question de forme non contractée est plus ouverte, alors qu'une question de forme contractée requiert davantage une réponse positive. On peut consulter toutes les formes contractées au tableau des contractions (p. 98-99).

On peut construire, en théorie, les voix passives du *present perfect* continu, du *pluperfect* continu, du futur continu, du futur antérieur continu, du conditionnel présent continu, du conditionnel passé continu, mais ces formes ne sont jamais utilisées. Vous trouverez ici plutôt des exemples de formes contractées (p. 90-95).

*Shall* est rarement employé en Amérique du Nord (voir le futur, p. 92). On ne l'emploie que dans des situations qui exigent un registre soutenu, ou pour s'exprimer avec une grande politesse : « *Shall I / we ask?* » (ou « *Should I / we ask?* »).

En Amérique du Nord, *should* n'est jamais employé pour exprimer le conditionnel (voir le conditionnel présent, p. 94) ; on emploie plutôt *would*. *Should*, en Amérique du Nord, exprime l'obligation.

# PRÉSENT

## VOIX ACTIVE

| Présent simple | Présent continu |
|---|---|
| **forme affirmative** | **forme affirmative** |
| I ask<br>he / she / it asks<br>we / you / they ask | I am asking<br>he / she / it is asking<br>we / you / they are asking |
| **forme interrogative** | **forme interrogative** |
| Do I ask?<br>Does he / she / it ask?<br>Do we / you / they ask? | Am I asking?<br>Is he / she / it asking?<br>Are we / you / they asking? |
| **forme négative** | **forme négative** |
| I do not ask<br>he / she / it does not ask<br>we / you / they do not ask | I am not asking<br>he / she / it is not asking<br>we / you / they are not asking |
| **forme interro-négative** | **forme interro-négative** |
| Do I not ask?<br>Does he / she / it not ask?<br>Do we / you / they not ask? | Am I not asking?<br>Is he / she / it not asking?<br>Are we / you / they not asking? |

## VOIX PASSIVE

| Présent simple | Présent continu |
|---|---|
| **forme affirmative** | **forme affirmative** |
| I am asked<br>he / she / it is asked<br>we / you / they are asked | I am being asked<br>he / she / it is being asked<br>we / you / they are being asked |
| **forme interrogative** | **forme interrogative** |
| Am I asked?<br>Is he / she / it asked?<br>Are we / you / they asked? | Am I being asked?<br>Is he / she / it being asked?<br>Are we / you / they being asked? |
| **forme négative** | **forme négative** |
| I am not asked<br>he / she / it is not asked<br>we / you / they are not asked | I am not being asked<br>he / she / it is not being asked<br>we / you / they are not being asked |
| **forme interro-négative** | **forme interro-négative** |
| Am I not asked?<br>Is he / she / it not asked?<br>Are we / you / they not asked? | Am I not being asked?<br>Is he / she / it not being asked?<br>Are we / you / they not being asked? |

À la forme interro-négative, la forme contractée de *am not* est *aren't*.

## VOIX ACTIVE

| Prétérit simple | Prétérit continu |
|---|---|
| **forme affirmative** | **forme affirmative** |
| I asked<br>he / she / it asked<br>we / you / they asked | I was asking<br>he / she / it was asking<br>we / you / they were asking |
| **forme interrogative** | **forme interrogative** |
| Did I ask?<br>Did he / she / it ask?<br>Did we / you / they ask? | Was I asking?<br>Was he / she / it asking?<br>Were we / you / they asking? |
| **forme négative** | **forme négative** |
| I did not ask<br>he / she / it did not ask<br>we / you / they did not ask | I was not asking<br>he / she / it was not asking<br>we / you / they were not asking |
| **forme interro-négative** | **forme interro-négative** |
| Did I not ask?<br>Did he / she / it not ask?<br>Did we / you / they not ask? | Was I not asking?<br>Was he / she / it not asking?<br>Were we / you / they not asking? |

## VOIX PASSIVE

| Prétérit simple | Prétérit continu |
|---|---|
| **forme affirmative** | **forme affirmative** |
| I was asked<br>he / she / it was asked<br>we / you / they were asked | I was being asked<br>he / she / it was being asked<br>we / you / they were being asked |
| **forme interrogative** | **forme interrogative** |
| Was I asked?<br>Was he / she / it asked?<br>Were we / you / they asked? | Was I being asked?<br>Was he / she / it being asked?<br>Were we / you / they being asked? |
| **forme négative** | **forme négative** |
| I was not asked<br>he / she / it was not asked<br>we / you / they were not asked | I was not being asked<br>he / she / it was not being asked<br>we / you / they were not being asked |
| **forme interro-négative** | **forme interro-négative** |
| Was I not asked?<br>Was he / she / it not asked?<br>Were we / you / they not asked? | Was I not being asked?<br>Was he / she / it not being asked?<br>Were we / you / they not being asked? |

# PRESENT PERFECT

## VOIX ACTIVE

| *Present perfect* simple | *Present perfect* continu |
|---|---|
| **forme affirmative** | **forme affirmative** |
| I have asked<br>he / she / it has asked<br>we / you / they have asked | I have been asking<br>he / she / it has been asking<br>we / you / they have been asking |
| **forme interrogative** | **forme interrogative** |
| Have I asked?<br>Has he / she / it asked?<br>Have we / you / they asked? | Have I been asking?<br>Has he / she / it been asking?<br>Have we / you / they been asking? |
| **forme négative** | **forme négative** |
| I have not asked<br>he / she / it has not asked<br>we / you / they have not asked | I have not been asking<br>he / she / it has not been asking<br>we / you / they have not been asking |
| **forme interro-négative** | **forme interro-négative** |
| Have I not asked?<br>Has he / she / it not asked?<br>Have we / you / they not asked? | Have I not been asking?<br>Has he / she / it not been asking?<br>Have we / you / they not been asking? |

## VOIX PASSIVE

### *Present perfect* simple

**forme affirmative**

I have been asked
he / she / it has been asked
we / you / they have been asked

**forme interrogative**

Have I been asked?
Has he / she / it been asked?
Have we / you / they been asked?

**forme négative**

I have not been asked
he / she / it has not been asked
we / you / they have not been asked

**forme interro-négative**

Have I not been asked?
Has he / she / it not been asked?
Have we / you / they not been asked?

## EXEMPLES

### Formes contractées

**forme interro-négative**

**Voix active**

| | |
|---|---|
| Don't I ask? | présent simple |
| Aren't I asking? | présent continu |
| Didn't I ask? | prétérit simple |
| Wasn't I asking? | prétérit continu |
| Haven't I asked? | *present perfect* simple |
| Haven't I been asking? | *present perfect* continu |

**Voix passive**

| | |
|---|---|
| Aren't I asked? | présent simple |
| Aren't I being asked? | présent continu |
| Wasn't I asked? | prétérit simple |
| Wasn't I being asked? | prétérit continu |
| Haven't I been asked? | *present perfect* simple |

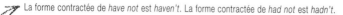 La forme contractée de *have not* est *haven't*. La forme contractée de *had not* est *hadn't*.

## VOIX ACTIVE

### *Pluperfect* simple

#### forme affirmative

I had asked
he / she / it had asked
we / you / they had asked

#### forme interrogative

Had I asked?
Had he / she / it asked?
Had we / you / they asked?

#### forme négative

I had not asked
he / she / it had not asked
we / you / they had not asked

#### forme interro-négative

Had I not asked?
Had he / she / it not asked?
Had we / you / they not asked?

### *Pluperfect* continu

#### forme affirmative

I had been asking
he / she / it had been asking
we / you / they had been asking

#### forme interrogative

Had I been asking?
Had he / she / it been asking?
Had we / you / they been asking?

#### forme négative

I had not been asking
he / she / it had not been asking
we / you / they had not been asking

#### forme interro-négative

Had I not been asking?
Had he / she / it not been asking?
Had we / you / they not been asking?

## VOIX PASSIVE

### *Pluperfect* simple

#### forme affirmative

I had been asked
he / she / it had been asked
we / you / they had been asked

#### forme interrogative

Had I been asked?
Had he / she / it been asked?
Had we / you / they been asked?

#### forme négative

I had not been asked
he / she / it had not been asked
we / you / they had not been asked

#### forme interro-négative

Had I not been asked?
Had he / she / it not been asked?
Had we / you / they not been asked?

## EXEMPLES

### Formes contractées

#### forme interro-négative

Voix active

Hadn't I asked?          *pluperfect* simple
Hadn't he/she/it asked?
Hadn't we/you/they asked?

Hadn't I been asking?   *pluperfect* continu
Hadn't he/she/it been asking?
Hadn't we/you/they been asking?

Voix passive

Hadn't I been asked?     *pluperfect* simple
Hadn't he/she/it been asked?
Hadn't we/you/they been asked?

# FUTUR

## VOIX ACTIVE

| **Futur simple** | **Futur continu** |
|---|---|

**forme affirmative**

| | |
|---|---|
| I / we will (shall) ask | I / we will (shall) be asking |
| he / she / it will ask | he / she / it will be asking |
| you / they will ask | you / they will be asking |

**forme interrogative**

| | |
|---|---|
| Will (Shall) I / we ask? | Will (Shall) I / we be asking? |
| Will he / she / it ask? | Will he / she / it be asking? |
| Will you / they ask? | Will you / they be asking? |

**forme négative**

| | |
|---|---|
| I / we will (shall) not ask | I / we will (shall) not be asking |
| he / she / it will not ask | he / she / it will not be asking |
| you / they will not ask | you / they will not be asking |

**forme interro-négative**

| | |
|---|---|
| Will (Shall) I / we not ask? | Will (Shall) I / we not be asking? |
| Will he / she / it not ask? | Will he / she / it not be asking? |
| Will you / they not ask? | Will you / they not be asking? |

## VOIX PASSIVE

**Futur simple**

**forme affirmative**

I / we will (shall) be asked
he / she / it will be asked
you / they will be asked

**forme interrogative**

Will (Shall) I / we be asked?
Will he / she / it be asked?
Will you / they be asked?

**forme négative**

I / we will (shall) not be asked
he / she / it will not be asked
you / they will not be asked

**forme interro-négative**

Will (Shall) I / we not be asked?
Will he / she / it not be asked?
Will you / they not be asked?

## EXEMPLES

**Formes contractées**

Voix active

| | |
|---|---|
| **forme négative** | futur simple |
| I/We won't ask. | |
| **forme interro-négative** | futur simple |
| Won't I/we ask? | |
| **forme négative** | futur continu |
| I/We won't be asking. | |
| **forme interro-négative** | futur continu |
| Won't I/we be asking? | |

Voix passive

| | |
|---|---|
| **forme négative** | futur simple |
| I/We won't be asked. | |
| **forme interro-négative** | futur simple |
| Won't I/we be asked? | |

La forme contractée de *will not* est *won't*.

# FUTUR ANTÉRIEUR

## VOIX ACTIVE

### Futur antérieur simple

**forme affirmative**

I / we will (shall) have asked
he / she / it will have asked
you / they will have asked

**forme interrogative**

Will (Shall) I / we have asked?
Will he / she / it have asked?
Will you / they have asked?

**forme négative**

I / we will (shall) not have asked
he / she / it will not have asked
you / they will not have asked

**forme interro-négative**

Will (Shall) I / we not have asked?
Will he / she / it not have asked?
Will you / they not have asked?

### Futur antérieur continu

**forme affirmative**

I / we will (shall) have been asking
he / she / it will have been asking
you / they will have been asking

**forme interrogative**

Will (Shall) I / we have been asking?
Will he / she / it have been asking?
Will you / they have been asking?

**forme négative**

I / we will (shall) not have been asking
he / she / it will not have been asking
you / they will not have been asking

**forme interro-négative**

Will (Shall) I / we not have been asking?
Will he / she / it not have been asking?
Will you / they not have been asking?

## VOIX PASSIVE

### Futur antérieur simple

**forme affirmative**

I / we will (shall) have been asked
he / she / it will have been asked
you / they will have been asked

**forme interrogative**

Will (Shall) I / we have been asked?
Will he / she / it have been asked?
Will you / they have been asked?

**forme négative**

I / we will (shall) not have been asked
he / she / it will not have been asked
you / they will not have been asked

**forme interro-négative**

Will (Shall) I / we not have been asked?
Will he / she / it not have been asked?
Will you / they not have been asked?

## EXEMPLES

### Formes contractées

Voix active

**forme négative**   futur antérieur simple
I/We won't be asked.

**forme interro-négative**   futur antérieur simple
Won't I/we have asked?

**forme négative**   futur antérieur continu
I/We won't have been asking.

**forme interro-négative**   futur antérieur continu
Won't I/we have been asking?

Voix passive

**forme négative**   futur antérieur simple
I/We won't have been asked.

**forme interro-négative**   futur antérieur simple
Won't I/we have been asked?

# CONDITIONNEL PRÉSENT

| VOIX ACTIVE | |
|---|---|
| **Conditionnel présent simple** | **Conditionnel présent continu** |
| **forme affirmative** | **forme affirmative** |
| I / we would (should) ask<br>he / she / it would ask<br>you / they would ask | I / we would (should) be asking<br>he / she / it would be asking<br>you / they would be asking |
| **forme interrogative** | **forme interrogative** |
| Would (Should) I / we ask?<br>Would he / she / it ask?<br>Would you / they ask? | Would (Should) I / we be asking?<br>Would he / she / it be asking?<br>Would you / they be asking? |
| **forme négative** | **forme négative** |
| I / we would (should) not ask<br>he / she / it would not ask<br>you / they would not ask | I / we would (should) not be asking<br>he / she / it would not be asking<br>you / they would not be asking |
| **forme interro-négative** | **forme interro-négative** |
| Would (Should) I / we not ask?<br>Would he / she / it not ask?<br>Would you / they not ask? | Would (Should) I / we not be asking?<br>Would he / she / it not be asking?<br>Would you / they not be asking? |

| VOIX PASSIVE | EXEMPLES |
|---|---|
| **Conditionnel présent simple** | **Formes contractées** |
| **forme affirmative** | Voix active |
| I / we would (should) be asked<br>he / she / it would be asked<br>you / they would be asked | **forme négative** conditionnel présent simple<br>I/We wouldn't ask.<br>**forme interro-négative** conditionnel présent simple<br>Wouldn't I/we ask? |
| **forme interrogative** | **forme négative** conditionnel présent continu<br>I/We wouldn't be asking. |
| Would (Should) I / we be asked?<br>Would he / she / it be asked?<br>Would you / they be asked? | **forme interro-négative** conditionnel présent continu<br>Wouldn't I/we be asking? |
| **forme négative** | Voix passive |
| I / we would (should) not  be asked<br>he / she / it would not be asked<br>you / they would not be asked | **forme négative** conditionnel présent simple<br>I/We wouldn't be asked.<br>**forme interro-négative** conditionnel présent simple<br>Wouldn't I/we be asked? |
| **forme interro-négative** | |
| Would (Should) I / we not be asked?<br>Would he / she / it not be asked?<br>Would you / they not be asked? | |

La forme contractée de *would not* est *wouldn't*.

# CONDITIONNEL PASSÉ

## VOIX ACTIVE

### Conditionnel passé simple

**forme affirmative**

I / we would (should) have asked
he / she / it would have asked
you / they would have asked

**forme interrogative**

Would (Should) I / we have asked?
Would he / she / it have asked?
Would you / they have asked?

**forme négative**

I / we would (should) not have asked
he / she / it would not have asked
you / they would not have asked

**forme interro-négative**

Would (Should) I / we not have asked?
Would he / she / it not have asked?
Would you / they not have asked?

### Conditionnel passé continu

**forme affirmative**

I / we would (should) have been asking
he / she / it would have been asking
you / they would have been asking

**forme interrogative**

Would (Should) I / we have been asking?
Would he / she / it have been asking?
Would you / they have been asking?

**forme négative**

I / we would (should) not have been asking
he / she / it would not have been asking
you / they would not have been asking

**forme interro-négative**

Would (Should) I / we not have been asking?
Would he / she / it not have been asking?
Would you / they not have been asking?

## VOIX PASSIVE

### Conditionnel passé simple

**forme affirmative**

I / we would (should) have been asked
he / she / it would have been asked
you / they would have been asked

**forme interrogative**

Would (Should) I / we have been asked?
Would he / she / it have been asked?
Would you / they have been asked?

**forme négative**

I / we would (should) not have been asked
he / she / it would not have been asked
you / they would not have been asked

**forme interro-négative**

Would (Should) I / we not have been asked?
Would he / she / it not have been asked?
Would you / they not have been asked?

## EXEMPLES

### Formes contractées

Voix active

**forme négative**    conditionnel passé simple
I/We wouldn't have asked.

**forme interro-négative**    conditionnel passé simple
Wouldn't I/we have asked?

**forme négative**    conditionnel passé continu
I/We wouldn't have been asking.

**forme interro-négative**    conditionnel passé continu
Wouldn't I/we have been asking?

Voix passive

**forme négative**    conditionnel passé simple
I/We wouldn't have been asked.

**forme interro-négative**    conditionnel passé simple
Wouldn't I/we have been asked?

# PRONONCIATION

## TERMINAISON DU PRÉSENT (TROISIÈME PERSONNE DU SINGULIER)

- Elle se prononce [s] :
  après les sons finaux des consonnes [f] *(laughs)*, [k] *(blinks)*, [p] *(grasps)*, [t] *(lifts)* et [θ] *(froths)*.

- Elle se prononce [z] :
  - après les sons finaux des consonnes [v] *(loves)*, [g] *(bags)*, [b] *(disturbs)*, [d] *(binds)*, [l] *(travels)*, [m] *(seems)*, [n] *(abandons)*, [ð] *(bathes)* ;
  - après une voyelle, le plus souvent [i], *(carries)* ;
  - après les diphtongues [ei] *(plays)*, [ai] *(sighs)*, [au] *(vows)*, [ɔi] *(annoys)*.

- Elles se prononce [iz] :
  - après les sons finaux des consonnes [s] *(convinces)*, [z] *(advises)*, [dʒ] *(changes)*, [ʃ] *(washes)*
  Dans certains cas, cela impliquera une **modification orthographique**.

## TERMINAISON DU PASSÉ DES VERBES RÉGULIERS *(-ED)*

- Elle se prononce [d] :
  - après les sons finaux des consonnes [v] *(loved)*, [g] *(bagged)*, [b] *(disturbed)*, [l] *(travelled)*, [m] *(seemed)*, [n] *(abandoned)*, [ð] *(bathed)* ;
  - après une voyelle, le plus souvent [i], *(carried)* ;
  - après les diphtongues [ei] *(played)*, [ai] *(sighed)*, [au] *(vowed)*, [ɔi] *(annoyed)*.

- Elle se prononce [id] :
  - après [t] *(lifted)* et [d] *(handed)*.

- Elle se prononce [t] :
  - après [f] *(laughed)*, [k] *(blinked)*, [p] *(grasped)*, [ʃ] *(convinced)*, [ʃ] *(washed)*.

# MODIFICATIONS ORTHOGRAPHIQUES

### TERMINAISON DE LA TROISIÈME PERSONNE DU SINGULIER

- La terminaison *-y* devient *-ies* : *carry* → *carries*.

- La prononciation [iz] se manifeste par l'ajout d'un *e* de soutien devant le *s* final :
  *pass* → *passes*, *watch* → *watches*, *buzz* → *buzzes*.

### TERMINAISON DES VERBES RÉGULIERS *(-ED)*

- La terminaison *-y* devient *-ied* : *carry* → *carried*.

- On n'ajoute que le *-d* après les verbes se terminant en *-e* : *love* → *loved*.

### TERMINAISON EN *-ING*

- La terminaison *-e* est remplacée par *-ing* : *love* → *loving*.

- La terminaison *-ie* devient *-ying* : *lie* → *lying*.

### REDOUBLEMENT DE LA CONSONNE FINALE

Le redoublement a lieu :

- quand le verbe ne comporte qu'une seule syllabe et que la consonne finale est précédée d'une seule voyelle courte :
  *beg* → *begged, begging*

- quand le verbe a plusieurs syllabes dont la dernière est accentuée et que la consonne est immédiatement précédée d'une seule voyelle courte :
  *admit* → *admitted, admitting*

Toutes ces modifications sont indiquées dans **l'Index général**, p. 115.

# TABLEAU DES CONTRACTIONS

| Forme affirmative | | Forme |
|---|---|---|
| **auxiliaire *be*** | | |
| I am | I'm | I am not |
| he/she/it is | he's/she's/it's | he/she/it is not |
| we/you/they are | we're/you're/they're | we/you/they are not |
| | | I was not |
| | | we were not |
| **auxiliaire *have*** | | |
| I have | I've | I have not |
| he/she/it has | he's/she's/it's | he/she/it has not |
| we/you/they have | we've/you've/they've | we/you/they have not |
| I had | I'd | I had not |
| **auxiliaire *do*** | | |
| | | I/you/we/they do not |
| | | he/she/it does not |
| | | I did not |
| **auxiliaires *will (shall)*** | | |
| I will (shall) | I'll | I will (shall) not |
| he/she will | he'll/she'll | he/she will not |
| **auxiliaires *would (should)*** | | |
| I would (should) | I'd | I would (should) not |
| he would | he'd | he/she would not |
| I would (should) have | I would've (should've) | I would (should) not have |
| he would have | he would've | he/she would not have |
| **auxiliaire *can*** | | I cannot |
| **auxiliaire *could*** | | I could not |
| **auxiliaire *must*** | | I must not |
| **auxiliaire *might*** | | I might not |
| **auxiliaire *ought to* [1]** | | I ought not to |

1. *Ought* n'est presque jamais employé en Amérique du Nord pour exprimer l'obligation. On lui préfère *should*.

| négative | Forme interro-négative | |
| --- | --- | --- |
| I'm not | Am I not? | Aren't I? (fam.) [2] |
| he/she isn't / he's/she's not | Is he/she not? | Isn't he/she? |
| we aren't / we're not | Are we not? | Aren't we? |
| I wasn't | Was I not? | Wasn't I? |
| we weren't | Were we not? | Weren't we? |
| I haven't | Have I not? | Haven't I? |
| he/she hasn't | Has he/she not? | Hasn't he/she? |
| we haven't | Have we not? | Haven't we? |
| I hadn't | Had I not? | Hadn't I? |
| I don't | Do I not? | Don't I? |
| he/she doesn't | Does he/she not? | Doesn't he/she? |
| he/she didn't | Did he/she not? | Didn't he/she? |
| I won't (shan't) [3] | Will (Shall) I not? | Won't (Shan't) I? |
| he/she won't | Will he/she not? | Won't he/she? |
| I wouldn't (shouldn't) | Would (Should) I not? | Wouldn't (Shouldn't) I? |
| he/she wouldn't (shouldn't) | Would he/she not? | Wouldn't he/she? |
| I wouldn't (shouldn't) have | Would (should) I not have? | Wouldn't (Shouldn't) I have? |
| he/she wouldn't have | Would he/she not have? | Wouldn't he/she have? |
| I can't | Can I not? | Can't I? |
| I couldn't | Could I not? | Couldn't I? |
| I mustn't | Must I not? | Mustn't I? |
| I mightn't | Might I not? | Mightn't I? |
| I oughtn't to | Ought I not to? | Oughtn't I to? |

2. Bien que *aren't I* soit la forme standard la plus courante, on pourrait entendre *ain't* dans certains milieux. Cette forme fautive est employée volontairement pour marquer l'emphase, ou dans des contextes populaires ou folkloriques, par exemple, dans des chansons.

3. *Shan't*, la forme contractée de *shall not*, n'est presque jamais employé en Amérique du Nord.

# COMMENT POSER UNE QUESTION

Il vous faudra faire la différence entre deux types de questions : les questions fermées, pour lesquelles on attend une réponse par *yes* ou *no,* et les questions ouvertes, qui suggèrent de répondre de façon circonstanciée.

## QUESTIONS FERMÉES

• Dans le cas d'un verbe ordinaire au présent ou au prétérit, l'ajout de l'auxiliaire *do* ou *did*, en début de question, est indispensable.

> *Do you go out mornings for coffee?*
> Est-ce que tu sors le matin pour prendre un café ?
> *Does she like this book?*
> Est-ce qu'elle aime ce livre ?
> *Did they write to him?*
> Lui ont-ils écrit ?

• Inutile d'ajouter un auxiliaire si la phrase en contient déjà un, qu'il s'agisse de *be*, de *have* ou d'un modal : une simple inversion suffit.

> *Are you going to Chicago?*
> Allez-vous à Chicago ?
> *Has she read this book?*
> A-t-elle lu ce livre ?
> *Must you really go now?*
> Vous devez vraiment partir maintenant ?

Dans le cas de plusieurs auxiliaires, l'inversion ne porte qu'entre le premier d'entre eux et le sujet.

> *Could they have missed their train?*
> Se pourrait-il qu'ils aient raté leur train ?

• Si vous attendez plutôt une réponse positive, utilisez la forme interro-négative, en accolant *n't* à l'auxiliaire.

> *Don't you like coffee?*
> Tu n'aimes pas le café ?
> *Hasn't she bought a new car?*
> N'a-t-elle pas acheté une nouvelle voiture ?
> *Shouldn't they be here now?*
> Ne devraient-ils pas être arrivés ?

Attention toutefois à la place de la négation, juste avant le verbe, si la forme n'est pas contractée (cf. tableau, p. 98).

> *Does he not like beer?*
> N'aime-t-il pas la bière ?

- Elles requièrent toujours un mot interrogatif, qui peut être :
  - **un adverbe ou une expression adverbiale :**

    *When do you go to Winnipeg?*
    Quand allez-vous à Winnipeg ?

    *Why didn't you tell him about it?*
    Pourquoi ne lui as-tu pas dit ?

    *How did you like the movie?*
    Qu'as-tu pensé du film ?

➤ *How* peut aussi être être placé devant un adjectif ou un adverbe.

    *How far is it to Montreal from here?*
    Montréal est à quelle distance d'ici ?

    *How long have they been working?*
    Depuis combien de temps travaillent-ils ?

    *How good are you at skating?*
    Êtes-vous bon patineur (bonne patineuse) ?

    *How well can she swim?*
    Est-ce qu'elle nage bien ?

  - **un pronom interrogatif complément :**

    *Who(m) did you meet in Paris?*
    Qui as-tu rencontré à Paris ?

    *What does he have to do in Paris?*
    Que doit-il faire à Paris ?

  - **un pronom interrogatif sujet** (il n'y a alors ni inversion du sujet, ni emploi de *do/does/did*) :

    *Who will go to Miami with me?*
    Qui ira à Miami avec moi ?

    *What happened?*
    Que s'est-il passé ?

- Si la question comporte un **verbe à particule**, celle-ci se place :
  - en début de question :

    *To whom will you offer this opportunity?*
    À qui offriras-tu cette occasion ?

  - ou, **de préférence**, en fin de question :

    *Who(m) will you offer this opportunity to?*

- Enfin, si la question porte sur un **choix** entre deux choses ou deux personnes, c'est le pronom *which* qui s'impose.

    *Which would you rather have, a blue scarf or a pink one?*
    Lequel préférerais-tu : un foulard bleu ou un foulard rose ?

# LES *TAGS*

Pour éviter de répéter inutilement un verbe, l'anglais possède une série de structures qui, toutes construites à partir d'auxiliaires, permettent aussi bien de répondre brièvement à une question que d'exprimer des réactions.

Elles se placent à la fin d'une question ou d'une phrase affirmative, d'où leur nom de *tag* qui désigne en anglais l'extrémité de quelque chose (par exemple, *the tag line* : le dernier vers d'un poème). On répond généralement à un *tag* comme si la question et l'énoncé étaient positifs. Par exemple, à « *It's raining, isn't it?* », on répondrait « *Yes, it is* » s'il pleuvait vraiment, ou « *No, it isn't* » s'il ne pleuvait pas. Ce sont aussi les réponses à la question « *Is it raining?* ».

## RÉPONSES COURTES

> *Do you know them? Yes, I do. / No, I don't.*
> Vous les connaissez ? Oui. / Non.
> *Haven't you already met them? Yes, I have. / No, I haven't.*
> Ne les avez-vous pas déjà rencontrés ? Oui. / Non.
> *Can you see that tree in the distance? Yes, I can. / No, I can't.*
> Vous voyez cet arbre au loin ? Oui. / Non.

## REPRISES INTERROGATIVES

C'est l'équivalent du français « n'est-ce pas ? » ou, dans une langue moins soutenue, « hein ? ».

- Phrase **affirmative** → *tag* **interro-négatif**.

> *She knows them, doesn't she?*      *You went with them, didn't you?*
> Elle les connaît, n'est-ce pas ?     Tu es allé avec eux, n'est-ce pas ?
> *You can hear me, can't you?*
> Vous m'entendez, n'est-ce pas ?

- Phase **négative** → *tag* **interrogatif**.

> *You won't go without us, will you?*   *He shouldn't be here, should he?*
> Tu ne partiras pas sans nous, hein ?   Il ne devrait pas être là, n'est-ce pas ?

- Phrase à **l'impératif** → *tag* **interrogatif**.

> *Open the door, will you?* [1]      *Let's have dinner, shall we?*
> Ouvre la porte, veux-tu ?           Et si nous dînions ?

---

1. *Open the door, will you?* est très péremptoire ; on comprendrait facilement que le locuteur s'exprime avec colère, avec urgence ou avec impatience. On s'exprimerait plus poliment en demandant *"Would / Could you open the door, please?"*

## Réactions

- **Étonnement**

  Le *tag* traduit des expressions comme « Tiens ? », « Vraiment ? », « Vous croyez ? », « Ah oui ? »...

  – Phrase **affirmative** → *tag* **interrogatif.**

    *"She can swim very fast." "Can she ?"*

    « Elle nage très vite. » « Ah bon ? »

  – Phrase **négative** → *tag* **interro-négatif.**

    *"He didn't know this." "Didn't he?"*

    « Il ne savait pas ça. » « Vraiment ? »

  L'auxiliaire du *tag* est accentué. L'intonation sera montante pour exprimer la surprise, descendante pour exprimer le doute ou l'indifférence.

- **Constatation**

  Le *tag* traduit des expressions comme « Eh oui ! », « C'est bien vrai », « Bien sûr ! »

    *"He adores her." "So he does."*

    « Il l'adore. » « Ça, tu peux le dire ! »

  À ne pas confondre avec le *tag* suivant : (*so* + auxiliaire + sujet).

- **« Moi aussi... » « Moi non plus... »**

  – Phrase **affirmative** → *so* + auxiliaire + sujet.

    *"I'd like a nice cup of coffee." "So would I."*

    « J'aimerais une bonne tasse de café. » « Moi aussi. »

    *"She travels a lot." "So do I."*

    « Elle voyage beaucoup. » « Moi aussi. »

  – Phrase **négative** → *neither* + auxiliaire + sujet.

    *"I can't see them." "Neither can I."*

    « Je ne les vois pas. » « Moi non plus. »

- **Contradiction**

  – Phrase **affirmative** → *tag* **négatif.**

    *"I'll buy some." "I won't."*

    « J'en achèterai quelques-uns. » « Pas moi. »

  – Phrase **négative** → *tag* **affirmatif.**

    *"I don't like this movie." "I do."*

    « Je n'aime pas ce film. » « Moi, si. »

  Attention à *never*, *hardly*, qui ont un sens négatif.

    *"I have never read such a good book." "Neither have I."*

    « Je n'ai jamais lu un aussi bon livre. » « Moi non plus. »

    *"I can hardly imagine anything better." "Neither can I."*

    « Je ne peux rien imaginer de mieux. » « Moi non plus. »

# TABLEAUX DES VERBES IRRÉGULIERS

## DÉFINITION

- La majorité des verbes anglais ont très régulièrement quatre formes : *like, likes, liked, liking*.

- Moins de deux cents verbes sont dit « irréguliers », parce qu'ils ont des formes spéciales pour le prétérit et le participe passé : *begin, begins, **began**, **begun**, beginning*.
  La voyelle centrale marque le changement essentiel : elle peut rester la même aux trois temps ; elle peut aussi changer une ou deux fois.

## CLASSEMENT

- C'est ce fait qui détermine notre classement et pourra aider à la mémorisation. On distinguera trois catégories, en symbolisant la voyelle (ou diphtongue) centrale du présent par A, celle du prétérit par B et celle du participe passé par C :

  | | | | |
  |---|---|---|---|
  | 1. Trois voyelles semblables : | *hit,* | *hit,* | *hit* | atteindre, frapper |
  | 2. Deux voyelles semblables : | *cling* | *clung* | *clung* | s'accrocher |
  | | *run* | *ran* | *run* | courir |
  | 3. Trois voyelles différentes : | *begin* | *began* | *begun* | commencer |

- Secondairement, la terminaison peut également varier.
  Le *d* de l'infinitif peut se changer en *t* : *build, built, built* (construire).
  Ou encore, on peut observer l'addition d'un *n* : *break, broke, broken* (casser).

## MÉMORISATION

Vous pourrez ainsi vous servir de ces groupements par ressemblance. Vous trouverez la liste complète, pages 209-219.

- Il peut vous être utile de savoir que les verbes irréguliers concernent généralement :
  – des activités vitales et quotidiennes, liées à la survie : *eat, drink, sleep, build, dwell...*
  – des mouvements et activités du corps : *see, smell, lie, run, swim, make...*
  – des relations humaines de communication : *say, speak, tell, teach, learn...*
  – des relations humaines de lutte pour la vie : *beat, fight, hit, strike...*
  – des relations humaines commerciales : *bid, buy, sell...*

- Sachez aussi que :
  – plusieurs de ces verbes sont rares (litt.) ;
  – l'usage en Amérique du Nord veut que le *simple past* et le *past participle* de certains verbes se construisent en *-ed*, alors que ces verbes seraient plutôt irréguliers en Grande-Bretagne. Quelques-uns de ces verbes (*smell*, par exemple) sont répertoriés ici ; leurs formes irrégulières se trouvent entre parenthèses ;
  – tous les verbes nouveaux – il en naît chaque année – rejoignent la forme rassurante des verbes réguliers en *-ed*.

# TROIS VOYELLES SEMBLABLES : AAA

| A | A | A | |
|---|---|---|---|
| [ɪ] | [ɪ] | [ɪ] | |
| *hit* | *hit* | *hit* | atteindre, frapper |
| *knit* | *knit (knitted)* | *knit (knitted)* | tricoter [1] |
| *quit* | *quit (quitted)* | *quit (quitted)* | quitter |
| *slit* | *slit* | *slit* | fendre, inciser |
| *split* | *split* | *split* | fendre |
| *rid* | *rid (ridded)* | *rid (ridded)* | débarrasser [2] |
| *bid* | *bid (bade)* | *bid (bidden)* | offrir (prix), ordonner |
| *build* | *built* | *built* | bâtir |
| *gild* | *gilded (gilt)* | *gilded (gilt)* | dorer (litt.) |
| *spill* | *spilled (spilt)* | *spilled (spilt)* | répandre (liquide) |
| [e] | [e] | [e] | |
| *bet* | *bet* | *bet* | parier |
| *let* | *let* | *let* | laisser, permettre, louer |
| *set* | *set* | *set* | placer |
| *shed* | *shed* | *shed* | verser (larmes, sang) |
| *spread* | *spread* | *spread* | étendre, répandre |
| *bend* | *bent* | *bent* | courber |
| *lend* | *lent* | *lent* | prêter |
| *rend* | *rent* | *rent* | déchirer (litt.) |
| *send* | *sent* | *sent* | envoyer |
| *spend* | *spent* | *spent* | dépenser, passer (temps) |
| *dwell* | *dwelled (dwelt)* | *dwelled (dwelt)* | habiter |
| *smell* | *smelled (smelt)* | *smelt (smelled)* | sentir (nez) |
| *spell* | *spelled (spelt)* | *spelled (spelt)* | épeler |
| [ʌ] | [ʌ] | [ʌ] | |
| *cut* | *cut* | *cut* | couper |
| *shut* | *shut* | *shut* | fermer |
| *thrust* | *thrust* | *thrust* | enfoncer |
| [ʊ] | [ʊ] | [ʊ] | |
| *put* | *put* | *put* | mettre |
| [D] | [D] | [D] | |
| *cost* | *cost* | *cost* | coûter |

---

1. **knit** : régulier au sens propre *(a knitted sweater)*, irrégulier au sens figuré *(a well-knit plot* : une conspiration bien ourdie).
2. **rid** : surtout employé au participe passé : *to get rid of* (se débarrasser de).

# TROIS VOYELLES SEMBLABLES : AAA

| A | A | A | |
|---|---|---|---|
| [iː] | [iː] | [iː] | |
| beat | beat | beaten | battre [1] |
| bereave | bereaved (bereft) | bereaved (bereft) | dépouiller |
| dream | dreamed (dreamt) | dreamed (dreamt) | rêver |
| lean | leaned (leant) | leaned (leant) | s'appuyer |
| kneel | kneeled (knelt) | kneeled (knelt) | s'agenouiller |
| beseech | beseeched (besought) | beseeched (besought) | implorer |
| [ɜr] | [ɜr] | [ɜr] | |
| burst | burst | burst | éclater |
| hurt | hurt | hurt | faire mal |
| burn | burned (burnt) | burned (burnt) | brûler |
| gird | girded (girt) | girded (girt) | ceindre (litt.) |
| learn | learned (learnt) | learned (learnt) | apprendre |
| [ɔi] | [ɔi] | [ɔi] | |
| spoil | spoiled (spoilt) | spoiled (spoilt) | gâter, gâcher |
| [æ] | [æ] | [æ] | |
| broadcast | broadcast (broadcasted) | broadcast | diffuser |
| cast | cast | cast | lancer |
| forecast | forecast (forecasted) | forecast (forecasted) | prévoir |
| have | had | had | avoir |
| [ai] | [ai] | [ai] | |
| thrive | thrived (throve] | thrived (thriven) | prospérer |
| [ei] | [ei] | [ei] | |
| lade | laded | laden | charger |
| make | made | made | fabriquer |
| lay | laid | laid | poser à plat |
| pay | paid | paid | payer |

---

1. **beat** : le participe passé est *beat* dans *(dead-)beat* (crevé de fatigue) et *deadbeat* (irresponsable financièrement) (fam.)

# TROIS VOYELLES SEMBLABLES : AAA

| A | A | A | |
|---|---|---|---|
| [ɒ] | [ɒ] | [ɒ] | |
| saw | sawed | sawed (sawn) | scier |
| [u:] | [u:] | [u:] | |
| strew | strewed | strewed (strewn) | joncher |
| [hju:] | [hju:] | [hju:] | |
| hew | hewed | hewn (hewed) | tailler à la hache |
| [o:] | [o:] | [o:] | |
| clothe | clothed (clad) | clothed (clad) | vêtir (litt.) |
| mow | mowed | mowed (mown) | faucher |
| show | showed | shown (showed) | montrer |
| sow | sowed | sown (sowed) | semer |
| sew | sewed | sewn (sewed) | coudre |

---

Dans cette catégorie, le participe passé est le plus souvent devenu aussi régulier. La forme irrégulière est quelquefois conservée pour l'adjectif.

On peut y ajouter des formes isolées comme :
– **wrought** (de *to work* : œuvrer) dans *wrought iron* : le fer forgé,
– **shaven** dans *a clean-shaven face* : un visage bien rasé,
– **molten** (de *to melt* : fondre) dans *molten lead* : plomb fondu,
– **rotten** (de *to rot* : pourrir) dans *rotten eggs* : œufs pourris,
– **sewn** (de *to sew* : coudre) dans *hand-sewn clothing* : vêtements cousus à la main,
  alors que les participes passés à valeur verbale sont réguliers.

# DEUX VOYELLES SEMBLABLES : ABB

| A | B | B | |
|---|---|---|---|
| [ɪ] | [ʌ] | [ʌ] | |
| cling | clung | clung | s'accrocher |
| dig | dug | dug | creuser |
| fling | flung | flung | lancer, jeter |
| sling | slung | slung | lancer (fronde) |
| slink | slunk | slunk | aller furtivement |
| spin | spun | spun | tournoyer |
| stick | stuck | stuck | coller |
| sting | stung | stung | piquer (insecte) |
| string | strung | strung | enfiler [1] |
| swing | swung | swung | (se) balancer |
| wring | wrung | wrung | tordre |
| win | won | won | gagner |
| [æ] | [ʌ] | [ʌ] | |
| hang | hung | hung | pendre [2] |
| [ai] | [ʌ] | [ʌ] | |
| strike | struck | struck (stricken) | frapper [3] |
| [ai] | [ɪ] | [ɪ] | |
| bite | bit | bitten / bit | mordre |
| chide | chid | chidden | gronder |
| hide | hid | hidden (hid) | cacher |
| light | lit (lighted) | lit (lighted) | allumer [4] |
| slide | slid | slid | glisser |
| [ai] | [D] | [D] | |
| shine | shone (shined) | shone (shined) | briller [5] |
| [ei] | [e] | [e] | |
| say | said | said | dire |

---

1. **string** : on utilise le participe passé régulier dans *stringed instruments* (instruments à cordes).
2. **hang** : le verbe est régulier dans le sens de : exécuter par pendaison.
3. **strike** : au sens figuré, le participe passé peut être *stricken*.
4. **light** : le participe régulier est employé comme un adjectif : *a lighted candle*. Le participe passé irrégulier s'emploie après *be* comme attribut du groupe sujet *(the candle is lit)* et dans les composés *(floodlit* : illuminé).
5. **shine** : le verbe est régulier dans : *to shine shoes* (cirer des chaussures).

# DEUX VOYELLES SEMBLABLES : ABB

| A | B | B | |
|---|---|---|---|
| [iː] | [e] | [e] | |
| lead | led | led | mener |
| read | read | read | lire |
| bleed | bled | bled | saigner |
| breed | bred | bred | élever (bêtes) [1] |
| feed | fed | fed | nourrir |
| flee | fled | fled | fuir [2] |
| speed | sped (speeded) | sped (speeded) | (se) hâter |
| leave | left | left | laisser, quitter |
| deal | dealt | dealt | distribuer |
| leap | leapt (leaped) | leapt (leaped) | sauter |
| mean | meant | meant | signifier |
| creep | crept | crept | ramper |
| feel | felt | felt | ressentir |
| keep | kept | kept | garder |
| meet | met | met | (se) rencontrer |
| sleep | slept | slept | dormir |
| sweep | swept | swept | balayer |
| weep | wept | wept | pleurer |
| [æ] | [ʊ] | [ʊ] | |
| stand | stood | stood | être debout |
| understand | understood | understood | comprendre |
| [e] | [oː] | [oː] | |
| sell | sold | sold | vendre |
| tell | told | told | raconter |
| [uː] | [ɒ] | [ɒ] | |
| shoe | shod (shoed) | shod (shoed) | ferrer [3] |
| lose | lost | lost | perdre |
| shoot | shot | shot | tirer (armes) |

---

1. **breed** : quand il s'agit d'enfants : *bring up* ou *raise*.
2. **flee** : à l'infinitif, on emploie plutôt *fly away*.
3. **shoe** : pour les personnes, s'emploie surtout au participe passé (*well shod* : bien chaussé).

# DEUX VOYELLES SEMBLABLES : ABB

| A | B | B | |
|---|---|---|---|
| [ai] | [au] | [au] | |
| *bind* | *bound* | *bound* | lier |
| *find* | *found* | *found* | trouver |
| *grind* | *ground* | *ground* | moudre |
| *wind* | *wound* | *wound* | enrouler |
| [ɔ:] | [e] | [e] | |
| *hold* | *held* | *held* | tenir |
| [i:] | [ɜr] | [ɜr] | |
| *hear* | *heard* | *heard* | entendre |
| [i:] | [ɒ] | [ɒ] | |
| *seek* | *sought* | *sought* | chercher |
| *teach* | *taught* | *taught* | enseigner |
| [ɪ] | [ɒ] | [ɒ] | |
| *bring* | *brought* | *brought* | apporter |
| *think* | *thought* | *thought* | penser |
| [ai] | [ɒ] | [ɒ] | |
| *buy* | *bought* | *bought* | acheter |
| *fight* | *fought* | *fought* | combattre |
| [æ] | [ɒ] | [ɒ] | |
| *catch* | *caught* | *caught* | attraper |
| [ɪ] | [æ] | [æ] | |
| *sit* | *sat* | *sat* | être assis |
| *spit* | *spat* | *spat* | cracher |
| [e] | [ɒ] | [ɒ] | |
| *forget* | *forgot* | *forgot (forgotten)* | oublier |
| *get* | *got* | *got* | obtenir [1] |
| *tread* | *trod* | *trodden* | piétiner |

---

1. **get** : *gotten = obtained, become.* Dans les composés : *forget* → *forgotten*, *beget* → *begotten* (litt.).

# DEUX VOYELLES SEMBLABLES : ABB / AAB

| A | B | B | |
|---|---|---|---|
| [iː] | [oː] | [oː] | |
| *heave* | *hove (heaved)* | *hove (heaved)* | soulever [1] |
| *speak* | *spoke* | *spoken* | parler |
| *steal* | *stole* | *stolen* | dérober |
| *weave* | *wove* | *woven* | tisser |
| *freeze* | *froze* | *frozen* | geler |
| [uː] | [oː] | [oː] | |
| *choose* | *chose* | *chosen* | choisir |
| [ei] | [oː] | [oː] | |
| *awake* | *awoke* | *awoken* | éveiller |
| *break* | *broke* | *broken* | casser [2] |
| *wake* | *woke (waked)* | *woken (waked)* | réveiller [3] |
| [ai] | [ei] | [ei] | |
| *lie* | *lay* | *lain* | être couché [4] |
| [e] | [ɔr] | [ɔr] | |
| *bear* | *bore* | *borne / born* | (sup)porter [5] |
| *tear* | *tore* | *torn* | déchirer |
| *swear* | *swore* | *sworn* | jurer |
| *wear* | *wore* | *worn* | porter, user (vêtements) |

| A | A | B | |
|---|---|---|---|
| [e] | [e] | [oː] | |
| *swell* | *swelled* | *swollen (swelled)* | enfler |
| [ai] | [ai] | [ɪ] | |
| *shrive* | *shrived* | *shriven (shrived)* | confesser (litt.) |
| [iː] | [iː] | [ɔr] | |
| *shear* | *sheared* | *shorn (sheared)* | tondre |
| [iː] | [iː] | [oː] | |
| *cleave* | *cleaved / clove (cleft)* | *cloven / cleft (cleaved)* | fendre [6] (litt.) |

1. **heave** : le verbe n'est irrégulier que dans la langue des marins (*to heave the anchor* : lever l'ancre).
2. **break** : le participe passé *broke* est employé dans un sens familier : fauché.
3. **wake** : régulier parfois en Amérique du Nord.
4. **lie** : régulier dans le sens de mentir.
5. **bear** : *to be born* = naître (verbe passif).
6. **cleave** : emplois courants du participe passé *cloven*, dans *cloven hoof* (sabot / pied fourchu), de *cleft* dans *to be in a cleft stick* (être dans une impasse).

# DEUX VOYELLES SEMBLABLES : ABA

| A | B | A | |
|---|---|---|---|
| [ʌ] | [æ] | [ʌ] | |
| *run* | *ran* | *run* | courir |
| [ʌ] | [ei] | [ʌ] | |
| *become* | *became* | *become* | devenir |
| *come* | *came* | *come* | venir |
| [ı] | [ei] | [ı] | |
| *forgive* | *forgave* | *forgiven* | pardonner |
| *give* | *gave* | *given* | donner |
| [i:] | [ei] | [i:] | |
| *eat* | *ate* | *eaten* | manger |
| [i:] | [ɒ] | [i:] | |
| *see* | *saw* | *seen* | voir |
| [i:] | [ɒ] | [i:] | |
| *be* | *was (were)* | *been* | être |
| [ɒ] | [e] | [ɒ] | |
| *fall* | *fell* | *fallen* | tomber |
| [ɒ] | [u:] | [ɒ] | |
| *draw* | *drew* | *drawn* | tirer |
| *withdraw* | *withdrew* | *withdrawn* | (se) retirer |
| [ei] | [ʊ] | [ei] | |
| *mistake* | *mistook* | *mistaken* | se tromper |
| *shake* | *shook* | *shaken* | secouer |
| *take* | *took* | *taken* | prendre |
| *undertake* | *undertook* | *undertaken* | entreprendre |
| [ei] | [u:] | [ei] | |
| *slay* | *slew (slayed)* | *slain* | assassiner |
| [o:] | [u:] | [o:] | |
| *blow* | *blew* | *blown* | souffler |
| *grow* | *grew* | *grown* | croître |
| *throw* | *threw* | *thrown* | jeter |
| [o:] | [nju:] | [o:] | |
| *know* | *knew* | *known* | savoir |

# TROIS VOYELLES DIFFÉRENTES : ABC

| A | B | C | |
|---|---|---|---|
| [ɪ] | [æ] | [ʌ] | |
| *begin* | *began* | *begun* | commencer |
| *swim* | *swam* | *swum* | nager |
| *ring* | *rang* | *rung* | sonner [1] |
| *sing* | *sang* | *sung* | chanter |
| *spring* | *sprang* | *sprung* | bondir |
| *drink* | *drank* | *drunk* | boire [2] |
| *shrink* | *shrank* | *shrunk* | se rétrécir [3] |
| *sink* | *sank / sunk* | *sunk* | sombrer [4] |
| *stink* | *stank* | *stunk* | puer |
| [ai] | [oː] | [ɪ] | |
| *arise* | *arose* | *arisen* | survenir |
| *drive* | *drove* | *driven* | conduire |
| *strive* | *strove (strived)* | *striven* | s'efforcer |
| *ride* | *rode* | *ridden* | chevaucher |
| *stride* | *strode* | *stridden* | enjamber |
| *smite* | *smote* | *smitten* | frapper |
| *write* | *wrote* | *written* | écrire |
| *rise* | *rose* | *risen* | se lever |
| [uː] | [ɪ] | [ʌ] | |
| *do* | *did* | *done* | faire |
| [oː] | [e] | [ɒ] | |
| *go* | *went* | *gone* | aller |
| [ai] | [uː] | [oː] | |
| *fly* | *flew* | *flown* | voler (air) |

---

1. ***ring*** : régulier dans le sens de : encercler.
2. ***drink*** : le participe passé *drunken* est utilisé comme adjectif *(a drunken man)* mais on dit : *he is drunk.*
3. ***shrink*** : de même *shrunken* : ratatiné.
4. ***sink*** : de même *sunken* : creux (joues, yeux).

# INDEX GÉNÉRAL

T   transitif
I   intransitif
A   auxiliaire
C   verbe à complémentation (voir liste des verbes à complémentation, p. 167-174)
◊   verbe pouvant s'associer avec 1 à 10 particules
◊◊   verbe pouvant s'associer avec 11 à 20 particules
◊◊◊   verbe pouvant s'associer avec plus de 20 particules (voir liste des verbes à particule, p. 175-208)

Les verbes irréguliers sont en couleur (voir liste des verbes irréguliers, p. 209-219).

Les modifications orthographiques sont indiquées entre parenthèses.

- **bb**, **gg**, **ll**, **rr**, **tt**... = redoublement de la consonne finale :
  *beg → begged / begged / begging*
- **ie** = **y** final remplacé par **ie** au présent (3ᵉ pers. du sing.) et au passé :
  *carry → carries / carried*
- **es** = **e** ajouté au présent (3ᵉ pers. du sing.) :
  *harrass → harrasses*
- **yi** = **ie** devient **y** devant **ing** :
  *die → dying*

*a*

abandon, ◊, T, C
abase, T
abash (es), ◊, T
abate, T/I
abbreviate, ◊, T
abdicate, T/I
abduct, T
abet (tt), ◊, T
abhor (rr), T, C
abide, ◊, T/I
abjure, T
abnegate, T
abolish (es), T
abominate, T, C
abort, T/I
abound, ◊, I
abrade, T
abridge, T
abrogate, T
absent, ◊, T
absolve, ◊, T
absorb, ◊, T, C
abstain, ◊, I, C
abstract, ◊, T
abuse, T
abut (tt), ◊, I
accede, ◊, I
accelerate, T/I
accent, T
accentuate, T
accept, ◊, T, C
access (es), ◊, I
acclaim, T
acclimatize (-ise), ◊, T/I
accommodate, ◊, T
accompany (ie), T

accomplish (es), T
accord, ◊, T/I
accost, T
account, ◊, T, C
accredit, ◊, T
accrue, ◊, I
accumulate, T/I
accuse, ◊, T, C
accustom, ◊, T, C
ache, ◊, I, C
achieve, T
acidify (ie), T
acidulate, T
acknowledge, ◊, T, C
acquaint, ◊, T
acquiesce, ◊, I
acquire, T
acquit (tt), ◊, T
act, ◊, T/I
activate, T
actuate, T
adapt, ◊, T/I
add, ◊, T/I, C
addict, ◊, T, C
addle, T/I
address (es), ◊, T
adduce, T
adhere, ◊, I
adjoin, T/I
adjourn, ◊, T/I
adjudge, T
adjudicate, ◊, T/I
adjure, T, C
adjust, ◊, T/I
ad-lib (bb), T/I
administer, ◊, T/I
administrate, T
admire, ◊, T
admit (tt), ◊, T, C
admix (es), T/I
admonish (es), T, C

adopt, ◊, T
adore, T, C
adorn, ◊, T
adulate, T
adulterate, T
adumbrate, T
advance, ◊, T/I
advantage, T
adventure, T/I
advert, ◊, I (litt.)
advertise, ◊, T/I, C
advise, ◊, T/I, C
advocate, T, C
aerate, T
affect, ◊, T
affiliate, ◊, T
affirm, ◊, T, C
affix (es), ◊, T
afflict, ◊, T
afford, T, C
afforest, T
affront, T
age, T/I
agglomerate, T/I
agglutinate, ◊, T/I
aggrandize (-ise), T
aggravate, T
aggregate, T/I
aggrieve, T
agitate, ◊, T/I
agonize (-ise), T/I
agree, ◊, T/I, C
aid, T, C
ail, T/I
aim, ◊, T/I, C
air, T
airmail, ◊, T
alarm, ◊, T
alert, ◊, T
alienate, ◊, T
alight, ◊, I

align, ◊, T / I

allay, T

allege, T, C

allegorize (-ise), T / I

alleviate, T

alliterate, T / I

allocate, ◊, T, C

allot (tt), ◊, T, C

allow, ◊, T, C

alloy, T

allude, ◊, I

allure, ◊, T

ally (ie), ◊, T / I

alphabetize (-ise), T

alter, T / I

alternate, ◊, T / I

amalgamate, ◊, T / I

amass, T

amaze, ◊, T

amble, ◊◊◊, I

ambush (es), T / I

ameliorate, T / I

amend, T / I

Americanize (-ise), T

amortize (-ise), T

amount, ◊, I, C

amplify (ies), T

amputate, T

amuse, ◊, T, C

anaesthetize / anesthetize (-ise), T

analyze (-yse), T

anathematize (-ise), T

anatomize (-ise), T

anchor, T / I

anger, T

angle, ◊, T / I

anglicize (-ise), T

animalize (-ise), T

animate, T

annex (es), ◊, T

annihilate, T

annotate, T

announce, ◊, T, C

annoy, ◊, T

annul (ll / l), T

annunciate, T, C

anoint, ◊, T

answer, ◊, T / I, C

antagonize (-ise), T

antedate, T

anticipate, T, C

ape, T

apologize (-ise), ◊, I, C

appall (-pal [ll]), ◊, T

apparel, T

appeal, ◊, I, C

appear, ◊, I

appease, T

append, ◊, T

appertain, ◊, I

applaud, T

apply (ie), ◊, T / I, C

appoint, ◊, T, C

apportion, ◊, T

appose, ◊, T

appraise, T

appreciate, T / I, C

apprehend, T

apprentice, ◊, T

apprise, ◊, T

approach (es), ◊, T / I

approbate, ◊, T

appropriate, ◊, T

approve, ◊, T, C

approximate, ◊, T / I

arbitrate, ◊, T / I

arc, ◊, I

arch (es), ◊, T / I

argue, ◊, T / I, C

arise, ◊, I

arm, ◊, T / I

armour (-or), T

arouse, ◊, T

arraign, ◊, T, C

arrange, ◊, T / I, C

array, T

arrest, T

arrive, ◊, I

arrogate, ◊, T

arrow, T / I

article, T

articulate, T / I

ascend, T / I

ascertain, T

ascribe, ◊, T

ask, ◊, T / I, C

aspirate, T

aspire, ◊, I, C

assail, ◊, T

assassinate, T

assault, T

assemble, T / I

assent, ◊, I

assert, T, C

assess (es), ◊, T

assign, ◊, T

assimilate, ◊, T / I

assist, ◊, T / I, C

associate, ◊, T / I, C

assort, ◊, T / I

assuage, T

assume, T, C

assure, ◊, T, C

asterisk, T

astonish (es), ◊, T, C

astound, T

atomize (-ise), T

atone, ◊, T, C

atrophy, (ies), I

attach (es), ◊, T / I

attack, T

attain, ◊, T / I

attempt, T, C
attend, ◊, T / I
attenuate, T / I
attest, ◊, T / I, C
attire, ◊, T
attitudinize (-ise), I
attract, ◊, T
attribute, ◊, T
attune, ◊, T
auction, ◊, T
audit, T
audition, ◊, T / I
augment, T / I
augur, T / I, C
authenticate, T
author, T
authorize (-ise), T, C
autograph, T
automate, T
automatize (-ise), T
avail, ◊, T / I
avalanche, I
avenge, ◊, T
aver (rr), T / I, C (litt.)
average, ◊, T / I
avert, ◊, T
avoid, T, C
await, T
awake, ◊, T / I
awaken, ◊, T / I
award, ◊, T
awe, ◊, T
axe, T

*b*

baa, I
babble, ◊, T / I

baby (ie), T
baby-sit (tt), T / I
back, ◊, T / I
backcomb, T
backdate, ◊, T
backfire, I
backslide, I
backspace, I
backtrack, I
badger, ◊, T, C
baffle, T
bag (gg), ◊, T / I
bail, ◊, T
bait, ◊, T, C
bake, T / I
balance, ◊, T / I
bale, ◊, T
balk, ◊, T / I
ballast, T
balloon, I
ballot, ◊, I
bamboozle, ◊, T, C
ban (nn), T
band, ◊, T / I
bandage, ◊, T
bandy (ie), ◊, T
bang, ◊, T / I
banish (es), ◊, T
bank, ◊, T / I
bankroll, T
bankrupt, T
banquet, T / I
banter, T / I
baptize (-ise), T
bar (rr), ◊, T, C
barb, T
barbarize (-ise), T / I
barbecue, T
barber, T
bare, ◊, T
bargain, ◊, I

barge, ◊◊◊, T / I
bark, ◊, T / I, C
barrel (ll), T / I
barricade, ◊, T
barter, ◊, T / I
base, ◊, T
bash (es), ◊, T
bask, ◊, I
bastardize (-ise), T
baste, T
bat (tt), ◊, T / I
batch (es), I
bath, T / I
bathe, ◊, T / I
batten, ◊, T / I
batter, ◊, T / I
battle, ◊, I
bawl, ◊, T / I
bay, ◊, I
bayonet (tt), T
be, ◊◊◊, I / A
beach (es), T / I
beacon, T
bead, T / I
beagle, I
beam, ◊, T / I
bear, ◊◊, T / I, C
beard, T
beat, ◊◊, T / I, C
beatify (ie), T
beautify (ie), T
beckon, ◊, T / I
become, ◊, T / I
bed (dd), ◊, T / I
bedaub, ◊, T
bedeck, ◊, T
bedevil (ll / l), T
bedew, ◊, T
beef, ◊, T / I
beep, T / I
beetle, ◊, I

befall, T/I

befit (tt), T

befoul, ◊, T

befriend, T

befuddle, ◊, T

beg (gg), ◊, T/I, C

beget (tt), T (litt.)

begin (nn), ◊, T/I, C

begrime, ◊, T

begrudge, T

beguile, ◊, T, C

behave, ◊, I

behead, T

behold, T

behoove, T, C (litt.)

belay, T/I

belch, ◊, T/I

belie (yi), T

believe, ◊, T/I, C

belittle, T

bell, T

bellow, ◊, T/I

belly (ie), ◊, T/I

belong, ◊, I

belt, ◊, T/I

bemoan, T

bemuse, T

bench (es), T

benchmark, T

bend, ◊, T/I

benefit, ◊, T/I, C

benumb, ◊, T

bequeath, ◊, T

berate, T

bereave, ◊, T

berth, T/I

beseech (es), T, C

beset (tt), ◊, T

besiege, ◊, T

besmear, ◊, T

besmirch (es), T

bespatter, ◊, T

bespeak, T (litt.)

best, ◊, T

bestir (rr), T (litt.)

bestow, ◊, T

bestrew, ◊, T

bestride, T (litt.)

bet (tt), ◊, T/I, C

betake, T (litt.)

bethink, ◊, T, C (arch.)

betide*, T/I

betray, ◊, T

betroth, ◊, T

better, T/I

bevel (ll / l), T/I

bewail, T

beware, ◊, T/I

bewilder, T

bewitch (es), T

bias (es), ◊, T

bicker, ◊, I

bicycle, ◊◊◊, I

bid (dd), ◊, T/I, C

bide, T/I

biff, T (fam.)

bifurcate, T/I

bike, ◊◊◊, I

bilk, ◊, T, C

bill, T

billet, ◊, T

billow, I

bind, ◊, T/I, C

birch (es), T

bisect, T/I

bite, ◊, T/I

bivouac, T (litt.)

blab (bb), ◊, T/I, C

blabber, ◊, T

black, ◊, T/I

blackball, T

blacken, ◊, T/I

blacklist, T

blackmail, ◊, T, C

blame, ◊, T

blanch (es), T/I

blank, ◊, T

blanket, ◊, T

blare, ◊, T/I, C

blaspheme, ◊, T/I

blast, ◊, T, C

blather, T/I

blaze, ◊, T/I

blazon, ◊, T

bleach (es), ◊, T/I

bleat, ◊, T/I, C

bleed, ◊, T/I

bleep, T/I

blemish (es), T

blench (es), T

blend, ◊, T/I

bless (es), ◊, T

blight, T

blind, ◊, T

blindfold, T

blink, ◊, T/I

blister, T/I

blitz (es), T

bloat, T/I

block, ◊, T/I

blockade, T

blood, T

bloom, ◊, I

blossom, ◊, I

blot (tt), ◊, T/I

blotch (es), T/I

blow, ◊◊, T/I

---

* *Betide* n'existe qu'à l'impératif et à la 3e personne du singulier : *Woe betide those who...* Malheur à ceux qui...

blubber, ◊, T/I, C

bludgeon, T

blue, T

bluff, ◊, T/I, C

blunder, ◊, T/I

blunt, T

blur (rr), ◊, T

blurt, ◊, T, C

blush (es), ◊, I, C

bluster, I

board, ◊, T/I

boast, ◊, T/I, C

boat, T/I

bob (bb), ◊, T/I

bobsled (dd), I

bode, T/I

bog (gg), ◊, T/I

boggle, ◊, I

boil, ◊, T/I

bolster, ◊, T

bolt, ◊, T/I

bomb, ◊, T/I

bombard, ◊, T

bond, T

bone, T

boo, T/I

book, ◊, T/I

boom, T/I

boomerang, I

boost, ◊, T

boot, ◊, T

bootleg (gg), T/I

bootstrap (pp), T

booze, I

border, ◊, T/I

bore, ◊, T/I

borrow, ◊, T

boss (es), ◊, T

botanize (-ise), I

botch (es), ◊, T

bother, ◊, T/I, C

bottle, ◊, T

bottle-feed, T

bottom, ◊, T/I

bounce, ◊◊◊, T/I

bound, ◊, T/I

bow, ◊, T/I

bowdlerize (-ise), T

bowl, ◊, T/I

box (es), ◊, T/I

brace, ◊, T/I

bracket, T

brag (gg), ◊, T/I, C

braid, T

brain, T

brake, I

branch (es), ◊, T/I

brand, ◊, T

brandish (es), T

brave, T

brawl, I

bray, I

braze, T

brazen, ◊, T

breach (es), T/I

bread, T

break, ◊◊, T/I

breakfast, ◊, I

breast, T

breast-feed, T

breathalyze (-lyse), T

breathe, ◊, T/I

breech (es), T

breed, ◊, T/I

breeze, ◊, I

brew, ◊, T/I

bribe, ◊, T, C

brick, ◊, T

bridge, ◊, T

bridle, ◊, T/I

brief, T

brigade, T

brighten, ◊, T/I

brim (mm), ◊, T/I

bring, ◊◊, T, C

brisk, ◊, T/I

bristle, ◊, T/I

broach (es), ◊, T

broadcast, T/I, C

broaden, ◊, T/I

brocade, T

broil, T/I

bronze, T/I

brood, ◊, I

brook, T

browbeat, ◊, T, C

brown, ◊, T/I

browse, ◊, T/I

bruise, T/I

brush (es), ◊, T/I

brutalize (-ise), ◊, T

bubble, ◊, I

buck, ◊, T/I

buckle, ◊, T/I

bud (dd), T/I

budge, T/I

budget, ◊, T

buffer, T

buffet, ◊, T/I

bug (gg), ◊, T

build, ◊, T/I

bulge, ◊,T/I

bulk, ◊, I

bull, T

bulldoze, ◊, T, C

bully (ie), ◊, T/I, C

bum (mm), ◊, T/I (fam.)

bump, ◊, T/I

bunch (es), ◊, T/I

bundle, ◊, T/I

bung, ◊, T

bungle, T/I

bunk, ◊, I

bunker, T

buoy, ◊, T

burble, I

burden, ◊, T

burgeon, I

burglarize (-ise), T

burgle, T/I

burn, ◊, T/I, C

burnish (es), T/I

burp, ◊, T

burr, T/I

burrow, ◊, T/I

burst, ◊, T/I, C

bury (ie), ◊, T

bus (ss/es), T/I

busk, T

bust, ◊, T/I, C

bustle, ◊, T/I

busy (ie) ◊, T/I, C

butcher, T

butt, ◊, T/I

butter, ◊, T

button, ◊, T

buttonhole, T

buttress (es), ◊, T

buy, ◊, T/I

buzz (es), ◊, T/I

bypass (es), T

# C

cable, ◊, T, C

cache, T

cackle, I

cadge, ◊, T/I

cage, ◊, T

cajole, ◊, T, C

cake, ◊, T/I

calcify (ie), T/I

calcine, T/I

calculate, ◊, T/I, C

calibrate, T

calk, T

call, ◊◊, T/I

calm, ◊, T/I

calve, T/I

camber, T/I

camouflage, T

camp, ◊, T/I

campaign, ◊, I

can* (nn), T

can, A

Canadianize (-ise), T

canalize (-ise), ◊, T

cancel (ll/l), ◊, T

cane, T

canker, T

cannibalize (-ise), T

cannon, ◊, I

canonize (-ise), T

canoodle, T/I

canopy (ie), T

cant, T/I

canter, T/I

canvass (es), ◊, T/I

cap (pp), ◊, T

capacitate, T

caper, I

capitalize (-ise), ◊, T/I

capitulate, I

capsize (-ise), T/I

captain, T

caption, T

captivate, T

capture, ◊, T

caramelize (-ise), T/I

carbonize (-ise), T

card, T

care, ◊, I, C

careen, T/I

career, ◊◊◊, I

caretake, T

carol (ll/l), T/I

carom, I

carouse, I

carp, ◊, I

carpenter, I

carpet, ◊, T

carry (ie), ◊◊, T/I

cart, T

cartoon, T

carve, ◊, T

cascade, ◊◊, T/I

case, T

cash (es), ◊, T

cashier, T

cast, ◊◊, T/I

castigate, T

castrate, T

catapult, T

catch (es), ◊, T/I

categorize (-ise), T

cater, ◊, I

caterwaul, I

catnap (pp), I

caulk, T

cause, T, C

cauterize (-ise), T

caution, ◊, T, C

cave, ◊, T/I

cavil (ll/l), ◊, I

cavort, I

caw, I

cease, ◊, T/I, C

cede, ◊, T

---

* Ne pas confondre l'auxiliaire modal *can* avec le verbe ordinaire *to can* : mettre en conserve.

celebrate, T/I
cellar, T
cement, T
censor, T
censure, ◊, T
centralize (-ise), T/I
centre (-ter), ◊, T/I
centuple, T
certificate, T
certify (ie), ◊, T, C
chafe, ◊, T/I
chaff, T
chagrin, ◊, T, C
chain, ◊, T
chain-smoke, T/I
chair, T
chalk, ◊, T
challenge, T, C
chamfer, T
champ, ◊, T/I
champion, T, C
chance, ◊, T/I, C
change, ◊◊, T/I
channel (ll/l), ◊, T
channelize (-ise), T
chant, T/I
chap (pp), T/I
chaperon, T
char (rr), T/I
characterize (-ise), T
charge, ◊, T/I, C
charm, ◊, T/I
chart, ◊, T
charter, T
chase, ◊, T
chasten, T
chastise, ◊, T, C
chat (tt), ◊, I
chatter, I
chauffeur, T
cheapen, T/I

cheat, ◊, T/I, C
check, ◊, T/I
checkmate, T
checkpoint, T
cheep, T/I
cheer, ◊, T/I, C
cheese, ◊, T
chequer (checker), T
cherish (es), T
chew, ◊, T/I
chide, ◊, T, C
chill, T/I
chime, ◊, T/I
chink, T/I
chip (pp), ◊, T/I
chirp, I
chirr, I
chisel (ll/l), ◊, T
chitter, I
chi(v)vy (ie), ◊, T, C
chlorinate, T
chloroform, T
chock, T
choke, ◊, T/I
chomp, T
choose, ◊, T/I, C
chop (pp), ◊, T/I
choreograph, T
chortle, I
chorus (es), T/I
christen, ◊, T
Christianize (-ise), T
chronicle, T
chuck, ◊, T
chuckle, ◊, I
chug (gg), ◊◊◊, I
chum (mm), ◊, I (fam.)
churn, ◊, T/I
cicatrize (-ise), T/I
cipher, T/I
circle, ◊, T/I

circularize (-ise), T
circulate, ◊, T/I
circumcise, T
circumnavigate, T
circumscribe, ◊, T
circumvent, T
cite, ◊, T
civilize (-ise), T
clack, T/I
claim, ◊, T, C
clamber, ◊, I
clamour (-or), ◊, I
clamp, ◊, T/I
clank, T/I
clap (pp), ◊, T/I
clarify (ies), T
clash (es), ◊, T/I
clasp, ◊, T
class (es), ◊, T
classify (ie), T
clatter, ◊, T/I
claw, ◊, T/I
clean, ◊, T/I
cleanse, T
clear, ◊, T/I
cleave, ◊, T/I
clench (es), T
clerk, I
click, ◊, T/I
climb, ◊, T/I
clinch (es), T/I
cling, ◊, I
clink, T/I
clip (pp), ◊, T
cloak, T
clobber, T
clock, ◊, T
clog (gg), ◊, T/I
cloister, T
clone, T
clop, ◊◊◊, I

close, ◊◊, T/I
closet, ◊, T
clot (tt), T/I
clothe, ◊, T
cloud, ◊, T/I
clout, T
clown, ◊, I
cloy, T/I
club (bb), ◊, T/I
cluck, ◊, T
clue, ◊, T
clump, T/I
cluster, ◊, T/I
clutch (es), ◊, T/I
clutter, ◊, T/I
coach (es), ◊, T/I
coagulate, T/I
coal, T/I
coalesce, I
coarsen, I
coast, ◊, T/I
coat, ◊, T
coax (es), ◊, T, C
cobble, T
cock, ◊, T
cockle, T/I
cocoon, T/I
coddle, T
code, T
codify (ie), T
coerce, ◊, T, C
coexist, ◊, I
cogitate, ◊, T/I, C
cohabit, ◊, I
cohere, I
coil, ◊, T/I
coin, ◊, T
coincide, ◊, I
cold-shoulder, T
collaborate, ◊, I
collapse, T/I

collar, T
collate, ◊, T
collect, ◊, T/I
collectivize (-ise), T
collide, ◊, I
collocate, ◊, T
colonize (-ise), T
colour (-or), ◊, T/I
comb, ◊, T/I
combat, ◊, T/I
combine, ◊, T/I
come, ◊◊◊, I, C
comfort, T
command, T/I, C
commandeer, T
commemorate, T
commence, ◊, T/I, C
commend, ◊, T
comment, ◊, T/I
commentate, ◊, T/I
commercialize (-ise), T
commingle (comingle), T/I
comminute, T
commiserate, ◊, T/I
commission, ◊, T, C
commit (tt), ◊, T, C
commune, ◊, I
communicate, ◊, T/I
communize (-ise), T
commutate, T
commute, ◊, T/I
compact, ◊, T
compare, ◊, T/I
compartmentalize (-ise), T
compass (es), ◊, T
compel (ll/l), ◊, T, C
compensate, ◊, T/I
compete, ◊, I
compile, T
complain, ◊, I, C
complement, T

complete, T
complicate, ◊, T
compliment, ◊, T
comply (ie), ◊, I
comport, ◊, T/I
compose, ◊, T
compost, T
compound, ◊, T/I
comprehend, T
compress (es), ◊, T
comprise, ◊, T
compromise, ◊, T/I
compute, T, C
computerize (-ise), T
con (nn), ◊, T, C
concatenate, ◊, T
conceal, ◊, T
concede, ◊, T/I, C
conceive, ◊, T/I
concentrate, ◊, T/I
concentre (concenter), T/I
concern, ◊, T
concert, ◊, T/I
conciliate, T
conclude, ◊, T/I, C
concoct, T
concrete, T/I
concur (rr), ◊, I, C
concuss (es), T
condemn, ◊, T, C
condense, T/I
condescend, ◊, I, C
condition, ◊, T, C
condole, ◊, I
condone, T
conduce, ◊, I
conduct, ◊, T
cone, T
confabulate, I
confect, T
confederate, ◊, T/I

confer (rr), ◊, T/I

confess (es), ◊, T/I, C

confide, ◊, T/I, C

configure, T

confine, ◊, T, C

confirm, ◊, T, C

confiscate, ◊, T

conflate, T

conflict, ◊, I

conform, ◊, T/I

confound, ◊, T

confront, ◊, T

confuse, ◊, T, C

confute, T

congeal, T/I

congest, T/I

conglomerate, T/I

congratulate, ◊, T, C

congregate, T/I

conjecture, T/I, C

conjoin, T/I

conjugate, T/I

conjure, ◊, T/I, C

conk, ◊, T/I

connect, ◊, T/I

connive, ◊, I

connote, T

conquer, T

conscript, ◊, T

consecrate, ◊, T, C

consent, ◊, I, C

conserve, T

consider, ◊, T, C

consign, ◊, T

consist, ◊, I, C

console, ◊, T

consolidate, T/I

consort, ◊, I

conspire, ◊, T/I, C

constipate, T

constitute, T

constrain, ◊, T, C

constrict, T

construct, ◊, T

construe, ◊, T/I

consult, ◊, T/I

consume, ◊, T

consummate, T

contact, T

contain, ◊, T

containerize (-ise), T

contaminate, T

contemplate, T, C

contend, ◊, T/I, C

content ◊, T, C

contest, ◊, T/I

continue, ◊, T/I, C

contort, T

contour, T

contract, ◊, T/I, C

contradict, T

contrast, ◊, T/I

contravene, T

contribute, ◊, T/I, C

contrive, T, C

control (ll/l), T

controvert, T

convalesce, ◊, I

convene, T/I

conventionalize (-ise), T

converge, ◊, T/I

converse, ◊, I

convert, ◊, T

convey, ◊, T, C

convict, ◊, T, C

convince, ◊, T, C

convoke, T

convoy, T

convulse, ◊, T

coo, T/I

cook, ◊, T/I

cool, ◊, T/I

coop, ◊, T

cooperate / co-operate, ◊, I

co-opt, ◊, T

coordinate / co-ordinate, T

cop (pp), ◊, T

cope, ◊, I, C

copper, T

copulate, ◊, I

copy (ie), ◊, T

copyright, T

cord, T

cordon, ◊, T

core, T

cork, ◊, T

corner, T/I

corral, T

correct, T

correlate, ◊, T/I

correspond, ◊, I

corroborate, T

corrode, T/I

corrugate, T

corrupt, T/I

coruscate, I

cosset, ◊, T, C

cost, ◊, T/I

co-star (rr), ◊, T/I

cotton, ◊, T/I

couch (es), ◊, T/I

cough, ◊, T/I

could, A

counsel (ll/l), T/I, C

count, ◊◊, T/I, C

counter, ◊, T/I

counteract, T

counterbalance, T

counterclaim, T/I

counterfeit, T

countermand, T

counterplot (tt), T/I

counterpoise, T

countersign, T

countersink, T

countervail, T / I

couple, ◊, T / I

course, ◊, T / I

court, ◊, T / I, C

court-martial (ll / l), T

covenant, ◊, T / I, C

cover, ◊, T / I

covet, T

cow, ◊, T, C

cower, ◊, I

cox (es), T / I

crab (bb), ◊◊, T / I

crack, ◊, T / I

crackle, T / I

cradle, T

cram (mm), ◊, T / I

cramp, T

crane, ◊, T / I

crank, ◊, T

crash (es), ◊, T / I

crate, T

crave, ◊, T / I

crawl, ◊, I

crayon, T

craze, T / I

creak, I

cream, ◊, T

crease, ◊, T / I

create, T

credit, ◊, T, C

creep, ◊◊, I

cremate, T

creosote, T

crepitate, I

crest, T

crew, T/I

crib (bb), ◊, T / I

crick, T

criminate, T

crimp, T

cringe, ◊, I

crinkle, T / I

cripple, ◊, T

crisp, ◊, T / I

crisscross (es), T / I

criticize (-ise), ◊, T, C

croak, T / I

crock, ◊, T / I

crook, T

croon, T / I

crop (pp), ◊, T / I

cross (es), ◊, T / I

crossbreed, T / I

cross-check, T

crosscut (tt), T

cross-examine, T

crosshatch (es), T

cross-question, T

cross-reference, T / I

crouch (es), ◊, I

crow, ◊, I

crowd, ◊, T / I

crown, ◊, T

crucify (ie), T

cruise, I

crumble, ◊, T / I

crumple, ◊, T / I

crunch (es), ◊, T / I

crusade, ◊, I

crush (es), ◊, T / I

crust, ◊, T / I

cry (ie), ◊, T / I

crystallize (-ise), T / I

cube, T

cuddle, ◊, T / I

cudgel (ll/l), T

cue, ◊, T

cuff, T

cull, ◊, T

culminate, ◊, I, C

cultivate, T

cup (pp), ◊, T

curb, ◊, T

curdle, T / I

cure, ◊, T

curl, ◊, T / I

curry (ie), T

curse, ◊, T / I

curtail, T

curtain, ◊, T

curve, T / I

cushion, T

customize (-ise), T

cut (tt), ◊◊, T / I

cycle, ◊◊◊, I

*d*

dab (bb), ◊, T

dabble, ◊, T / I

dally (ie), ◊, I

dam (mm), ◊, T

damage, T

damn, T

damp, ◊, T

dampen, ◊, T / I

dance, ◊◊◊, T / I

dandle, T

dangle, ◊, T / I

dapple, T / I

dare*, T / A, C

darken, T / I

---

* *Dare* se comporte ou bien comme auxiliaire, ou bien comme verbe à part entière (voir p. 43).

darn, T

dart, ◊◊◊, T/I

dash (es), ◊◊, T/I

date, ◊, T/I

daub, ◊, T

daunt, T

dawdle, ◊, T/I

dawn, ◊, I, C

daydream, ◊, I

daze, T

dazzle, T

deactivate, T

deaden, ◊, T

deafen, T

deal, ◊, T/I

debar (rr), ◊, T, C

debark, T/I

debase, T

debate, ◊, T/I, C

debauch (es), T

debilitate, T

debit, ◊, T

debouch (es), I

debrief, T

debug (gg), T

debunk, T

decaffeinate, T

decalcify (ie), T

decamp, ◊, I

decant, T

decapitate, T

decapsulate, T

decarbonize (-ise), T

decay, T/I

decease, I

deceive, ◊, T/I, C

decelerate, T/I

decentralize (-ise), T/I

decide, ◊, T/I, C

decimalize (-ise), T,

decimate, T

decipher, T

deck, ◊, T

declaim, ◊, T/I

declare, ◊, T/I, C

declassify (ie), T

decline, T/I, C

declutch (es), I

decode, T

decolonize, T

decolourize (-ise, -orize), T

decompose, T/I

decompress (es), T

deconfigure, T

deconsecrate, T

decontaminate, T

decontrol (ll), T

decorate, ◊, T

decorticate, T

decouple, T/I

decoy, ◊, T, C

decrease, ◊, T/I

decree, T, C

decrement, T

decript, T

decry (ie), T

dedicate, ◊, T, C

deduce, ◊, T, C

deduct, ◊, T

deed, ◊, T

deem, T, C

de-emphasize (-ise), T

de-energize (-ise), T

deepen, T/I

deep-fry, (ie), T

de-expedite, T

deface, ◊, T

defalcate, I (litt.)

defame, T

default, ◊, T/I

defeat, T

defecate, I

defect, ◊, I

defend, ◊, T, C

defer (rr), T/I, C

defile, I

define, ◊, T

deflagrate, T/I

deflate, T

deflect, ◊, T/I

deflower, T

defoliate, T

deforest, T

deform, T

defraud, ◊, T

defray, T

defreeze, T

defrock, T

defrost, T

defuse, T

defy (ie), T, C

degauss (es), T

degenerate, ◊, I

degrade, T

dehumanize (-ise), T

dehumidify (ie), T

dehydrate, T

de-ice, T

deify (ie), T

deign, T, C

deinstall, T

deject, T

delay, ◊, T/I, C

delegate, ◊, T

delete, ◊, T

deliberate, ◊, T/I, C

delight, ◊, T/I, C

delimit, T

delineate, T

deliver, ◊, T

delouse, T

delude, ◊, T, C

deluge, ◊, T

delve, ◊, I
demagnetize (-ise), T
demand, ◊, T, C
demarcate, T
demean, T / I
demilitarize (-ise), T
demise, ◊, T
demist, T
demobilize (-ise), T
democratize (-ise), T / I
demolish (es), T
demonetize (-ise), T
demonstrate, ◊, T / I, C
demoralize (-ise), T
demote, ◊, T
demount, T
demur (rr), ◊, I
denationalize (-ise), T
denature, T
denazify (ie), T
denigrate, T
denominate, T
denote, T
denounce, ◊, T
dent, T
denude, ◊, T
deny (ie), ◊, T, C
deodorize (-ise), T
deoxidize (-ise), T
deoxygenate, T
depart, ◊, T / I
depend, ◊, I, C
depersonalize (-ise), T
depict, T
depilate, T
deplete, ◊, T
deplore, T, C
deploy, T / I
depolarize (-ise), T
depopulate, T
deport, T

depose, ◊, T / I, C
deposit, ◊, T
deprave, T
deprecate, T
depreciate, T / I
depress (es), T
deprive, ◊, T
depute, ◊, T, C
deputize (-ise), ◊, T / I
derail, T
derange, T
deregulate, T
deride, T
derive, ◊, T / I
derogate, ◊, I
desalinate, T
descale, T
descant, ◊, I
descend, ◊, T / I, C
describe, ◊, T
descry (ie), T (litt.)
desecrate, T
desegregate, T
desensitize (-ise), T
desert, T / I
deserve, T / I, C
design, ◊, T
designate, ◊, T
desire, T, C
desist, ◊, I, C
deskill, T
desolate, T
despair, ◊, I, C
despatch (es), ◊, T
despise, ◊, T, C
despoil, ◊, T
despond, I (arch.)
desquamate, T / I
destine, ◊, T
destroy, T
destruct, T / I

desulfurize (-ise), T
detach (es), ◊, T / I
detail, ◊, T
detain, T
detect, T
deter (rr), ◊, T, C
deteriorate, T / I
determine, ◊, T / I, C
detest, T, C
dethrone, T
detonate, T / I
detour, I
detract, ◊, T / I
detrain, T / I
detune, T
devalue, T
devastate, T
develop, ◊, T / I
deviate, ◊, I
devil (ll / l), T
devise, T
devitalize (-ise), T
devolve, ◊, T / I
devote, ◊, T, C
devour, ◊, T
dew, T
dewater, T
diagnose, T
dial (ll / l), T
dice, ◊, T / I
dictate, ◊, T / I
die (yi), ◊◊, I
diet, T / I
differ, ◊, I
differentiate, ◊, T / I
diffract, T
diffuse, T / I
dig (gg), ◊, T / I
digest, T / I
digitalize (-ise), T
digitize (-ise), T

dignify (ie), T

digress (es), ◊, I

dilate, ◊, T / I

dilly-dally (ie), I

dilute, ◊, T

dim (mm), ◊, T / I

diminish (es), T / I

dimple, T / I

din (nn), ◊, T / I

dine, ◊, T / I

dip (pp), ◊, T / I

diphthongize (-ise), T / I

direct, ◊, T

dirty (ie), ◊, T / I

disable, T

disabuse, ◊, T

disadvantage, T

disagree, ◊, I, C

disallow, T

disappear, ◊, I

disappoint, ◊, T, C

disappropriate, T

disapprove, ◊, T / I, C

disarm, T / I

disarrange, T

disassemble, T

disavow, T

disband, T / I

disbar (rr), ◊, T

disbelieve, ◊, T / I

disbud (dd), T

disburden, ◊, T

disburse, T

discard, T / I

discern, ◊, T

discharge, ◊, T / I

discipline, T

disclaim, T

disclose, T

discolour (-or), T / I

discomfit, T

discommode, T

discompose, T

disconcert, T

disconnect, ◊, T

discontinue, T / I

discord, ◊, I

discount, T

discourage, ◊, T, C

discourse, ◊, I

discover, T, C

discredit, T

discriminate, ◊, T / I

discuss (es), ◊, T

disdain, T, C

disembark, ◊, T / I

disembowel, T

disempower, T

disenchant, T

disencumber, ◊, T

disenfranchise, T

disengage, ◊, T / I

disentail, T

disentangle, ◊, T / I

disentitle (es), T

disfigure, T

disfranchise, T

disgorge, T / I

disgrace, T

disguise, ◊, T

disgust, ◊, T, C

dish (es), ◊, T

dishonour (-or), T

disillusion, T

disincline, T / I

disinfect, T

disinherit, T

disintegrate, T / I

disinter (rr), T

disjoin, T / I

dislike, T, C

dislocate, T

dislodge, ◊, T

dismantle, ◊, T

dismast, T

dismay, ◊, T, C

dismember, T

dismiss (es), ◊, T, C

dismount, ◊, T / I

disobey, T

disorder, T

disorganize (-ise), T

disorientate, T

disown, T

disparage, T

dispatch (es), ◊, T

dispel (ll), T

dispense, ◊, T / I, C

disperse, T / I

dispirit, T

displace, T

display, T

displease, ◊, T

disport, T / I

dispose, ◊, T / I

dispossess (es), ◊, T

disprove, T

dispute, ◊, T / I, C

disqualify (ie), ◊, T, C

disquiet, T

disregard, T

disremember, T, C

disrobe, T / I

disrupt, T

dissatisfy (ie), ◊, T, C

dissect, T

dissemble, T / I

disseminate, T

dissent, ◊, I, C

dissimulate, T / I

dissipate, T / I

dissociate, ◊, T

dissolve, ◊, T / I

dissuade, ◊, T, C

distance, T

distemper, T

distend, T/I

distill (-til [ll]), T/I

distinguish (es) ◊, T/I

distort, T

distract, ◊, T, C

distrain, ◊, I

distress (es), T

distribute, ◊, T

distrust, T

disturb, T

disunite, T

ditch (es), T/I

dither, I

divagate, ◊, I (litt.)

dive, ◊, I

diverge, ◊, I

diversify (ie), T

divert, ◊, T

divest, ◊, T

divide, ◊, T/I

divine, T

divorce, ◊, T

divulge, ◊, T

dizzy, (ie), T

do (es), ◊◊, T/A, C

dock, ◊, T/I

docket, T

doctor, T

document, T

dodder, ◊, I

dodge, T/I

doff, T (litt.)

dog (gg), T

dogmatize (-ise), I

dogsled (dd), I

dole, ◊, T

doll, ◊, T

dolly (ie), ◊, T/I

domesticate, T

domicile, T

dominate, ◊, T/I

domineer, ◊, I

don (nn), T

donate, ◊, T

doodle, I

doom, ◊, T

dope, ◊, T

dose, ◊, T

dot (tt), ◊, T

dote, ◊, I

double, ◊, T/I

double-check, T/I

double-park, T/I

doubt, ◊, T/I, C

douse, T/I

dovetail, ◊, T/I

dowel (ll/l), T

down, T

downgrade, T

download, T

downshift, T

dowse, I

doze, ◊, I

draft, ◊, T

drag (gg), ◊, T/I

draggle, T/I

dragoon, ◊, T, C

drain, ◊, T/I

dramatize (-ise), T

drape, ◊, T

draw, ◊◊, T/I

drawl, ◊, T/I

dread, T, C

dream, ◊, T/I, C

dredge, ◊, T/I

drench (es), ◊, T

dress (es), ◊, T/I

dribble, T/I

drift, ◊, I

drill, ◊, T/I, C

drink, ◊, T/I

drip (pp), T/I

drive, ◊◊◊, T/I

drivel (ll/l), ◊, I

drizzle, ◊, I

drone, ◊, T/I

drool, ◊, I

droop, ◊, T/I

drop (pp), ◊◊, T/I

drown, ◊, T/I

drowse, ◊, T/I

drub (bb), T

drudge, I

drug (gg), T

drum (mm), ◊, T/I

dry (ie), ◊, T/I

dry-clean, T

dub (bb), ◊, T

duck, ◊, T/I

duel (ll/l), I

dull, ◊, T/I

dumbfound, T

dummy (ie), T/I

dump, ◊, T

dun (nn), ◊, T

dunk, ◊, T/I

dupe, T

duplicate, T

dust, ◊, T

dwarf, T

dwell, ◊, I

dwindle, ◊, I

dye, T/I

dyke, T

dynamite, T

*e*

earmark, ◊, T
earn, T
earth, ◊, T/I
ease, ◊, T/I
eat, ◊, T/I
eavesdrop (pp), ◊, I
ebb, ◊, I
echo (es), ◊, T/I
eclipse, T
economize (-ise), ◊, T/I
eddy (ie), I
edge, ◊, T/I
edify (ie), T
edit, ◊, T
editorialize (-ise), I
educate, ◊, T
educe, ◊, T
efface, T
effect, T
effervesce, I
egg, ◊, T, C
ejaculate, T
eject, ◊, T
eke, ◊, T
elaborate, ◊, T/I
elapse, I
elate, ◊, T
elbow, ◊, T/I
elect, ◊, T
electrify (ie), T
electrocute, T
electrolyze (-yse), T
electroplate, T
electrotype, T
elevate, ◊, T
elicit, T
elide, T

eliminate, ◊, T
elongate, T/I
elope, ◊, I
elucidate, T
elude, T
emaciate, T
emanate, ◊, I
emancipate, ◊, T
emasculate, T
embalm, T
embank, T
embargo (es), T
embark, ◊, T/I
embarrass (es), T
embattle, T
embed (dd), ◊, T
embellish (es), ◊, T
embezzle, T
embitter, T
emblazon, ◊, T
embody (ie), ◊, T
embolden, T, C
embosom, ◊, T
emboss (es), T
embower, T (litt.)
embrace, ◊, T/I
embroider, T
embroil, ◊, T
emcee, T
emend, T
emerge, ◊, I
emigrate, ◊, I
emit (tt), ◊, T
emote, I
empanel (ll/l), T
empathize (-ise), I
emphasize (-ise), T
employ, ◊, T, C
empower, T, C
empty (ie), ◊, T/I
emulate, T

emulsify (ie), T
enable, T, C
enact, T
enamel (ll/l), T
enamour (-or), ◊, T
encage, T
encamp, T/I
encapsulate, T
encase, ◊, T
enchain, T
enchant, ◊, T
encipher, T
encircle, T
enclose, ◊, T
encode, T
encompass (es), ◊, T
encounter, T
encourage, ◊, T, C
encroach (es), ◊, I
encrust, ◊, T
encumber, ◊, T
end, ◊, T/I, C
endanger, T
endear, ◊, T
endeavour (-or), I, C
endorse, ◊, T
endow, ◊, T
endue, ◊, T
endure, T/I, C
energize (-ise), T
enervate, T
enfeeble, T
enfilade, T
enfold, ◊, T
enforce, ◊, T
enfranchise, T/I
engage, ◊, T/I, C
engender, T
engineer, T
engorge, ◊, T/I
engrave, ◊, T

engross (es), ◊, T

engulf, ◊, T

enhance, T

enjoin, ◊, T

enjoy, T, C

enlarge, ◊, T/I

enlighten, ◊, T

enlist, ◊, T/I

enliven, T

enmesh (es), ◊, T

ennoble, T

enquire, ◊, T/I

enrage, T

enrapture, T

enrich (es), ◊, T

enrol (-roll [ll]), ◊, T/I

ensconce, ◊, T

enshrine, ◊, T

enshroud, T

enslave, T

ensnare, ◊, T, C

ensue, ◊, I

ensure, ◊, T

entail, ◊, T

entangle, ◊, T

enter, ◊, T/I

entertain, ◊, T

enthrall (-ral [ll]), ◊, T, C

enthrone, ◊, T

enthuse, ◊, I

entice, ◊, T, C

entitle, ◊, T, C

entomb, ◊, T

entrain, T/I

entrance, T

entrap (pp), ◊, T, C

entreat, ◊, T, C

entrench (es), T

entrust, ◊, T

entwine, ◊, T/I

enucleate, T

enumerate, T

enunciate, T

envelop, ◊, T

envenom, T

envisage, T

envy (ie), T

epitomize (-ise), T

equal (ll/l), ◊, T

equalize (-ise), T

equate, ◊, T

equilibrate, T/I

equip (pp), ◊, T

equivocate, I

eradicate, T

erase, ◊, T

erect, T

erode, T

err, ◊, I

error, I

erupt, ◊, I

escalate, T

escape, ◊, T/I, C

eschew, T

escort, ◊, T

espouse, T

espy (ie), T

essay, T, C (litt.)

establish (es), ◊, T

esteem, T

estimate, ◊, T

estrange, ◊, T

etch (es), ◊, T/I

eternize (-ise), T

etherize (-ise), T

eulogize (-ise), T

evacuate, ◊, T

evade, T

evaluate, ◊, T

evanesce, I

evangelize (-ise), T

evaporate, ◊, T/I

even, ◊, T

evict, ◊, T

evince, T

eviscerate, T

evoke, T

evolve, ◊, T/I

exacerbate, T

exact, ◊, T

exaggerate, T/I

exalt, T

examine, ◊, T

exasperate, ◊, T

excavate, T

exceed, ◊, T/I

excel (ll), ◊, T/I, C

except, ◊, T

excerpt, ◊, T

exchange, ◊, T

excise, T

excite, ◊, T

exclaim, ◊, T/I, C

exclude, ◊, T

excogitate, T

excommunicate, T

excoriate, T

excrete, T

exculpate, T (litt.)

excuse, ◊, T, C

execrate, T/I

execute, T

exemplify (ie), T

exempt, ◊, T, C

exercise, ◊, T/I, C

exert, T, C

exfoliate, T

exhale, T/I

exhaust, T

exhibit, T

exhilarate, T

exhort, T, C

exhume, T

exile, ◊, T

exist, ◊, I

exit, T/I

exonerate, ◊, T

exorcise (-ize), ◊, T

expand, ◊, T/I

expatiate, ◊, I

expatriate, ◊, T

expect, ◊, T, C

expectorate, T/I

expedite, T

expel (ll), ◊, T

expend, ◊, T, C

experience, T

experiment, ◊, I

expiate, T

expire, T/I

explain, ◊, T, C

explicate, T

explode, ◊, T/I

exploit, T

explore, T

export, ◊, T

expose, ◊, T

expostulate, ◊, I

expound, ◊, T

express (es), ◊, T

expropriate, ◊, T

expunge, ◊, T

expurgate, ◊, T

extemporize (-ise), T/I

extend, ◊, T/I, C

extenuate, T

exteriorize (-ise), T

exterminate, T

externalize (-ise), T

extinguish (es), ◊, T

extirpate, T

extol (ll), T

extort, ◊, T

extract, ◊, T

extradite, ◊, T

extrapolate, T

extravasate, T/I

extricate, ◊, T

extrude, ◊, T

exude, T/I

exult, ◊, I, C

eye, ◊, T

∫

fabricate, T

face, ◊, T/I

facet, T

facilitate, T

factorize (-ise), T

fade, ◊, T/I

fail, ◊, T/I, C

faint, ◊, I

fake, ◊, T/I

fall, ◊◊, I

falsify (ie), T

falter, ◊, T/I

familiarize (-ise), ◊, T, C

fan (nn), ◊, T

fancy (ie), T, C

fantasize (-ise), ◊, I

fare, ◊, I

farm, ◊, T/I

farrow, T/I

fascinate, T

fashion, ◊, T

fast, I

fasten, ◊, T/I

father, ◊, T

fathom, ◊, T, C

fatigue, T

fatten, ◊, T/I

fault, T

favour (-or), ◊, T

fawn, ◊, T/I

fax, ◊, T, C

fear, ◊, T/I, C

feast, T/I

feather, ◊, T/I

feature, ◊, T

federate, T/I

feed, ◊, T/I

feel, ◊, T/I, C

feign, T/I

feint, I

felicitate, T

fell, T

fence, ◊, T/I

fend, ◊, T/I

ferment, T/I

ferret, ◊, T/I

ferry (ie), ◊, T/I

fertilize (-ise), T

fester, T/I

festoon, ◊, T

fetch (es), ◊, T

fete, T

fetter, T

feud, ◊, I

fib (bb), I

fictionalize (-ise), T

fiddle, ◊, I

fiddle-faddle, I

fidget, ◊, I

field, T/I

field-test, T

fight, ◊◊, T/I

figure, ◊, T/I

filch (es), ◊, T

file, ◊, T

filibuster, I

fill, ◊, T/I

fillet, T

fillip, T

film, ◊, T / I

filter, ◊, T / I

finalize (-ise), T

finance, T

find, ◊, T, C

fine, ◊, T

finesse, T / I

fine-tune, T

finger, T / I

finish (es), ◊, T / I, C

fire, ◊, T / I

firm, ◊, T / I

fish (es), ◊, T / I

fissure, T / I

fit (tt), ◊, T / I

fix (es), ◊, T / I

fizz (es), ◊, I

fizzle, ◊, I

flabbergast, ◊, T

flag (gg), ◊, T / I

flagellate, ◊, T

flail, T / I

flake, ◊, T / I

flambé, T

flame, ◊, I

flank, ◊, T

flap (pp), ◊, T / I

flare, ◊, T / I

flash (es), ◊, T / I

flatten, ◊, T / I

flatter, ◊, T, C

flaunt, T / I

flavour (-or), ◊, T

flay, T

fleck, ◊, T

flee, ◊, T / I

fleece, T

fleet, I

flesh (es), ◊, T / I

flex (es), T / I

flick, ◊, T / I

flicker, ◊, I

flinch (es), I

fling (◊◊), T / I

flip (pp), ◊, T / I

flirt, ◊, T / I

flit (tt), ◊, I

float, ◊, T / I

flock, ◊, I

flog (gg), ◊, T

flood, ◊, T / I

floor, T

flop (pp), ◊, I

flounce, ◊, I

flounder, ◊, I

flour, T

flourish (es), T / I

flout, T

flow, ◊, I

flowchart, T

flower, I

fluctuate, I

fluff, ◊, T

flummox, T

flunk, ◊, T / I

fluoresce, I

flurry (ie), T

flush (es), ◊, T / I

fluster, ◊, T / I

flute, T

flutter, ◊◊◊, T / I

fly (ie), ◊◊◊, T / I

foal, T / I

foam, ◊, I

fob (bb), ◊, T

focus (s / ss [es]), ◊, T / I

fodder, T

fog (gg), T / I

foil, T

foist, ◊, T

fold, ◊, T / I

follow, ◊, T / I

foment, T

fondle, T

fool, ◊, T / I, C

foot, T

footle, ◊, I

forage, T / I

foray, I

forbear, ◊, T / I, C (litt.)

forbid (dd), T, C

force, ◊, T, C

force-feed, T

ford, T

forebode, T

forecast, T

foreclose, ◊, T / I

foregather, ◊, I

foreordain, T

foresee, T, C

foreshadow, T

foreshorten, T

forestall, T

foretell, T, C (litt.)

forewarn, T

forfeit, T

forgather, ◊, I

forge, T / I

forget (tt), ◊, T / I, C

forgive, ◊, T, C

forgo (forego), (es), T

fork, ◊, T / I

form, ◊, T / I

formalize (-ise), T

format, T

formulate, T

fornicate, I

forsake, T

forswear, T

fortify (ie), ◊, T

forward, ◊, T

fossilize (-ise), T/I
foster, T
foul, ◊, T/I
found, ◊, T
founder, I
fox (es), T/I
fracture, T/I
fragment, T/I
frame, ◊, T/I
frank, T
fraternize (-ise), I
fray, T/I
frazzle, T
freak, ◊, I
freckle, T/I
free, ◊, T
freeze, ◊, T/I
freight, T
Frenchify (ie), T/I
frequent, T
freshen, ◊, T/I
fret (tt), ◊, T/I
frighten, ◊, T, C
frill, T
fringe, ◊, T
frisk, ◊, T/I
fritter, ◊, T
frizz (es), T/I
frizzle, ◊, T/I
frog-march, (es), ◊, T
frolic, ◊, I
front, ◊, T/I
frost, ◊, T
froth, ◊, I
frown, ◊, T/I
fructify (ie), I
fruit, I
frustrate, T
fry (ie), ◊, T/I
fuddle, T
fudge, ◊, T/I

fuel (ll/l), T/I
fulfil (ll/l), T
fulminate, ◊, T/I
fumble, ◊, T/I
fume, ◊, T/I, C
function, I
fund, T
funk, ◊, T/I
funnel, ◊, T
fur (rr), ◊, T/I
furbish (es), ◊, T
furl, T
furnish (es), ◊, T
furrow, T
further, T
fuse, ◊, T/I
fuss (es), ◊, T/I
fuzz (es), ◊, T/I

# *g*

gab (bb), I
gabble, ◊, T/I
gad (dd), ◊, I
gaff, T/I
gag (gg), T/I
gage, T
gaggle, I
gain, ◊, T/I
gainsay, T (litt.)
gall, T
gallivant, ◊, I
gallop, ◊◊◊, T/I
galumph, ◊◊, I
galvanize (-ise), ◊, T
gamble, ◊, T/I
gambol, ◊◊◊, I
game, ◊, T/I

gang, ◊, I
gangrene, T/I
gape, ◊, I
garb, ◊, T
garble, T
garden, I
gargle, T/I
garland, T
garner, T
garnish (es), ◊, T
garrison, T
garrotte (-ote), T
gas (ss), ◊, T/I
gash (es), T
gasify (ie), T/I
gasp, ◊, T/I
gate, T
gatecrash (es), T/I
gather, ◊, T/I
gauge, T
gawk, ◊, I
gawp, I
gaze, ◊, I
gazette, T
gear, ◊, T/I
gel (ll), I
geld, T
generalize (-ise), ◊, T/I
generate, ◊, T
genuflect, I
germinate, T/I
gesticulate, T/I
get (tt), ◊◊◊, T/I, C
ghost, T
ghost-write, T
gibber, I
gibe, ◊, T/I
giggle, ◊, I
gild, T
ginger, T
gird, ◊, T

girdle, ◊, T
give, ◊◊, T/I, C
gladden, T
glamorize (-ise), T
glance, ◊, I
glare, ◊, I
glass (es), ◊, T
glaze, ◊, T/I
gleam, ◊, I
glean, ◊, T/I
glide, ◊◊◊, T/I
glimmer, I
glimpse, T
glint, I
glissade, I
glisten, ◊, I
glitter, ◊, I
gloat, ◊, I
glorify (ie), T
glory (ie), ◊, I, C
gloss (es), ◊, T
glove, T
glow, ◊, I
glower, ◊, I
glue, ◊, T
glut (tt), ◊, T
gnash (es), T
gnaw, ◊, T/I
go (es), ◊◊◊, I, C
goad, ◊, T, C
gobble, ◊, T/I
goggle, ◊, I
golf, I
gong, T
goof, ◊, I
goose, ◊, T
gore, ◊, T
gorge, ◊, T/I
gossip, ◊, I
gouge, ◊, T
govern, T/I

gown, T/I
grab (bb), ◊, T/I
grace, ◊, T
gradate, T/I
grade, ◊, T
graduate, ◊, T/I
graft, ◊, T/I
grain, T
grant, ◊, T, C
granulate, T
graph, ◊, T
grapple, ◊, T/I
grasp, ◊, T/I
grass (es), T
grate, ◊, T/I
gratify (ie), T
gravel (ll/l), T
gravitate, ◊, I
graze, ◊, T/I
grease, T
greet, ◊, T
grey, I
grieve, ◊, T/I
grill, T
grimace, I
grin (nn), ◊, T/I
grind, ◊, T/I
grip (pp), T/I
gripe, ◊, T/I
grit (tt), T/I
grizzle, T/I
groan, ◊, I
groom, ◊, T
groove, T
grope, ◊, I
grouch (es), I
ground, ◊, T/I
group, ◊, T/I
grouse, ◊, I
grout, T
grovel (ll/l), ◊, I

grow, ◊◊, T/I
growl, ◊, T/I
grub (bb), ◊, T/I
grudge, T
grumble, ◊, T/I
grunt, T/I
guarantee, ◊, T
guard, ◊, T/I
guess (es), ◊, T/I, C
guffaw, T/I
guide, T
guillotine, T
gull, ◊, T, C
gully (ie), T/I
gulp, ◊, T/I
gum (mm), ◊, T/I
gun (nn), ◊, T/I
gurgle, ◊, T/I
gush (es), ◊, I
gussy (ie), ◊, T
gut (tt), T
gutter, T/I
guy, T
guzzle, ◊, T/I
gyp (pp), T (fam.)
gyrate, I

habituate, ◊, T, C
hack, ◊, T/I
hackle, T/I
hemorrage (haemorrage), I
haggle, ◊, I
hail, ◊, T/I
hallmark, T
halloo, I
hallucinate, T/I

halo (es), T

halt, T/I

halve, T

ham (mm), ◊, T/I

hammer, ◊, T/I

hamper, T

hand, ◊, T

handicap (pp), T

handle, T/I

hang, T/I

hanker, ◊, I

happen, ◊, I, C

harangue, T/I

harass (es), T

harbour (-or), T

harden, ◊, T/I

hare, ◊, I

hark, ◊, I

harm, T

harmonize (-ise), ◊, T/I

harness (es), ◊, T

harp, ◊, I

harpoon, T

harrow, T

harry (ie), T

harvest, T/I

hash (es), ◊, T

hasten, T/I, C

hatch (es), ◊, T/I

hate, T, C

haul, ◊, T/I

haunt, T

have, ◊◊, T/A

hawk, ◊, T/I

hazard, T

haze, ◊, T

head, ◊, T/I

headline, T

heal, ◊, T/I

heap, ◊, T

hear, ◊, T/I, C

hearten, ◊, T/I

heat, ◊, T/I

heave, ◊, T/I

heckle, T

hector, T, C

hedge, ◊, T/I

heed, T

hee-haw, I

heel, ◊, T/I

heighten, T

Hellenize (-ise), T/I

help, ◊◊, T/I, C

hem (mm), ◊, T

henna, T

herald, T

herd, ◊, T/I

hesitate, ◊, I, C

hew, ◊, T

hex (es), T

hibernate, I

hiccup (pp), I

hide, ◊, T/I

higgle, I

highlight, T

hijack, T

hike, T/I

hinder, ◊, T, C

hinge, ◊, T/I

hint, ◊, T/I, C

hire, ◊, T

hiss (es), ◊, T/I

hit (tt), ◊, T/I

hitch (es), ◊, T/I

hitch-hike, ◊◊, T/I

hive, ◊, T/I

hoard, ◊, T

hoax (es), ◊, T, C

hobble, ◊◊, T/I

hobnob (bb), ◊, I

hock, T

hocus (ss), T

hoe, T

hog (gg), T/I

hoist, ◊, T

hoke, ◊, T (fam.)

hold, ◊◊, T/I

hole, ◊, T/I

holiday, I

hollow, ◊, T/I

home, ◊, T

homogenize (-ise), T

hone, T

honeymoon, I

honour (-or), ◊, T, C

hoodwink, ◊, T, C

hoof, T/I

hook, ◊, T/I

hoop, T

hoot, ◊, T/I

hop (pp), ◊◊◊, T/I

hope, ◊, T/I, C

horn, ◊, I

horrify (ie), T

horse, ◊, I

horsewhip (pp), T

hose, ◊, T

hospitalize (-ise), T

hound, ◊, T

house, ◊, T

housetrain, T

hover, ◊, I

howl, ◊, T/I

huckster, T/I

huddle, ◊, T/I

huff, T/I

hug (gg), T

hulk, I

hull, T

hum (mm), ◊, T/I

humanize (-ise), T

humble, T

humbug (gg), ◊, T, C

humidify, T

humiliate, ◊, T, C

humour (-or), T

hump, ◊, T

hunch (es), ◊, T

hunger, ◊, I

hunker, ◊, I

hunt, ◊, T/I

hurdle, T/I

hurl, ◊, T

hurrah, T/I

hurry (ie), ◊◊, T/I

hurt, T/I

hurtle, ◊, T/I

husband, T

hush (es), ◊, T/I

husk, T

hustle, ◊, T/I, C

hybridize (-ise), T

hydrate, T

hydrogenate, T

hydrogenize (-ise), T

hydroplane, I

hype, ◊, T

hyphen, T

hyphenate, T

hypnotize (-ise), ◊, T, C

hypothesize (-ise), T/I

*i*

ice, ◊, T

ice-skate, I

idealize (-ise), T

identify (ie), ◊, T

idle, ◊, I

idolize (-ise), T

ignite, T/I

ignore, T

illuminate, ◊, T

illumine, T

illustrate, ◊, T

imagine, T, C

imbibe, T/I

imbricate, T/I

imbue, ◊, T

imitate, T

immaterialize (-ise), T

immerse, ◊, T

immigrate, ◊, I

immobilize (-ise), T

immolate, T

immortalize (-ise), T

immunize (-ise), ◊, T

immure, T

impair, T

impale, ◊, T

impanel (ll/l), T

impart, ◊, T

impeach (es), ◊, T, C

impede, T

impel (ll), ◊, T, C

impend, ◊, I

imperil (ll/l), T

impersonate, T

impinge, ◊, I

implant, ◊, T

implement, T

implicate, ◊, T

implode, T/I

implore, T, C

imply (ie), T, C

import, ◊, T, C

importune, T/I

impose, ◊, T/I

impound, T

impoverish (es), T

impregnate, ◊, T

impress (es), ◊, T, C

imprint, ◊, T

imprison, ◊, T

improve, ◊, T/I

improvise, T/I

impugn, T

impute, ◊, T

inaugurate, T

incapacitate, ◊, T, C

incarcerate, ◊, T

incarnate, T

incense, T

inch (es), T

incinerate, T

incise, T

incite, ◊, T

incline, ◊, T/I

include, ◊, T, C

incommode, T

inconvenience, T

incorporate, ◊, T/I

increase, ◊, T/I

increment, T

incubate, T/I

inculcate, ◊, T

inculpate, T/I

incur (rr), T

indemnify (ie), ◊, T

indent, ◊, T/I

index (es), T

indicate, T

indict, ◊, T, C

indispose, ◊, T, C

individualize (-ise), T

indoctrinate, ◊, T

indorse, T

induce, ◊, T, C

induct, T

indulge, ◊, T/I, C

industrialize (-ise), T

inebriate, T

infantilize (-ise), T

infatuate, ◊, T

infect, ◊, T

infer (rr), ◊, T, C

infest, ◊, T

infill, T

infiltrate, ◊, T/I

inflame, T/I

inflate, ◊, T

inflect, T

inflict, ◊, T

influence, T

inform, ◊, T/I, C

infringe, ◊, T/I

infuriate, T

infuse, ◊, T

ingest, T

ingraft, ◊, T

ingratiate, ◊, T

ingurgitate, T

inhabit, T

inhale, T/I

inhere, ◊, I

inherit, ◊, T

inhibit, ◊, T, C

inhume, T

initial, T

initialize (-ise), T

initiate, ◊, T

inject, ◊, T

injure, T

ink, ◊, T

inlay, ◊, T

innovate, ◊, T/I

inoculate, ◊, T

input, T, ◊◊

inquire, ◊, T/I, C

inscribe, ◊, T

inseminate, T

insert, ◊, T

inset (tt), ◊, T

insinuate, ◊, T, C

insist, ◊, I, C

inspect, T

inspire, T, C

install, ◊, T

instantiate, T

instigate, T, C

instill (-il [ll]), ◊, T

institute, ◊, T

institutionalize (-ise), T

instruct, ◊, T, C

instrument, T

insufflate, T

insulate, ◊, T

insult, T

insure, ◊, T

integrate, ◊, T/I

intend, ◊, T, C

intensify (ie), T/I

inter (rr), T

interact, ◊, I

interbreed, ◊, T/I

intercalate, T

intercede ◊, I

intercept, T

interchange, ◊, T

intercommunicate, I

interconnect, T/I

interdepend, I

interdict, ◊, T, C

interest, ◊, T, C

interfere, ◊, I

interfile, T

interfold, T

interject, T

interlace, ◊, T/I

interlard, ◊, T

interleave, ◊, T

interline, T

interlink, ◊, T/I

interlock, T/I

interlope, I

intermarry (ie), ◊, I

intermediate, ◊, I

intermingle, ◊, T/I

intermit (tt), T/I

intermix (es), T

intern, ◊, T

internalize (-ise), T

internationalize (-ise), T

interpenetrate, T

interpolate, T

interpose, ◊, T/I

interpret, ◊, T/I

interrelate, T

interrogate, ◊, T

interrupt, T

intersect, ◊, T/I

intersperse, ◊, T

intertwine, T/I

intervene, ◊, I

interview, ◊, T

interweave, ◊, T/I

intimate, ◊, T, C

intimidate, ◊, T

intone, T

intoxicate, ◊, T

intrigue, ◊, T/I

introduce, ◊, T

intrude, ◊, T/I

intrust, ◊, T

inundate, ◊, T

inure, ◊, T

invade, T

invalid, T

invalidate, T

inveigh, ◊, I

inveigle, ◊, T, C

invent, T

invert, T

invest, ◊, T/I

investigate, T

invigilate, I

invigorate, T
invite, ◊, T, C
invoice, T
invoke, ◊, T
involve, ◊, T, C
iodize (-ise), T
ionize (-ise), T
irk, T, C
iron, ◊, T / I
irradiate, T / I
irrigate, ◊, T
irritate, T
isolate, ◊, T
issue, ◊, T / I
italicize (-ise), T
itch (es), ◊, I, C
itemize (-ise), T
iterate, T
itinerate, I

# j

jab (bb), ◊, T / I
jabber, T / I
jack, ◊, T
jacket, T
jackknife, T / I
jag (gg), T
jam (mm), ◊, T / I
jangle, ◊, T / I
japan (nn), T
jar (rr), ◊, T / I
jaunt, ◊, T
jaw, ◊, T / I (fam.)
jazz (es), ◊, T / I
jeer, ◊, T / I
jell, I

jelly (ie), T / I
jeopardize (-ise), T
jerk, ◊, T / I
jest, ◊, I
jet (tt), T / I
jettison, T
jib (bb), ◊, I, C (arch.)
jibe, I
jig (gg), T / I
jigger, ◊, T
jiggle, T
jilt, T
jingle, T / I
jink , ◊◊◊, I
jitter, I
job (bb), ◊, T / I
jockey, ◊, T / I, C
jog (gg), ◊◊◊, T / I
joggle, T / I
join, ◊, T / I, C
joint, T
joke, ◊, I
jolly (ie), ◊, T
jolt, T/I
josh (es), T / I
jostle, ◊, T / I
jot (tt), ◊, T
journalize (-ise), T / I
journey, I
joust, I
jubilate, I
judder, I
judge, ◊, T / I
jug (gg), T
juggle, ◊, T / I
jumble, ◊, T
jump, ◊, T / I
junk, T
justify (ie), ◊, T, C
jut (tt), ◊, I
juxtapose, T

# k

kedge, T
keel, ◊, T / I
keep, ◊◊, T / I, C
key, T
keyboard, T
keypunch, T
kick, ◊◊, T / I
kid (dd), ◊, T / I
kidnap (pp), T
kill, ◊, T
kindle, ◊, T / I
kink, T/I
kiss (es), ◊, T / I
kit (tt), ◊, T
knead, T
kneecap (pp), T
kneel, ◊, I
knife, T
knight, T
knit (tt), ◊, T / I
knock, ◊◊, T / I
knot (tt), ◊, T / I
know, ◊, T / I, C
knuckle, ◊, I
KO ('s), T
kosher, ◊, T
kowtow, ◊, I

*l*

label (ll / l), ◊, T
labour (-or), ◊, T / I, C
lace, ◊, T / I
lacerate, T
lack, ◊, T / I
lacquer, T
lactate, I
ladder, T / I
lade, ◊, T
ladle, ◊, T
lag (gg), ◊, T / I
laicize (-ise), T
lallygag (gg), I (fam.)
lam (mm), ◊, T / I
lamb, I
lambast/e, T
lame, T
lament, T / I
laminate, T / I
lampoon, T
lance, T
land, ◊, T / I
languish (es), ◊, I
lap (pp), ◊, T / I
lapse, ◊, I
lard, ◊, T
lark, ◊, I
lash (es), ◊, T / I
lasso (es), T
last, ◊, T / I
latch (es), ◊, T / I
lath, T
lather, ◊, T / I
Latinize (-ise), T
laud, T
laugh, ◊, T / I, C

launch (es), ◊, T / I
launder, T / I
lavish (es), ◊, T
lay, ◊◊, T / I, C
layer, T
laze, ◊, T / I
leach (es), ◊, T / I
lead, ◊◊, T / I, C
leaf, ◊, T / I
league, ◊, T / I
leak, ◊, T / I
lean, ◊, T / I
leap, ◊, T / I
learn, ◊, T / I, C
lease, ◊, T
leash (es), T
leather, T
leave, ◊◊, T / I, C
leaven, ◊, T
lecture, ◊, T / I
leer, ◊, I
left-justify (ie), T / I
legalize (-ise), T
legislate, ◊, I
legitimate (legitimize [-ise]), T
lend, ◊, T
lengthen, ◊, T / I
lessen, T / I
let (tt), ◊, T / A, C
letter, T
level (ll / l), ◊, T / I
lever, ◊, T
levigate, T
levitate, T / I
levy (ie), ◊, T
liaise, ◊, I
libel (ll / l), T
liberate, ◊, T
license, ◊, T, C
lick, ◊, T
lie (yi), ◊◊, T / I

lie (yi), ◊, I
lift, ◊, T / I
ligature, T
light, ◊, T / I
lighten, T / I
like, T, C
liken, ◊, T
lilt, T / I
limber, ◊, T / I
lime, T
limit, ◊, T, C
limp, ◊, I
line, ◊, T / I
linearize (-ise), T
linger, ◊, I
link, ◊, T / I
lionize (-ise), T
liquefy (-uify), (ie), T / I
liquidate, T
liquidize (-ise), T
lisp, ◊, T / I
list, T / I
listen, ◊, T / I
litigate, T / I
litter, ◊, T / I
live, ◊◊, T / I
liven, ◊, T / I
load, ◊, T / I
loaf, ◊, I
loan, ◊, T
loathe, T, C
lob (bb), ◊, T / I
lobby (ie), ◊, T / I
localize (-ise), T
locate, T / I
lock, ◊, T / I
lodge, ◊, T / I
loft, T
log (gg), ◊, T / I
loiter, ◊, I
loll, ◊, T / I

long, ◊, I, C
look, ◊◊, T/I, C
loom, ◊, I
loop, T/I
loose, ◊, T/I
loosen, ◊, T/I
loot, T/I
lop (pp), ◊, T/I
lope, ◊◊◊, I
lord, T
lose, ◊, T/I
lot (tt), T/I
louden, T
lounge, ◊, I
louse, ◊, T
love, T, C
low, T/I
lower, ◊, T/I
lubricate, T
luff, ◊, T/I
lug (gg), ◊◊◊, T
lull, ◊, T/I, C
lumber, ◊, T
lump, ◊, T/I
lunch (es), ◊, T/I
lunge, ◊, T/I
lurch (es), I
lure, ◊, T, C
lurk, ◊, I
lust, ◊, I
lustre (-ter), T/I
lute, T/I
luxuriate, ◊, I
lynch (es), T

# M

macadamize (-ise), T
mace, T

macerate, T/I
machinate, T/I
machine, T
madden, ◊, T
magnetize (-ise), T
magnify (ie), T
mail, ◊, T
maim, T
maintain, ◊, T, C
major, ◊, I
make, ◊◊, T/I, C
malign, T
malinger, I
maltreat, T
man (nn), ◊, T
manacle, T
manage, ◊, T/I, C
mandate, T
manducate, I (litt.)
mangle, ◊, T
manhandle, T
manicure, T
manifest, T
manifold, T
manipulate, T
manoeuvre (maneuver,
   manoeuver), ◊, T/I
mantle, ◊, T
manufacture, T
manumit (tt), T (arch.)
manure, T
map (pp), ◊, T
mar (rr), T
maraud, T/I
marble, T
march (es), ◊, T/I
margin, T
marinate, T
mark, ◊, T/I, C
market, T/I
maroon, T

marry (ie), ◊, T/I
marshal (ll/l), ◊, T
martyr, T
martyrize (-ise), T
marvel (ll/l), ◊, I, C
mash (es), ◊, T
mask, ◊, T
masquerade, ◊, I
mass (es), T/I
massacre, T
massage, T
mast, T
master, T
masticate, T/I
masturbate, T/I
mat (tt), T/I
match (es), ◊, T/I
mate, ◊, T/I
materialize (-ise), T/I
matriculate, I
matter, ◊, I, C
mature, T/I
maul, ◊, T
maunder, I
maximize (-ise), T
may, A
mean, ◊, T, C
meander, I
measure, ◊, T
mechanize (-ise), T
meddle, ◊, I
mediate, ◊, T/I
medicate, T
meditate, ◊, T/I, C
meet, ◊, T/I
meld, T/I
mellow, T/I
melt, ◊, T/I
memorialize (-ise), T
memorize (-ise), T
menace, T

mend, T/I

menstruate, I

mention, ◊, T, C

meow (miaow), I

merchandise, T/I

merge, ◊, T/I

merit, T

mesh (es), ◊, T/I

mesmerize (-ise), ◊, T, C

mess (es), ◊, T/I

message, T

metabolize (-ise), T

metal (ll/l), T

metallize (-ise), T

metamorphose, ◊, T/I

mete, ◊, T

meter, T

mew, I

microfilm, T

micturate, T/I (litt.)

miff, T

might, A

migrate, ◊, I

mike, I

mildew, T/I

militarize (-ise), T

militate, ◊, I

milk, T/I

mill, ◊, T/I

mime, T/I

mimic, T

mince, ◊, T/I

mind, ◊, T/I, C

mine, ◊, T/I

mingle, ◊, T/I

miniaturize (-ise), T

minimize (-ise), T

minister, ◊, I

minor, ◊, I

mint, T

minute, T

mire, T/I

mirror, T

misapply (ie), T

misapprehend, T

misappropriate, T

misbehave, I

miscalculate, ◊, T/I

miscall, T

miscarry (ie), I

miscast, T

misconceive, ◊, T/I

misconduct, T

misconstrue, T

miscount, T/I

miscue, T

misdeal, T/I

misdescribe, T

misdirect, T

misdo (es), T

misdoubt, T

misfire, I

misgovern, T/I

mishandle, T

mishear, T

mis-hit (tt), T

misinform, T

misinterpret, T

misjudge, T

mislabel (ll), T

mislay, T

mislead, T

mismanage, T

mismatch (es), T

mismeasure, T

misname, T

misperceive, T

misplace, T

misplay, T

misprint, T

misprize, T (litt.)

mispronounce, T

misquote, T

misread, T

misremember, T

misreport, T

misrepresent, T

misrule, T

miss (es), ◊, T/I, C

misspeak, I

misspell, T

misspend, T

misstate, T

mist, ◊, T/I

mistake, ◊, T

mistime, T

mistranslate, T

mistreat, T

mistrust, T

mistype, T

misunderstand, T

misuse, T

mitigate, T

mitre (-ter), T/I

mix (es), ◊, T/I

moan, ◊, T/I

mob (bb), T

mobilize (-ise), T/I

mock, ◊, T/I

model (ll/l), ◊, T

moderate, T/I

modernize (-ise), T

modify (ie), T

modularize (-ise), T

modulate, ◊, T/I

moil, I

moisten, ◊, T/I

moisturize (-ise), T

molest, T

mollify (ie), T

mollycoddle, T

monetize (-ise), T

monitor, T

monkey, ◊, I
monopolize (-ise), T
moo, I
mooch (es), ◊◊, I
moon, ◊, T / I
moor, T / I
moot, T
mop (pp), ◊, T
mope, ◊, I
moralize ( -ise), ◊, T / I
mortar, T
mortgage, T
mortify (ie), T
mortise (-ice), T
moss, T
mother, T
motion, ◊, T / I, C
motivate, T
motor, T / I
motorize (-ise), T
mottle, T
mould (mold), ◊, T / I
moulder (molder), I
moult, T / I
mount, ◊, T / I
mountaineer, I
mourn, ◊, T / I
mouse, T / I
mouth, T / I
move, ◊◊◊, T / I
mow, ◊, T
muck, ◊, T / I
mud (dd), T
muddle, ◊, T
muddy (ie), ◊, T
muff, T / I
muffle, ◊, T
mug (gg), ◊, T
mulch (es), T
mulct, ◊, T
mull, ◊, T

multiplex (es), T
multiply (ie), ◊, T / I
mumble, T / I
mummify (ie), T
munch (es), T / I
munition, T
murder, T
murmur, ◊, T / I
muscle, ◊, I
muse, ◊, T / I
mushroom, I
muss (es), ◊, T
must, A
muster, ◊, T / I
mutate, T / I
mute, T
mutilate, T
mutiny (ie), ◊, I
mutter, T / I
muzzle, T
mystify (ie), T

# *n*

nab (bb), T
nag (gg), ◊, T / I
nail, ◊, T
name, ◊, T
nap (pp), I
narcotize (-ise), T
narrate, T
narrow, ◊, T / I
nasalize (-ise), T
nationalize (-ise), T
natter, I
naturalize (-ise), T / I
nauseate, T / I
navigate, ◊◊◊, T / I
nazify (ie), T

near, T
neaten, T
necessitate, T
neck, T / I
need, T / A, C
needle, T
negate, T
negative, T
neglect, T, C
negotiate, ◊, T / I
neigh, I
neighbour (-or), ◊, I
nest, ◊, T / I
nestle, ◊, I
net (tt), T
nettle, ◊, T
neuter, T
neutralize (-ise), T
nibble, ◊, T / I
nick, ◊, T
nickel (ll / l), T
nickname, T
nictitate, I
niggle, ◊, I
nip (pp), ◊, T / I
nitrate, T
nod (dd), ◊, T / I
noise, ◊, T
nominate, ◊, T
nonplus (ss), T
nonsuit, T
noodge, T
noose, T
normalize (-ise), T
nose, ◊, T / I
nosh (es), I (fam.)
notarize (-ise), T
notch (es), ◊, T
note, ◊, T, C
notice, T, C
notify (ie), ◊, T

nourish (es), ◊, T

nudge, T

nullify (ie), T

numb, ◊, T

number, ◊, T / I

nurse, ◊, T

nurture, ◊, T

nuzzle, ◊, I

# O

obey, T / I

obfuscate, T

object, ◊, T / I, C

objectify, (ie), T

obligate, T, C

oblige, ◊, T, C

oblique, I

obliterate, T

obscure, ◊, T

observe, ◊, T, C

obsess (es), ◊, T

obstruct, T

obtain, ◊, T / I

obtrude, ◊, T / I

obvert, I

obviate, T

occasion, T

occlude, T / I

occupy (ie), ◊, T, C

occur (rr), ◊, I, C

off, T / I

offend, ◊, T / I

offer, ◊, T / I, C

officer, T

officiate, ◊, I

offset (tt), T / I

ogle, ◊, T / I

oil, T

okay, I

omen, T

omit (tt), ◊, T, C

ooze, ◊, T / I

open, ◊, T / I

operate, ◊, T / I

opine, T / I, C

oppose, ◊, T, C

oppress (es), T

opt, ◊, I

orate, I

orbit, T / I

orchestrate, T

ordain, T

order, ◊, T / I, C

organize (-ise), T / I

orient, T / I

orientate, T / I

originate, ◊, T / I

ornament, T

orphan, T

oscillate, ◊, I

osculate, ◊, T / I

ossify (ie), T / I

ostracize (-ise), T

oust, ◊, T

out, T / I

outbid (dd), T

outbrave, T

outbreed, T

outclass (es), T

outcrop (pp), I

outcross (es), T

outdistance, T

outdo (es), T

outface, T

outfight, T

outfit (tt), T

outflank, T

outfox (es), T

outgas (es), I

outgo (es), T (arch.)

outgrow, T

outguess (es), T

outgun (nn), T

outlast, T

outlaw, T

outline, T

outmanoeuvre (-maneuver, -manoeuver), T

outmatch (es), T

outnumber, T

outpace, T

outperform, T

outplay, T

outrage, T

outrank, T

outreach, T

outride, T

outrun (nn), T

outscore, T

outshine, T

outsmart, T

outspeak, T

outspend, T

outspread, T

outstay, T

outstretch (es), T

outstrip (pp), T

out-talk, T

out-think, T

outvote, T

outwear, T

outweigh, T

outwit (tt), T

outwork, T

over, T

overachieve, T

overact, T / I

overawe, T

overbalance, T / I

overbear, T

overbid (dd), T / I

overbook, T

overbuild, T

overburden, ◊, T

overcall, T

overcast, T

overcharge, T / I

overcloud, T / I

overcome, ◊, T

overcrowd, ◊, T / I

overdo (es), T

overdose, T

overdraw, T

overdress (es), T

overdrive, T

overeat, I

overestimate, T

overexcite, T

overexert, T

overextend, I

overfeed, T / I

overflow, ◊, T / I

overfly (ie), T

overgraze, T

overgrow, T / I

overhang, T / I

overhaul, T

overhear, T

overheat, T / I

overindulge, T

overkill, I

overlap (pp), T / I

overlay, ◊, T

overleap, I

overlie (yi), T

overload, T

overlook, T

overmaster, T

overmatch (es), T

overpay, T

overplay, T

overpower, ◊, T

overprice, T

overproduce, T

overrate, T

overreach (es), T / I

override, T

overrule, T

overrun (nn), ◊, T / I

oversee, T

oversell, T

overset (tt), T

oversew, T

overshadow, T

overshoot, T

oversimplify (ie), T / I

oversleep, I

overspend, T

overspill, I

overstate, T

overstay, T

oversteer, I

overstep (pp), T

overstock, ◊, T

overstrain, T

overstress (es), T

overstuff, T

overtake, T

overtask, T

overtax (es), T

overthrow, T

overtire, T

overtop (pp), T

overtrain, T / I

overtrump, T

overturn, T / I

overvalue, T

overweight, T

overwhelm, ◊, T

overwind, T

overwinter, I

overwork, T / I

overwrite, T

owe, ◊, T, C

own, ◊, T

oxidize (-ise), T / I

oxygenate, T

*p*

pace, ◊◊◊, T / I

pacify (ie), T

pack, ◊, T / I

package, T

pad (dd), ◊◊◊, T

paddle, T / I

padlock, T

page, ◊, T

paginate, T

pain, T, C

paint, ◊, T / I

pair, ◊, T / I

pal (ll), ◊, I

palatalize (-ise), T

palaver, I

pale, ◊, I

palisade, T

pall, ◊, I

palliate, T

palm, ◊, T

palpate, T

palpitate, I

palter, ◊, I

pamper, T

pan (nn), ◊, T / I

pancake, I

pander, ◊, T / I

panel (ll / l), T

panhandle, T / I

panic, T / I

pant, ◊, T/I

pantomime, T/I

paper, ◊, T

parachute, ◊, T/I

parade, T/I

paragraph, T

parallel, T

paralyze (-ise), T

paraphrase, T

parboil, T

parcel (ll/l), ◊, T/I

parch (es), ◊, T/I

pardon, ◊, T, C

pare, ◊, T

parenthesize (-ise), T

park, T/I

parlay, ◊, T

parley, ◊, I

parody (ie), T

parole, T

parry (ie), T/I

parse, T

part, ◊, T/I

partake, ◊, I

participate, ◊, I

particularize (-ise), T/I

partition, ◊, T

partner, ◊, T

pass (es), ◊◊, T/I

paste, ◊, T

pasteurize (-ise), T

pasture, T/I

pat (tt), ◊, T

patch (es), ◊, T

patent, T

patrol (ll/l), T/I

patronize (-ise), T

patter, ◊, I

pattern, ◊, T

pauperize (-ise), T

pause, ◊, I

pave, ◊, T

paw, ◊, T

pawn, T

pay, ◊◊, T/I, C

peach (es), T (arch.)

peak, ◊, I

peal, ◊, T/I

pearl, I

pebble, T

peck, ◊, T

peculate, I

pedal (ll/l), T/I

peddle, T/I

pee, I

peek, ◊, I

peel, ◊, T/I

peep, ◊, I

peer, ◊, I

peeve, T

peg (gg), ◊, T/I

pelt, ◊, T/I

pen (nn), ◊, T

penalize (-ise), ◊, T, C

pencil (ll/l), T

penetrate, ◊, T/I

pension, ◊, T

people, ◊, T

pep (pp), ◊, T

pepper, ◊, T

perambulate, T/I

perceive, T, C

perch (es), ◊, T/I

percolate, ◊, T/I

percuss (es), T/I

perfect, T

perforate, ◊, T/I

perform, ◊, T/I

perfume, T

perish (es), ◊, T/I

perjure, T

perk, ◊, T/I

permeate, ◊, T/I

permit (tt), ◊, T/I, C

permute, T

perorate, I

peroxide, T

perpetrate, T

perpetuate, T

perplex (es), T

persecute, T

persevere, ◊, I, C

persist, ◊, I, C

personalize (-ise), T

personate, T

personify (ie), T

perspire, I

persuade, ◊, T, C

pertain, ◊, I

perturb, T

peruse, T

pervade, ◊, T

pervert, T

pester, ◊, T, C

pestle, T/I

pet (tt), T

peter, ◊, I

petition, ◊, T

petrify (ie), T/I

pettifog (gg), I

phase, ◊, T

philander, ◊, I

philosophize ( -ise), ◊, I

phone, ◊, T/I

photograph, T/I

Photostat (tt), T

phrase, T

pick, ◊, T/I

picket, T/I

pickle, T

picnic, I

picture, ◊, T

piddle, I

piece, ◊, T

pierce, ◊, T/I

pig (gg), ◊, I (fam.)

pigment, T

pile, ◊, T/I

pilfer, ◊, T/I

pillage, T/I

pillory (ie), T

pillow, ◊, T

pilot, ◊, T

pimp, ◊, I

pin (nn), ◊, T

pinch (es), ◊, T/I

pine, ◊, I

ping, I

pinion, ◊, T

pink, ◊, T

pioneer, T/I

pipe, ◊, T/I

pique, T

pirate, T

pirouette, I

piss (es), ◊, T/I (fam.)

pit (tt), ◊, T

pitch (es), ◊, T/I

pitchfork, T

pith, T

pity (ie), T

pivot, ◊, T/I

placard, T

placate, T

place, ◊, T

plagiarize (-ise), T

plague, ◊, T

plait, T

plan (nn), ◊, T/I, C

plane, ◊, T/I

planish (es), T

plank, ◊, T (fam.)

plant, ◊, T

plash (es), I

plaster, ◊, T

plasticize (-ise), T

plate, ◊, T

platinize (-ise), T

platitudinize (-ise), I

play, ◊◊◊, T/I, C

pleach (es), T

plead, ◊, T/I

please, T

pleat, T

pledge, ◊, T, C

plink, T

plod (dd), ◊◊◊, I

plonk, ◊, T

plop (pp), I

plot (tt), ◊, T/I, C

plow (plough), ◊, T/I

pluck, ◊, T

plug (gg), ◊, T/I

plumb, T

plume, ◊, T/I

plummet, T/I

plump, ◊, T/I

plunder, T

plunge, T/I

plunk, ◊, T

ply (ie), ◊, T/I

poach (es), ◊, T/I

pocket, T

pod (dd), T/I

poeticize (-ise), T

point, ◊, T/I, C

poise, ◊, T/I

poison, ◊, T

poke, ◊◊, T/I

polarize (-ise), T

pole, T

poleaxe, T

polemize (-ise), I

police, T

polish (es), ◊, T

poll, T/I

pollard, T

pollinate, T

pollute, ◊, T

pommel (ll/l), T

ponder, ◊, T/I

pontificate, I

pony (ie), T/I

pooh-pooh, T/I

pool, T

poop, ◊, T

pop (pp), ◊◊, T/I

popularize (-ise), T

populate, T

pore, ◊, I

portend, T

portion, ◊, T

portray, T

pose, ◊, T/I

position, T

possess (es), ◊, T

post, ◊, T/I

postdate, T

postpone, ◊, T, C

postulate, ◊, T/I

posture, T/I

pot (tt), ◊, T

potter, ◊, I

pouch (es), T

poultice, T

pounce, ◊, I

pound, ◊, T/I

pour, ◊◊, T/I

pout, I

powder, ◊, T

power, ◊, T

powwow, ◊, I

practise (-tice), ◊, T/I

praise, ◊, T, C

prance, ◊, I

prate, I (litt.)

prattle, ◊, I

pray, ◊, T / I, C

preach (es), ◊, T / I

prearrange, T

precede, T

precipitate, ◊, T / I

preclude, ◊, T, C

preconceive, T

precondition, T

precook, T

precool, T

predate, T

predecease, T

predestinate, ◊, T

predestine, ◊, T

predetermine, T

predict, T / I, C

predispose, ◊, T

predominate, ◊, I

pre-empt, T

preen, ◊, T

pre-establish (es), T

pre-exist, I

prefabricate, T

preface, ◊, T

prefer (rr), ◊, T, C

prefigure, T

prefix (es), ◊, T

preheat, T

prejudge, T

prejudice, ◊, T, C

prelude, ◊, T / I

premeditate, T

premiere, T

premise, T, C

preoccupy (ie), T

preordain, T

prepackage, T

prepare, ◊, T / I, C

prepay, T

preponderate, ◊, I

prepose, T

prepossess (es), ◊, T

pre-record, T

presage, ◊, T, C (litt.)

prescribe, ◊, T, C

present, ◊, T

preserve, ◊, T

pre-shrink, T

preside, ◊, I

presort, T

press (es), ◊◊, T / I, C

pressure, ◊, T, C

pressurize (-ise), T

presume, ◊, T / I, C

presuppose, T, C

pretend, ◊, T / I, C

prettify (ie), T

prevail, ◊, I

prevaricate, I

prevent, ◊, T, C

prey, ◊, I

price, ◊, T

prick, ◊, T / I

prickle, T / I

pride, ◊, T, C

prim (mm), ◊, T

prime, ◊, T

primp, ◊, T / I

prink, ◊, T / I

print, ◊, T / I, C

prioritize (-ise), T

prize, ◊, T

privilege, T, C

probate, T

probe, ◊, T

proceed, ◊, I, C

process (es), T

proclaim, T

procrastinate, I

procreate, T

procure, ◊, T

prod (dd), ◊, T, C

produce, ◊, T / I

profane, T

profess (es), T, C

proffer, T

profile, T

profit, ◊, T / I, C

profiteer, I

prognosticate, T

program (-amme [mm / m]),T / I

progress (es), ◊, I

prohibit, ◊, T, C

project, ◊, T / I

prolapse, I

proletarianize (-ise), T

proliferate, I

prolong, T

promenade, I

promise, ◊, T / I, C

promote, ◊, T

prompt, T, C

promulgate, T

pronounce, ◊, T

proof, T

prop (pp), ◊, T

propagandize (-ise), T / I

propagate, T / I

propel (ll / l), T

prophesy (ie), T / I, C

propitiate, T

proportion, T

propose, ◊, T, C

proposition, T

propound, T

prorate, T

prorogue, T

proscribe, T, C

prosecute, ◊, T, C

proselytize (-ise), T / I

prospect, ◊, T / I

prosper, ◊, T / I

prostitute, T
prostrate, ◊, T
protect, ◊, T
protest, ◊, T/I, C
protract, T
protrude, ◊, T/I
prove, ◊, T/I, C
provide, ◊, T/I
provision, ◊, T
provoke, ◊, T, C
prowl, ◊, I
prune, ◊, T/I
pry (ie), ◊, T/I
psych, ◊, T/I
psychoanalyze (-yse), T
publicize (-ise), T
publish (es), T
pucker, ◊, T/I
puddle, T/I
puff, ◊◊◊, T/I
pug (gg), T
pule, I (litt.)
pull, ◊◊◊, T
pullulate, I
pulp, T
pulsate, I
pulse, ◊, I
pulverize (-ise), T/I
pummel (ll/l), T
pump, ◊, T/I
pun (nn), I
punch (es), ◊, T
punctuate, ◊, T
puncture, T/I
punish (es), ◊, T, C
punt, T/I
pup (pp), I
pupate, I
purchase, T
purge, ◊, T
purify (ie), ◊, T

purl, T
purloin, T
purport, T, C
purpose, T, C
purr, I
purse, ◊, T
pursue, T
purvey, T
push (es), ◊◊◊, T/I
pussyfoot, ◊◊, I
put (tt), ◊◊◊, T/I
putrefy (ie), T/I
putt, T/I
putter, ◊, I
putty (ie), ◊, T
puzzle, ◊, T/I, C

# *q*

quack, I
quadrate, T/I
quadruple, T/I
quaff, T
quail, ◊, I
quake, ◊, I
qualify (ie), ◊, T/I
quantify (ie), T
quantize (-ise), T
quarantine, T
quarrel (ll/l), ◊, I, C
quarry (ie), T
quarter, T
quash (es), T
quaver, I
queen, T/I
queer, T (fam.)
quell, T
quench (es), T

query (ie), ◊, T, C
question, ◊, T, C
queue, ◊, I
quibble, ◊, I
quicken, ◊, T/I
quiet, ◊, T/I
quieten, ◊, T/I
quilt, T
quintuple, T/I
quip (pp), T/I
quirt, T
quit (tt), ◊, T/I, C
quiver, ◊, T/I
quiz (zz), T
quoin, T
quote, ◊, T

# *r*

rabbet, T
rabbit, I
race, ◊◊◊, T/I
rack (wrack), ◊, T
racket, ◊, I
radiate, ◊, T/I
radio, T/I
radiograph, T
raffle, T
raft, ◊, T/I
rag (gg), T
rage, ◊, I
raid, T
rail, ◊, T/I
railroad, ◊, T, C
rain, ◊, T/I
rainproof, T
raise, ◊, T
rake, ◊, T
rally (ie), ◊, T/I

ram (mm), ◊, T

ramble, ◊, I

ramify (ie), T/I

ramp, ◊, I

rampage, ◊, I

ranch (es), I

randomize (-ise), T

range, ◊, T/I

rank, ◊, T/I

rankle, I

ransack, ◊, T

ransom, T

rant, I

rap (pp), ◊, T/I

rape, T

rarefy (ie), T/I

rase, T

rasp, ◊, T/I

rat (tt), ◊, I

rate, ◊, T/I

ratify (ie), T

ratiocinate, I (litt.)

ration, ◊, T

rationalize (-ise), T

rattle, ◊◊◊, T/I

ravage, T

rave, ◊, I

ravel (ll/l), ◊, T/I

ravish (es), T

raze, T

razz (es), T (fam.)

reabsorb, T

reach (es), ◊, T/I

reacquaint, T

react, ◊, I

read, ◊◊, T/I, C

readjust, T

ready (ie), T

realign, T

realize (-ise), ◊, T, C

ream, ◊, T

reanimate, T

reap, ◊, T

reappear, I

reapply (ie), ◊, T/I

reappoint, T

reapportion, T

rear, ◊, T/I

rearm, T

rearrange, T

reason, ◊, T/I, C

reassemble, T/I

reassert, T

reassess (es), T

reassign, T

reassure, ◊, T

reawaken, T/I

rebate, I

rebel (ll/l), ◊, I, C

rebind, T

reboot, T

rebore, T

rebound, ◊, I

rebroadcast, T

rebuff, T

rebuild, T

rebuke, ◊, T, C

recalculate, T

recalibrate, T

recall, ◊, T, C

recant, T/I

recap (pp), T/I

recapitulate, T/I

recapture, T

recast, ◊, T

recede, ◊, I

receipt, T

receive, ◊, T

recess (es), T/I

recharge, T/I

rechristen, T

reciprocate, T/I

recite, ◊, T/I

reckon, ◊, T/I, C

reclaim, ◊, T

recline, ◊, T/I

reclothe, T

recognize (-ise), ◊, T

recoil, ◊, I, C

recollect, T/I, C

recommence, T/I

recommend, ◊, T, C

recommission, T

recommit (tt), T

recompense, ◊, T, C

recompute, T

reconceptualize (-ise), T

reconcile, ◊, T

recondition, T

reconfigure, T

reconnect, T

reconnoitre, T/I

reconquer, T

reconsider, T, C

reconsolidate, T

reconstitute, T

reconstruct, ◊, T

reconvene, T

reconvert, T

recopy (ie), T

record, ◊, T

recount, ◊, T, C

recoup, ◊, T

recover, ◊, T/I

recreate, T

recriminate, ◊, I

recross (es), T/I

recrudesce, I

recruit, ◊, T

rectify (ie), T

recultivate, T

recuperate, ◊, T/I

recur (rr), ◊, I

recut (tt), T

redact, T

redden, T / I

redecorate, T

redeem, ◊, T

redefine, T

redeploy, T

redevelop, T

redial (ll / l), T

redirect, ◊, T

rediscover, T

redistribute, T

redo (es), T

redouble, T / I

redound, ◊, I

redraft, T

redraw, T

redress (es), T

reduce, ◊, T / I, C

reduplicate, T

re-echo (es), T / I

re-edit, T

re-educate, T

reef, ◊, T

reek, ◊, I

reel, ◊, T / I

re-elect, T

re-embark, T / I

re-emerge, I

re-employ, T

re-enact, T

re-enlist, T / I

re-enter, T / I

re-equip (pp), ◊, T

re-erect, T

re-establish (es), ◊, T

re-evaluate, T

reeve, ◊, T

re-examine, T

ref (ff), T (fam.)

reface, T

refashion, T

refasten, T

refer (rr), ◊, T / I

referee, T / I

refile, T

refill, ◊, T

refine, T / I

refit (tt), T

reflate, T

reflect, ◊, T / I, C

refloat, T

refocus (s / ss [es]), ◊, T

reforge, T

reform, T / I

refract, T

refrain, ◊, I, C

refresh (es), ◊, T / I

refrigerate, T

refuel (ll / l), ◊, I

refund, ◊, T

refurbish (es), T

refurnish (es), T

refuse, ◊, T / I, C

refute, T

regain, ◊, T

regale, ◊, T

regard, ◊, T

regenerate, T / I

regild, T

register, ◊, T / I

regrade, T

regress (es), ◊, I

regret (tt), T, C

regroup, T / I

regularize (-ise), T

regulate, T

regurgitate, T / I

rehabilitate, T

rehash (es), T

rehear, T

rehearse, T

reheat, T

rehouse, T

reign, ◊, I

reignite, T

reimburse, ◊, T

reimport, T

reimpose, T

rein, ◊, T

reincarnate, T / I

reincorporate, T

reinfect, T

reinforce, ◊, T

reinsert, T

reinstall, T

reinstate, ◊, T

reinsure, T

reintegrate, ◊, T

reinter (rr), T

reintepret, T

reintroduce, T

reinvent, T

reinvest, T / I

reinvigorate, T

reissue, T

reiterate, T

reject, T

rejoice, ◊, T / I, C

rejoin, ◊, T / I

rejuvenate, T / I

rekey, T

rekindle, T / I

relabel (ll / l), T

relapse, I

relate, ◊, T / I, C

relax (es), ◊, T / I

relay, ◊, T

re-lay, T

relearn, T

release, ◊, T

relegate, ◊, T

relent, I

relieve, ◊, T
relight, T/I
reline, T
relinquish (es), T
relish (es), T, C
relive, T
reload, T
relocate, T
rely (ie), ◊, I
remain, ◊, I, C
remainder, T
remake, T
remand, T
remark, ◊, T/I, C
remarry (ie), I
remaster, T
rematch, T
remedy (ie), T
remember, ◊, T/I, C
remind, ◊, T, C
reminisce, ◊, I
remit (tt), ◊, T
remodel (ll), T
remold (-mould), T
remonstrate, ◊, T/I, C (litt.)
remount, T/I
remove, ◊, T/I
remunerate, ◊, T
rename, T
rend, ◊, T
render, ◊, T
rendezvous (es), I
renege, ◊, I
renew, T/I
renounce, T
renovate, T
rent, ◊, T
renumber, T
reoccupy (ie), T
reopen, T/I
reorder, T

reorganize (-ise), T/I
reorient, T
repackage, T
repaginate, T
repaint, T
repair, T
repaper, T
repatriate, T
repay, ◊, T
repeal, T
repeat, T/I, C
repel (ll/l), ◊, T
repent, ◊, T/I, C
repeople, T
rephrase, T
repine, ◊, I
replace, ◊, T
replant, T
replaster, T
replay, T
replenish (es), ◊, T
replicate, T
reply (ie), ◊, T/I, C
repopulate, T
report, ◊, T/I, C
repose, ◊, T/I
reposition, T
repossess (es), T
repot (tt), T
reprehend, ◊, T, C
represent, ◊, T, C
repress (es), T
reprieve, T
reprimand, ◊, T, C
reprint, ◊, T
reprise, T
reproach (es), ◊, T, C
reprobate, T
reprocess (es), T
reproduce, ◊, T/I
reprogram (-amme [mm/m]), T

reproof, T
reprove, ◊, T, C
republish (es), T
repudiate, T
repulse, ◊, T
repurchase, T
repute, T, C
request, ◊, T, C
require, ◊, T, C
requisition, ◊, T
requite, ◊, T
reread, T
reroute, T
rerun (nn), T
reschedule, T
rescind, T
rescue, ◊, T
reseal, T
research (es), ◊, T/I
reseat, T
resect, T
resell, T
resemble, T
resent, T, C
reserve, ◊, T
reset (tt), T
resettle, ◊, T/I
reshape, T
reshoot, T/I
reshuffle, T
reside, ◊, I
resign, ◊, T/I, C
re-sign, T/I
resist, T/I, C
resolve, ◊, T/I, C
resort, ◊, I, C
resound, ◊, I
resource, T
respect, ◊, T
respire, T/I
respite, T

respond, ◊, T/I

respray, T

rest, ◊, T/I

restage, T

restart, T/I

restate, T

restock, ◊, T

restore, ◊, T

restrain, T, C

restrict, ◊, T, C

restring, T

result, ◊, I, C

resume, T/I, C

resurface, T

resurge, I

resurrect, T

resuscitate, T/I

ret (tt), T

retail, ◊, T

retain, T

retake, T

retaliate, ◊, I

retard, T

retch (es), I

retell, T

rethink, T

reticulate, T/I

retire, ◊, T/I

retool, T

retort, T, C

retouch (es), T

retrace, T

retract, T/I

retrain, T/I

retransmit (tt), T

retread, T

retreat, ◊, T/I

retrench (es), T

retrieve, ◊, T

retrofit (tt), T

retrograde, I

retrogress (es), I

retry (ie), T

retune, T/I

return, ◊, T/I

reunite, ◊, T/I

rev (vv), ◊, T/I

revaccinate, T

revalue, T

revarnish (es), T

reveal, ◊, T, C

revel (ll/l), ◊, I, C

revenge, ◊, T

reverberate, T/I

revere, T

reverence, T

reverse, T/I

revert, ◊, I, C

review, T

revile, ◊, T/I

revise, T

revisit, T

revitalize (-ise), T

revive, T/I

revivify (ie), T

revoke, T/I

revolt, ◊, T/I, C

revolutionize (-ise), T

revolve, ◊, T/I

reward, ◊, T, C

reweigh, T

rewind, T

rewire, T

reword, T

rewrite, T

rhapsodize (-ise), ◊, I

rhyme, ◊, T/I

rib (bb), T

rice, T

rick, T

ricochet (tt), I

rid (dd), ◊, T

riddle, ◊, T

ride, ◊◊◊, T/I

ridge, T/I

ridicule, T

riffle, T

rifle, ◊, T

rig (gg), ◊, T

right, T

right-justify (ie), T/I

rile, T

rind, T

ring, ◊, T/I

ring, ◊, T/I

rinse, ◊, T

riot, I

rip (pp), ◊, T/I

ripen, T/I

riposte, I

ripple, T/I

rise, ◊, I

risk, ◊, T

rival (ll/l), T

rive, T/I (litt.)

rivet, ◊, T

roam, ◊, T/I

roar, ◊, T/I

roast, T/I

rob (bb), ◊, T

robe, T/I

rock, ◊, T/I

rocket, ◊, I

roister, I

roll, ◊◊, T/I

rollick, I

romance, I

romanize (-ise), T

romanticize (-ise), T/I

romp, ◊, I

roof, ◊, T

rook, T

room, ◊, I

roose, T

roost, I

root, ◊, T / I

rope, ◊, T / I

roster, T

rot (tt), ◊, T / I

rotate, T / I

rototill, T

rouge, T

rough, ◊, T

round, ◊, T / I

rouse, ◊, T / I

rout, ◊, T / I

route, ◊, T

rove, ◊, T / I

row, ◊◊◊, T / I

rub (bb), ◊◊, T / I

rubberize (-ise), T

rubberneck, I

ruck, ◊, T / I

rue, T (litt.)

ruff, T / I

ruffle, ◊, T

ruin, T

rule, ◊, T / I

rumble, ◊, I

ruminate, ◊, T / I

rummage, ◊, T / I

rumple, T

run (nn), ◊◊◊, T / I

rupture, T / I

rush (es), ◊◊◊, T / I, C

Russianize (-ise), T

rust, ◊, T / I

rusticate, T / I

rustle, ◊, T / I

rut (tt), T / I

*S*

sabotage, T

sack, T

sacrifice, ◊, T

sadden, T / I

saddle, ◊, T

safeguard, ◊, T

sag (gg), ◊, I

sail, ◊◊◊, T / I

salaam, T / I

salivate, I

sally (ie), ◊, I

salt, ◊, T

salute, ◊, T

salvage, ◊, T

salve, T

sample, T

sanctify (ie), T

sanction, T

sand, ◊, T

sandbag (gg), T

sandpaper, T

sandwich (es), ◊, T

sanitize, T

sap (pp), T / I

saponify (ie), T / I

sashay, ◊◊◊, I

sass (es), T

sate, T

satiate, ◊, T

satin, T

satirize (-ise), T

satisfy (ie), ◊, T / I

saturate, ◊, T

sauce, T

saunter, ◊, I

sauté, T

savage, T

save, ◊, T / I

savour (-or), ◊, T / I

savvy (ie), T

saw, ◊, T / I

say, ◊, T / I, C

scab (bb), ◊, I

scaffold, T

scald, T

scale, ◊, T / I

scallop, T

scalp, T

scam (mm), T / I

scamp, T

scamper, ◊◊◊, I

scan (nn), T / I

scandalize (-ise), ◊, T

scant, T / I (arch.)

scar (rr), ◊, T / I

scare, ◊, T, C

scarf, T

scarify (ie), T

scat (tt), T

scatter, ◊, T / I

scavenge, T / I

scent, ◊, T

s(c)hlep (pp), T (fam.)

s(c)hmooze, I

schedule, ◊, T, C

schematize (-ise), T / I

scheme, ◊, T / I, C

school, ◊, T, C

scintillate, I

scissor, T

scoff, ◊, I

scold, ◊, T / I, C

scoop, ◊, T

scoot, ◊, I

scope, ◊, T

scorch (es), T / I

score, ◊, T / I

scorn, T, C

scotch (es), T

scour, ◊, T / I

scourge, T

scout, ◊, T / I

scowl, ◊, I
scrabble, ◊, I
scram (mm), I
scramble, ◊◊◊, T/I
scrap (pp), T
scrape, ◊, T/I
scratch (es), ◊, T/I
scrawl, ◊, T/I
scream, ◊, T/I
screech (es), T/I
screen, ◊, T
screw, ◊, T/I
scribble, ◊, T/I
scribe, T/I
scrimmage, T
scroll, ◊, T/I
scrounge, ◊, T/I
scrub (bb), ◊, T/I
scrummage, T
scrumple, T
scrunch (es), T/I
scruple, I, C (litt.)
scrutinize (-ise), T
scud (dd), ◊◊◊, I
scuff, ◊, T/I
scuffle, ◊, I
scull, T/I
sculpt, T/I
sculpture, ◊, T
scum (mm), T/I
scupper, T
scurry (ie), ◊◊◊, I
scutter, T
scuttle, ◊◊◊, I
scythe, T
seal, ◊, T
seam, ◊, T
sear, T
search (es), ◊, T/I
season, ◊, T/I
seat, ◊, T

secede ◊, I
seclude, ◊, T
second, ◊, T
second-guess (es), T/I, C
secrete, T/I
section, ◊, T
secularize (-ise), T
secure, ◊, T/I
sedate, T
seduce, ◊, T, C
see, ◊◊, T/I, C
seed, T/I
seek, ◊, T/I, C
seem, I, C
seep, ◊, I
seesaw, I
seethe, ◊, I
segment, T/I
segregate, ◊, T/I
seize, ◊, T/I
select, ◊, T
sell, ◊, T/I
send, ◊◊, T/I
sense, T, C
sensitize (-ise), T
sentence, ◊, T
sentimentalize (-ise), T/I
separate, ◊, T/I
sequester, T
sequestrate, T
serenade, T
serialize (-ise), T
sermonize (-ise), T/I
serrate, T
serve, ◊, T/I
service, T
set (tt), ◊◊◊, T/I, C
settle, ◊, T/I
sever, T/I
sew, ◊, T/I
sex (es), T

sextuple, T/I
shack, ◊, T/I (fam.)
shackle, ◊, T
shade, ◊, T/I
shadow, T
shaft, ◊, T, C
shake, ◊, T/I
shall, A
sham (mm), T/I
shamble, ◊, I
shame, ◊, T, C
shampoo, T
shanghai, ◊, T, C
shape, ◊, T/I
share, ◊, T/I
sharp, T
sharpen, T/I
shatter, T/I
shave, ◊, T/I
shear, ◊, T/I
sheathe, ◊, T
shed (dd), ◊, T
sheer, ◊, I
sheet, ◊, T
shell, ◊, T/I
shelter, ◊, T/I
shelve, T/I
shepherd, ◊, T
shield, ◊, T, C
shift, ◊, T/I
shilly-shally (ie), I
shimmer, I
shimmy (ie), I
shin (nn), ◊, I
shine, ◊, T/I
shine, T
shingle, T
ship (pp), ◊, T/I
shipwreck, T
shirk, T/I
shiver, ◊, T/I

shoal, T/I
shock, ◊, T, C
shoe, ◊, T
shoo, ◊, T/I
shoot, ◊◊, T/I
shop (pp), ◊, T/I
shore, ◊, T
short, T
shorten, T/I
should, A
shoulder, ◊, T
shout, ◊, T/I
shove, ◊◊, T/I
shovel (ll/l), ◊, T
show, ◊◊, T/I, C
shower, ◊, T/I
shred (dd), T
shriek, ◊, T/I
shrill, T/I
shrimp, I
shrink, ◊, T/I, C
shrive, T (arch.)
shrivel (ll/l), ◊, T/I
shroud, ◊, T
shrug (gg), ◊, T/I
shuck, ◊, T
shudder, ◊, I
shuffle, ◊◊◊, T/I
shun (nn), T
shunt, T/I
shush (es), T
shut (tt), ◊, T/I
shuttle, ◊, T/I
shy (ie), ◊, I
sicken, ◊, T/I, C
side, ◊, I
sidle, ◊◊◊, I
sieve, ◊, T/I
sift, ◊, T/I
sigh, ◊, I
sight, T

sign, ◊, T/I
signal (ll/l), ◊, T/I, C
signify (ie), T/I
signpost, T
silence, T
silhouette, ◊, T
silt, ◊, T/I
silver, T
simmer, ◊, T/I
simper, I
simplify (ie), T
simulate, T
sin (nn), ◊, I
sing, ◊, T/I
singe, T
single, ◊, T
singularize (-ise), T
sink, ◊, T/I
sip (pp), T
siphon, ◊, T
sire, T
sit (tt), ◊◊, T/I
site, T
situate, T
size, ◊, T
sizzle, I
skate, ◊, I
skedaddle, I
sketch (es), ◊, T
skew, T/I
skewer, T
ski, I
skid (dd), I
skim (mm), ◊, T/I
skimp, ◊, T/I
skin (nn), ◊, T
skip (pp), ◊◊◊, T/I
skirmish (es), ◊, I
skirt, ◊, T/I
skitter, ◊◊◊, T/I
skulk, I

skunk, T
skydive, I
skyjack, T
skylark, I
skyrocket, I
slack, ◊, T/I
slacken, ◊, T/I
slake, T/I
slam (mm), ◊, T/I
slander, T
slang, T/I
slant, ◊, T/I
slap (pp), ◊, T
slash (es), T/I
slate, T
slaughter, T
slave, ◊, I
slaver, I
slay, T
sled / sledge (dd), ◊◊◊, T/I
sleep, ◊, T/I
sleigh, I
slenderize (-ise), T
sleuth, ◊, I
slew, ◊, T/I
slice, ◊, T
slick, ◊, T
slide, ◊◊◊, T/I
slight, T
slim (mm), ◊, T/I
sling, ◊, T
slink, ◊, I
slip (pp), ◊◊, T/I
slit (tt), ◊, T
slither, ◊◊◊, T/I
sliver, T/I
slobber, ◊, I
slog (gg), ◊◊◊, T/I
slop (pp), ◊, T/I
slope, ◊, T/I
slosh (es), ◊, T/I

slot (tt), ◊, T

slouch (es), ◊◊◊, T/I

slough (sluff), ◊, T

slow, ◊, T/I

slug (gg), T

sluice, ◊, T/I

slum, I

slumber, I

slump, ◊, I

slur (rr), ◊, T/I

slurp, ◊, T/I

slush, ◊◊, T/I

smack, ◊, I

smack, ◊, T/I

smarm, I

smart, ◊, I

smarten, ◊, T/I

smash (es), ◊, T/I

smatter, T

smear, ◊, T/I

smell, ◊, T/I

smelt, T

smile, ◊, T/I

smirch (es), T

smirk, I

smite, ◊, T

smoke, ◊, T/I

smooch (es), I

smooth, ◊, T

smother, ◊, T/I

smoulder (-molder), ◊, I

smudge, T/I

smuggle, ◊, T/I

snaffle, T

snag (gg), T

snake, I

snap (pp), ◊, T/I

snare, T

snarl, ◊, T/I

snatch (es), ◊, T/I

sneak, ◊◊◊, T/I

sneer, ◊, I

sneeze, ◊, I

snick, T/I

sniff, ◊, T/I

sniffle, I

snigger, I

snip (pp), ◊, T

snipe, ◊, I

snitch (es), ◊, I

snivel (ll/l), I

snoop, ◊, I

snooze, I

snore, I

snort, ◊, T/I

snow, ◊, T/I

snowball, T/I

snub (bb), T

snuff, ◊, T/I

snuffle, I

snug (gg), ◊, T/I

snuggle, ◊, T/I

soak, ◊, T/I

soap, ◊, T

soar, I

sob (bb), ◊, T/I

sober, ◊, T/I

socialize (-ise), T/I

sock, ◊, T

sod (dd), ◊, T

soften, ◊, T/I

solace, T

solder, T

soldier, ◊, I

sole, T

solemnize (-ise), T

solicit, ◊, T/I

solidify (ie), T/I

soliloquize (-ise), I

solve, T

soot, ◊, T

soothe, T

sop (pp), ◊, T

sorrow, ◊, I

sort, ◊, T

sough, I

sound, ◊, T/I

soup, ◊, T

sour, T/I

souse, ◊, T/I

sow, ◊, T/I

space, ◊, T

spade, ◊, T

span (nn), T

spangle, ◊, T

spank, T

spar (rr), ◊, I

spare, ◊, T

sparge, T

spark, ◊, T/I

sparkle, ◊, I

spatter, ◊, T/I

spawn, ◊, T/I

spay, T

speak, ◊, T/I

spear, ◊, T

specialize (-ise), ◊, T/I

specify (ie), T, C

speck, T

speckle, T

speculate, ◊, I

speechify (ie), I

speed, ◊, T/I

spell, ◊, T

spend, ◊, T

spew, ◊, T/I

spice, ◊, T

spiel, ◊, T/I (fam.)

spike, T/I

spill, ◊, T/I

spin (nn), ◊, T/I

spiral (ll/l), ◊, I

spirit, ◊, T

spit (tt), ◊, T/I

spit (tt), T

spite, T

splash (es), ◊, T/I

splatter, ◊, T

splay, ◊, T/I

splice, T

spline, T

splint, T

splinter, ◊, T/I

split (tt), ◊, T/I

splotch (es), ◊, T

splurge, ◊, I

splutter, ◊, T/I

spoil, ◊, T/I

spoke, T

sponge, ◊, T/I

sponsor, T

spook, T

spool, T

spoon, ◊, T/I

spoon-feed, T

spoor, T/I

sport, ◊, T/I

spot (tt), T

spotlight, T

spout, ◊, T/I

sprain, T

sprawl, ◊, I

spray, ◊, T/I

spread, ◊, T/I

sprig (gg), T

spring, ◊, T/I

sprinkle, ◊, T

sprint, ◊◊◊, I

sprout, ◊, T/I

spruce, ◊, T

spur (rr), ◊, T

spurn, T

spurt, ◊, T/I

sputter, ◊, T/I

spy (ie), ◊, T/I

squabble, ◊, T/I

squall, I

squander, ◊, T

square, ◊, T/I

squash (es), ◊, T/I

squat (tt), ◊, I

squawk, T/I

squeak, ◊, T/I

squeal, I

squeeze, ◊, T/I

squelch (es), T/I

squiggle, T/I

squint, ◊, T/I

squire, T (litt.)

squirm, ◊, I

squirrel, ◊, T

squirt, ◊, T/I

squish (es), T/I

stab (bb), ◊, T/I

stabilize (-ise), T

stable, T

stack, ◊, T

staff, T

stage, T

stagger, ◊◊◊, T/I

stagnate, I

stain, ◊, T/I

stake, ◊, T

stale, T/I

stalk, ◊, T/I

stall, T/I

stammer, ◊, T/I

stamp, ◊, T/I

stampede, ◊, T/I

stand, ◊◊◊, T/I, C

standardize (-ise), T

staple, T

star (rr), ◊, T/I

starch (es), ◊, T

stare, ◊, T/I

start, ◊◊, T/I, C

startle, ◊, T

starve, ◊, T/I, C

stash (es), ◊, T

state, T, C

station, ◊, T

stave, ◊, T

stay, ◊◊, T/I

steady (ie), ◊, T/I

steal, ◊, T/I

steam, ◊, T/I

steel, ◊, T

steep, ◊, T/I

steepen, T/I

steer, ◊, T/I

stem (mm), ◊, T/I, C

stencil (ll/l), T

stenotype, T

step (pp), ◊◊, T/I

stereotype, T

sterilize (-ise), T

stet (tt), T

stew, ◊, T/I

stick, ◊◊, T/I, C

stiff, T

stiffen, ◊, T/I

stifle, T/I

stigmatize (-ise), T

still, T/I

stimulate, ◊, T

sting, ◊, T/I

stink, ◊, T/I

stint, ◊, T

stipple, T

stipulate, ◊, T/I

stir (rr), ◊, T/I

stitch (es), ◊, T/I

stock, ◊, T

stockade, T

stockpile, T/I

stoke, ◊, T/I

stomach, T

stomp, ◊◊◊, I

stone, T

stonewall, I

stoop, ◊, T/I

stop (pp), ◊◊, T/I, C

stopper, T

store, ◊, T

storm, ◊, T/I

stow, ◊, T/I

straddle, T/I

strafe, T

straggle, ◊◊◊, I

straighten, ◊, T/I

strain, ◊, T/I

strand, ◊, T/I

strangle, T

strangulate, T

strap (pp), ◊, T

stratify (ie), T

stray, ◊◊◊, I

streak, ◊◊◊, T/I

stream, ◊◊◊, T/I

streamline, T

strengthen, T

stress (es), T

stretch (es), ◊, T/I

strew, ◊, T

stride, ◊◊◊, T/I

stridulate, I

strike, ◊◊, T/I, C

string, ◊, T

strip (pp), ◊, T/I

stripe, T

strive, ◊, I, C

stroke, T

stroll, ◊◊◊, I

strop (pp), T

struggle, ◊◊◊, I

strum (mm), ◊, T/I

strut (tt), ◊◊◊, I

stub (bb), ◊, T

stucco (es), T

stud (dd), ◊, T

study (ie), ◊, T/I

stuff, ◊, T

stultify (ie), T

stumble, ◊◊◊, I

stump, ◊◊◊, T/I

stun (nn), T

stunt, T/I

stupefy (ie), ◊, T

stutter, ◊, T/I

style, T

stylize (-ise), T

stymie (-mying), T

sub (bb), T

subcontract, T/I

subdivide, ◊, T/I

subdue, T

subject, ◊, T

subjugate, T

sublease, T/I

sublet (tt), ◊, T/I

sublimate, T

submerge, ◊, T/I

submit (tt), ◊, T/I, C

subordinate, ◊, T

suborn, T

subpoena, T, C

subrogate, T

subscribe, ◊, I

subserve, T

subside, ◊, I

subsidize (-ise), T

subsist, ◊, I

substantiate, T

substitute, ◊, T/I

subsume, T

subtend, T

subtilize (-ise), T/I

subtitle, T

subtract, ◊, T

suburbanize (-ise), T

subvert, T

succeed, ◊, T/I, C

succour (-cor), T

succumb, ◊, I

succuss (es), T

suck, ◊, T/I

suckle, T/I

sue, ◊, T/I

suffer, ◊, T/I

suffice, ◊, T/I

suffix (es), ◊, T

suffocate, T/I

suffuse, ◊, T

sugar, T

suggest, ◊, T, C

suit, ◊, T

sulk, I

sully (ie), T (litt.)

sulphurize / sulfurize (-ise), T

sum (mm), ◊, T

summarize (-ise), T

summer, I

summon, ◊, T, C

summons (es), T

sun (nn), T

sunbathe, I

sunder, ◊, T

sup (pp), ◊, T/I

superabound, ◊, I

superannuate, T/I

superheat, T

superimpose, ◊, T

superintend, T

superpose, ◊, T

supersaturate, T

superscribe, T

supersede, T

supervene, ◊, I

supervise, T/I

supplant, T

supple, T

supplement, ◊, T

supplicate, T/I (litt.)

supply (ie), ◊, T

support, T

suppose, T, C

suppress (es), T

suppurate, I

surcharge, ◊, T

surf, I

surface, ◊, T/I

surfeit, ◊, T/I

surge, ◊, I

surmise, T, C

surmount, ◊, T

surname, T

surpass (es), ◊, T

surprise, ◊, T, C

surrender, ◊, T/I

surround, ◊, T

surtax (es), T

survey, T

survive, T/I

suspect, ◊, T, C

suspend, ◊, T

suss (es), ◊, T, C

sustain, T

swab (bb), ◊, T

swaddle, ◊, T

swagger, ◊◊◊, I

swallow, ◊, T/I

swamp, ◊, T

swank, ◊, I

swap (swop [pp]), ◊, T/I

swarm, ◊, I

swat (tt), T

swathe, ◊, T

sway, ◊◊◊, T/I

swear, ◊, T/I, C

sweat, ◊, T/I

sweep, ◊◊◊, T

sweeten, T/I

swell, ◊, T/I

swelter, I

swerve, ◊, T/I

swig (gg), ◊, T

swill, ◊, T

swim (mm), ◊◊◊, T/I

swindle, ◊, T

swing, ◊◊◊, T/I

swipe, ◊, T/I

swirl, ◊◊◊, T/I

swish (es), ◊, T/I

switch (es), ◊, T/I

swivel (ll), ◊, T/I

swoon, I

swoop, ◊, I

syllogize (-ise), I

symbolize (-ise), T

sympathize (-ise), ◊, I

synchronize (-ise), T/I

syncopate, T

syndicate, T

synthesize (-ise), T

syringe, T

systematize (-ise), T

tab (bb), T

table, T

taboo, T

tabulate, T

tack, ◊, T/I

tackle, ◊, T

tag (gg), ◊, T/I

tail, ◊, T/I

tailor, ◊, T

taint, ◊, T

take, ◊◊◊, T/I, C

talk, ◊◊, T/I, C

tally (ie), ◊, T/I

tame, T

tamp, ◊, T

tamper, ◊, I

tan (nn), T/I

tangle, ◊, T/I

tango, I

tank, ◊, I

tantalize (-ise), T

tap (pp), ◊, T/I

tape, T

taper, ◊, T/I

tar (rr), T

tarnish (es), T/I

tarry (ie), I

tart, ◊, I (fam.)

task, ◊, T

taste, ◊, T/I

tat (tt), T/I

tattle, I

tattoo, T

tauten, T/I

tax (es), ◊, T, C

taxi, ◊, I

teach (es), T/I, C

team, ◊◊, T/I

tear, ◊◊, T/I

tease, ◊, T

tee, ◊, T/I

teem, ◊, I

teeter, I

teethe, I

telecast, T/I

telecopy, ◊, T

telegraph, ◊, T/I

telephone, ◊, T/I

telescope, ◊, T/I

televise, T

telex, ◊, T

tell, ◊◊, T, C

temper, ◊, T

temporize (-ise), ◊, I

tempt, ◊, T, C

tend, ◊, I, C

tend, T

tender, ◊, T/I

tense, ◊, T/I

term, T

terminate, ◊, T/I

terrace, T

terrify (ie), ◊, T, C

test, ◊, T

testify (ie), ◊, T/I, C

tether, T

thank, ◊, T, C

thatch (es), T

thaw, ◊, T/I

theorize (-ise), ◊, T/I

thicken, ◊, T/I

thieve, T/I

thin (nn), ◊, T/I

think, ◊◊, T/I, C

thirst, ◊, I

thrash (es), ◊, T/I

thread, ◊, T

threaten, ◊, T/I, C

thresh (es), T

thrill, ◊, T/I

thrive, ◊, I

throb (bb), ◊, I

throng, ◊, T/I

throttle, ◊, T

throw, ◊◊, T/I

thrust, ◊◊, T/I

thud (dd), ◊, I

thumb, ◊, T

thump, ◊, T/I

thunder, ◊, T/I

thwart, T

tick, ◊, T/I

ticket, T

tickle, T/I

tide, ◊, I

tidy (ie), ◊, T/I

tie (yi), ◊, T/I

tighten, ◊, T/I

tile, T

till, T

tilt, ◊, T/I

timber, T

time, T, C

tin (nn), T

tincture, T

ting, T/I

tinge, ◊, T

tingle, ◊, I

tinker, ◊, T/I

tinkle, T/I

tinsel (ll/l), T

tint, T

tip (pp), ◊, T/I

tipple, I

tiptoe, ◊◊◊, I

tire, ◊, T/I, C

tithe, T

titillate, T

titivate, T/I

title, T

titrate, T

titter, I

tittle-tattle, I

toady (ie), ◊, T/I

toast, T

toboggan, I

toddle, ◊, I

toe, T

tog (gg), ◊, T/I

toil, ◊◊◊, I

tolerate, T, C

toll, ◊, T/I

tomahawk, T

tone, ◊, T/I

tongue, T

tool, ◊, T/I

toot, T/I

tooth, T

top (pp), ◊, T/I

topple, ◊, T/I

torch, T

torment, ◊, T

torpedo (es), T

torrefy (ie), T

torture, T

toss (es), ◊◊, T/I

tot (tt), ◊, T/I

total (ll/l), T/I

totalize (-ise), T

tote, T

totter, ◊, I

touch (es), ◊, T/I

toughen, ◊, T/I

tour, T/I

tourney, T

tousle, T

tout, ◊, I

tow, ◊, T

towel (ll/l), ◊, T

tower, ◊, I

toy, ◊, I

trace, ◊, T

track, ◊, T

trade, ◊, T/I

traduce, T

traffic, ◊, T/I

trail, ◊◊◊, T/I

train, ◊, T/I, C

traipse, ◊◊◊, I

tramp, T/I

trample, ◊, T/I

tranquilize (-ise), T

transact, ◊, T

transcend, T

transcribe, T

transfer (rr), ◊, T/I

transfigure, T

transfix (es), ◊, T

transform, ◊, T

transfuse, T

transgress (es), T/I

translate, ◊, T/I

transliterate, T

transmit (tt), ◊, T

transmogrify (ie), T

transmute, ◊, T

transpierce, T

transpire, T/I

transplant, T

transport, ◊, T

transpose, ◊, T

transship (pp), T/I

transude, I

trap (pp), ◊, T, C

trash, T/I

travel (ll/l), ◊, T/I

traverse, T/I

travesty (ie), T

trawl, T/I

tread, ◊, T/I

treasure, ◊, T

treat, ◊, T/I

treble, T/I

tree, T/I

trek (kk), ◊, I

tremble, ◊, I

trench (es), T

trend, ◊, I

trepan (nn), T

trespass (es), ◊, I

trick, ◊, T, C

trickle, ◊, I

trifle, ◊, T/I

trigger, ◊, T

trill, T/I

trim (mm), ◊, T

trip (pp), ◊◊◊, T/I

triple, T/I

triplicate, T

trisect, T

triumph, ◊, I

troll, T/I

troop, ◊, T/I

trot (tt), ◊◊◊, T/I

trouble, ◊, T/I, C

trounce, T

truck, ◊, T/I

truckle, ◊, I

trudge, ◊◊◊, I

true, ◊, T

trump, ◊, T

trumpet, ◊, T/I

truncate, T

trundle, ◊◊◊, T/I

truss (es), ◊, T

trust, ◊, T/I, C

try (ie), ◊, T/I, C

tub (bb), T/I

tube, T

tuck, ◊, T/I

tuft, T

tug (gg), ◊, T/I

tumble, ◊, T/I

tumefy (ie), T/I

tune, ◊, T/I

tunnel (ll), ◊, T/I

turf, ◊, T

turn, ◊◊, T/I

tussle, ◊, I

tutor, ◊, T

twaddle, I

twang, T/I

tweak, T

tweet, I

twiddle, ◊, T

twig (gg), T

twin (nn), T

twine, ◊, T/I

twinge, I

twinkle, ◊, I

twirl, T/I

twist, ◊, T/I

twit (tt), T

twitch (es), T/I

twitter, I

two-time, T

type, ◊, T/I

typecast, T

typeset, (tt) T

typify (ie), T

tyrannize (-ise), ◊, T/I

# *U*

ulcerate, T/I

ululate, I

umpire, T/I

unbalance, T

unbar (rr), T/I

unbend, T/I

unbind, T

unblock, T

unbolt, T

unbosom, ◊, T

unbuckle, T

unburden, ◊, T

unbutton, T/I

uncap (pp), T

unchain, T

unclasp, T

unclench (es), T

uncloak, T

unclog (gg), T

unclothe, T

uncoil, T/I

uncork, T

uncouple, T

uncover, T

uncross (es), T

uncurl, T / I

undeceive, ◊, T

underbid (dd), T

undercharge, T

undercut (tt), T

underestimate, T

undergird, T

undergo (es), T

underlie (yi), T

underline, T

undermine, T

underpin (nn), T

underplay, T

underprice, T

underrate, T

underscore, T

undersell, T

undershoot, T

understand, ◊, T / I, C

understate, T

understudy (ie), T

undertake, T

undervalue, T

underwrite, T

undo (es), T

undock, T / I

undress (es), T / I

undulate, T / I

unearth, T

unfasten, ◊, T

unfold, ◊, T / I

unfreeze, T

unfurl, T / I

unhand, T (arch.)

unharness (es), T

unhinge, T

unhook, T

unhorse, T

unify (ie), ◊, T

unite, ◊, T / I

unkink, T / I

unknot (tt), T

unlace, T

unlash (es), ◊, T

unlatch (es), T

unleash (es), ◊, T

unload, ◊, T / I

unlock, T

unloose, T

unman (nn), T

unmask, T / I

unmoor, T / I

unnerve, T

unpack, T / I

unpick, T

unpin (nn), ◊, T

unplug (gg), T

unravel (ll / l), T / I

unreel, T / I

unriddle, T

unrobe, T / I

unroll, T / I

unsaddle, T

unsay, T

unscramble, T

unscrew, T / I

unseal, T

unseat, T

unsettle, T

unsex (es), T

unshackle, T

unsheathe, T

unship (pp), T

unsling, ◊, T

unsnarl, T

unstick, T

unstitch (es), T

unstop (pp), T

unstrap (pp), ◊, T

unstring, T

untangle, T

untether, T

unthread, T

untie (yi), T

untuck, T

untwine, T

untwist, T / I

unveil, T

unwind, T / I

unwrap (pp), T

unyoke, ◊, T

up (pp), T

upbraid, ◊, T

upchuck, T (fam.)

update, T

upend, T

upgrade, ◊, T

uphold, T

upholster, ◊, T

uplift, T

uproot, ◊, T

upset (tt), T / I

upshift, T / I

upstage, T

upturn, T

urbanize (-ise), T

urge, ◊, T, C

urinate, I

use, ◊, T, C

usher, ◊, T

usurp, ◊, T / I

utilize (-ise), ◊, T

utter, T

## V

vacate, T
vaccinate, ◊, T
vacillate, ◊, I
vacuum, T / I
valet, T
validate, T
value, ◊, T
vamoose, I
vamp, ◊, T / I
vandalize (-ise), T
vanish (es), ◊, I
vanquish (es), T
vaporize (-ise), T / I
vapour (-or), I
variegate, T
varnish (es), T
vary (ie), ◊, T / I
vat (tt), T
vaticinate, T / I, C (litt.)
vault, ◊, T
vaunt, T / I, C
veer, ◊, T / I
veg (gg), ◊, I (fam.)
vegetate, I
veil, T
vein, T
vend, T
veneer, T
venerate, T
vent, ◊, T
ventilate, T
venture, ◊, T / I, C
verbalize (-ise), T
verge, ◊, I
verify (ie), T
versify (ie), T / I
vest, ◊, T / I

vet (tt), T
veto (es), T
vex (es), ◊, T
vibrate, T / I
victimize (-ise), T
victual (ll / l), T / I
vie (yi), ◊, T / I
view, T
vilify (ie), T
vindicate, T
violate, T
visa, T
visit, ◊, T
visualize (-ise),
vitalize (-ise), T,
vitiate, T
vitrify (ie), T / I
vituperate, T / I
vivify (ie), T
vivisect, T
vocalize (-ise), T / I
vociferate, ◊, T / I
voice, T
void, T
volatilize (-ise), T / I
volley, T / I
volunteer, ◊, T / I, C
vomit, ◊, T / I
vote, ◊, T / I, C
vouch (es), ◊, T / I
vouchsafe, T (litt.)
vow, T, C
voyage, T / I
vulcanize (-ise), T / I
vulgarize (-ise), T

## W

wad (dd), T
waddle, ◊◊◊, I
wade, ◊◊◊, T / I
waffle, ◊, I
wag (gg), T / I
wage, T
wager, ◊, T, C
waggle, T / I
wail, ◊, I
wainscot (tt), T
wait, ◊, T / I, C
waive, T
wake, ◊, T / I
waken, ◊, T / I
walk, ◊◊◊, T / I
wall, ◊, T
wallop, T
wallow, ◊, I
waltz (es), ◊◊◊, I
wander, ◊, T / I
wane, I
wangle, ◊, T / I
want, ◊, T / I, C
war (rr), ◊, I
warble, T / I
ward, ◊, T
warehouse, T
warm, ◊, T / I
warn, ◊, T, C
warp, T / I
warrant, T
wash (es), ◊, T / I
wassail, T (arch.)
waste, ◊, T / I
watch (es), ◊, T / I, C
water, ◊, T / I
waterproof, T
wave, ◊, T / I

waver, I
wax (es), T
waylay, T
weaken, T / I
wean, ◊, T
wear, ◊, T / I
weary (ie), ◊, T / I, C (litt.)
weather, ◊, T / I
weatherize (-ise), T
weave, ◊, T / I
wed (dd), ◊, T / I
wedge, ◊, T
weed, ◊, T
weep, ◊, T / I
weigh, ◊, T / I
weight, ◊, T
weird, ◊, I (fam.)
welcome, ◊, T
weld, ◊, T / I
well, ◊, I
welsh (es), T / I
welt, T
welter, ◊, I
wend, ◊◊◊, T / I
westernize (-ise), T
wet (tt), ◊, T
whack, ◊, T
whale, I
wharf, T / I
wheedle, ◊, T, C
wheel, ◊, T / I
wheeze, ◊, I
whelp, T / I
whet (tt), T
whicker, T
whiff, T / I
while, ◊, T
whimper, T / I
whine, T / I

whip (pp), ◊◊◊, T / I
whirl, ◊◊◊, T / I
whirr, ◊◊◊, I
whisk, ◊, T / I
whisper, ◊, T / I, C
whistle, ◊, T / I
white, ◊, T
whiten, T / I
whitewash (es), T
whittle, ◊, T / I
whizz (es), ◊, I
whomp, T
whoop, ◊, T / I
whop (pp), T
whore, I
wick, ◊, T
widen, ◊, T / I
wield, T
wig, ◊, T
wiggle, T / I
wile, T
will*, T, C
wilt, I
win (nn), ◊, T / I
wince, ◊, I
wind, ◊, T / I
wind, T
wing, T / I
wink, ◊, T / I
winkle, ◊, T
winnow, ◊, T
winter, ◊, T / I
wipe, ◊, T
wire, ◊, T
wise, ◊, T
wish (es), ◊, T / I, C
withdraw, ◊, T / I
wither, ◊, T / I
withhold, ◊, T

withstand, T
witness (es), ◊, T / I
wobble, ◊, I
wolf, ◊, T
womanize (-ise), I
wonder, ◊, T / I, C
woo, ◊, T, C
woof, I
word, T
work, ◊◊, T / I, C
worm, ◊, T
worry (ie), ◊, T / I
worsen, I
worship (pp), T / I
worst, T
would, A
wound, ◊, T
wrangle, ◊, I
wrap (pp), ◊, T
wreak, T
wreathe, ◊, T / I
wreck, T
wrench (es), ◊, T
wrest, ◊, T
wrestle, ◊, T / I
wriggle, ◊◊◊, T / I
wring, ◊, T
wrinkle, ◊, T / I
write, ◊◊, T / I, C
writhe, ◊, I
wrong, T

x, ◊, T
xerox, T
x-ray, T

---

* Ne pas confondre l'auxiliaire modal *will* et le verbe *to will* (vouloir, léguer). Voir p. 38.

yacht, I
yackety-yak, I
yak ([kk], -ack), I (fam.)
yammer, ◊, I
yank, ◊, T / I
yap (pp), ◊, I
yarn, I
yaw, I
yawn, T / I
yawp, I
yearn, ◊, I, C
yell, ◊, T / I
yellow, T / I
yelp, I
yen (nn), I, C
yield, ◊, T / I
yip (pp), I
yodel (ll), I
yoke, T
yowl, I

zap (pp), ◊◊◊, T / I
zero (es), ◊, T / I
zigzag (gg), ◊◊◊, T / I
zing, ◊, T / I
zip (pp), ◊◊◊, T / I
zone, ◊, T
zonk, ◊, T / I
zoom, ◊◊◊, T / I

# VERBES À COMPLÉMENTATION

| Type | Exemple | Abréviation |
|---|---|---|
| • forme en *-ing* | *I like reading.* | + *-ing* |
| • infinitif (forme infinitive avec ou sans *to*) proposition infinitive | *I want to go.* *I want you to come.* | + inf. |
| • proposition complétive introduite par *that* | *I know that I can speak English well.* | + that |
| • prétérit modal | *I wish (that) he were here.* | + prét. mod. |
| • double passif | *I was given a book.* | db. pass. |
| • passif impersonnel | *He is said to...* | pass. imp. |
| • interrogative indirecte | *I asked him what he was doing.* | + int. ind. |
| • particule *into* ou *out of* + *-ing* | *She coaxed the cat into coming down the tree.* | + into + *-ing* |
| • autres particules + *-ing* | *I agree about doing this.* | + part. |

Pour la grammaire des verbes à complémentation, voir p. 76-85.

abandon + ing
abhor + ing / + inf.
abominate + ing
absorb + part.
abstain + part.
accept + inf. / + that
account + part.
accuse + part.
accustom + part.
ache + inf.
acknowledge + ing / + inf. / +
   that / pass. imp.
add + that
addict + part.
adjure + inf.
admit + ing / + that
admonish + inf.
adore + ing / + inf.
advertise + that / pass. imp.
advise + ing / + inf. / + that
advocate + ing / + inf. / + that
affirm + that
afford + inf.
agree + inf. / + that / + part.
aid + inf. / + part.
aim + inf. / + part.
allege + that / pass. imp.
allocate db. pass.
allot db. pass.
allow + inf. / db. pass.
amount + part.
amuse + part.
announce + that / pass. imp.
annunciate + that
answer + that / db. pass. / +
   part.

anticipate + ing
apologize + part.
appeal + inf.
apply + inf. / + part.
appoint + inf.
appreciate + ing / + inf. /
   + that
approve + part.
argue + that / + part.
arraign + part.
arrange + inf.
ask + inf. / + that / db. pass.
aspire + inf.
assert + that
assist + part.
associate + part.
assume + that / pass. imp.
assure + that / db. pass.
astonish + that / + part.
atone + part.
attempt + inf.
attest + that / pass. imp.
augur + that
authorize + inf.
aver + that
avoid + ing

badger + into + ing
bait + into + ing
bamboozle + into + ing
bar + part.
bark + that
bear + ing
beat + into + ing
beg + inf.
beguile + into + ing

begin + ing / + inf. / + part.
behoove + inf
believe + that / pass. imp. / +
   part.
benefit + part.
beseech + inf.
bet + that
bethink + that
bid + inf.
bind + inf.
blab + that
blackmail + into. / + ing
blare + that
blast + that
bleat + that
blubber + that
bluff + into + ing
blurt out + that
blush + inf.
boast + that
bother + inf.
brag + that
bribe + into + ing
bring + inf. / db. pass.
broadcast + that
browbeat + into + ing
bulldoze + into + ing
bully + into + ing
burn + inf.
burst + inf.
bust + part.
busy + ing

# C

cable + that
calculate + that / + part.
care + inf. / + int. ind.
cause + inf.

**caution** + inf. / + that / + part.
**cease** + ing / + inf.
**certify** + that / pass. imp.
**chagrin** + part.
**challenge** + inf. / pass. imp.
**champion** + ing
**chance** + inf.
**charge** + part.
**chastise** + part.
**cheat** + into + ing
**cheer** + inf.
**chide** + part.
**chi(v)vy** + into + ing
**choose** + inf.
**claim** + inf. / + that / pass. imp.
**coax** + into + ing
**coerce** + into + ing
**cogitate** + that
**come** + inf.
**command** + inf.
**commence** + ing / + inf.
**commission** + inf.
**commit** + inf. / + part.
**compel** + inf.
**complain** + that / + part.
**compute** + that
**con** + into + ing
**concede** + that
**conclude** + that / + part.
**concur** + that
**condemn** + inf.
**condescend** + inf.
**condition** + inf.
**confess** + that / + part.
**confide** + that
**confine** + part.
**confirm** + that / pass. imp.
**confuse** + part.
**congratulate** + part.

**conjecture** + that
**conjure** + inf.
**consecrate** + part.
**consent** + inf. / + part.
**consider** + ing / + that / pass. imp.
**consist** + part.
**conspire** + inf.
**constrain** + inf.
**contemplate** + ing
**contend** + that
**content** + part.
**continue** + ing / + inf.
**contract** + inf.
**contribute** + part.
**contrive** + inf.
**convey** + that
**convict** + part.
**convince** + inf.
**cope** + part.
**counsel** + inf.
**count** + part.
**court** + into + ing
**covenant** + inf.
**cow** + into + ing
**credit** + part.
**criticize** + part.
**culminate** + part.

*d*

**dare** + inf.
**dawn** + that / + int. ind.
**debar** + part.
**debate** + int. ind.
**deceive** + into + ing
**decide** + inf. / + that / + int. ind. / + part.

**declare** + that / pass. imp.
**decline** + inf.
**decoy** + into + ing
**decree** + that
**dedicate** + part.
**deduce** + that
**deem** + inf. / pass. imp.
**defend** + part.
**defer** + ing
**defy** + inf.
**deign** + inf.
**delay** + part.
**deliberate** + int. ind.
**delight** + part.
**delude** + into + ing
**demand** + inf. / + that
**demonstrate** + that
**deny** + ing / + that / db. pass.
**depend** + int. ind.
**deplore** + that
**depose** + that
**depute** + inf.
**descend** + part.
**deserve** + inf.
**desire** + inf.
**desist** + part.
**despair** + that / + part.
**despise** + ing / + part.
**deter** + part.
**determine** + inf. / + that / + int. ind.
**detest** + ing
**devote** + part.
**disagree** + that / + int. ind. / + part.
**disappoint** + part.
**disapprove** + part.
**discourage** + part.
**discover** + that
**disdain** + inf.

**disgust** + that / + part.
**dislike** + ing
**dismay** + part.
**dismiss** + part.
**dispense** + part.
**dispute** + int. ind.
**disqualify** + part.
**disremember** + inf. / + that
**dissatisfy** + part.
**dissuade** + part.
**distract** + part.
**do** + part.
**doubt** + that / + int. ind.
**dragoon** + into + ing
**dread** + ing / + inf. / + that
**dream** + that
**drill** + int. ind.

*e*

**egg** + inf.
**embolden** + inf.
**employ** + inf. / + part.
**empower** + inf.
**enable** + inf.
**encourage** + inf.
**end** + part.
**endeavour** + inf.
**endure** + ing
**engage** + inf. / + part.
**enjoy** + ing
**ensnare** + into + ing
**enthral** + into + ing
**entice** + inf.
**entitle** + inf.
**entrap** + into + ing
**entreat** + inf.
**escape** + ing
**essay** + inf.

**excel** + part.
**exclaim** + that
**excuse** + part.
**exempt** + part.
**exercise** + part.
**exert** + inf.
**exhort** + inf.
**expect** + inf. / + that / pass. imp.
**expend** + part.
**explain** + that / + int. ind.
**extend** + inf.
**exult** + part.

**fail** + inf.
**familiarize** + part.
**fancy** + ing / + that
**fathom** + int. ind.
**fax** + that
**fear** + ing / + that
**feel** + that / + part.
**find** + that / pass. imp.
**finish** + ing
**flatter** + that / + part.
**fool** + into + ing
**forbear** + inf. / + part.
**forbid** + ing / + inf. / db. pass.
**force** + inf. / + into + ing
**foresee** + that / db. pass. / + int. ind.
**foretell** + that / db. pass. / + int. ind.
**forget** + ing / + inf. / + that / + int. ind.
**forgive** + part.

**frighten** + into + ing / + part.
**fume** + part.

**get** + ing / + inf.
**give** db. pass. / + part.
**glory** + part.
**go** + inf.
**goad** + into + ing
**grant** + that / db. pass.
**guess** + that / + int. ind.
**gull** + into + ing

**habituate** + part.
**happen** + inf. / + that
**hasten** + inf.
**hate** + ing / + inf.
**hear** + ing / + inf. / + that / pass. imp. / + int. ind.
**hector** + into + ing
**help** + inf.
**hesitate** + inf.
**hint** + that
**hoax** + into + ing
**honour** + inf.
**hoodwink** + into + ing
**hope** + inf. / + that
**humbug** + into + ing
**humiliate** + into + ing
**hustle** + into + ing
**hypnotize** + into + ing

# i

**imagine** + ing / + that / + int. ind.
**impeach** + part.
**impel** + inf.
**implore** + inf.
**imply** + that
**import** + that
**impress** + that
**include** + ing
**indict** + part.
**indispose** + part.
**induce** + inf.
**indulge** + part.
**infer** + that
**inform** + that
**inhibit** + part.
**inquire** + int. ind.
**insinuate** + that
**insist** + that / + part.
**inspire** + inf.
**instigate** + inf.
**instruct** + inf. / pass. imp.
**intend** + ing / + inf.
**interdict** + part.
**interest** + inf. / + part.
**intimate** + that
**inveigle** + into + ing
**invite** + inf.
**involve** + ing / + part.
**irk** + inf.
**itch** + inf.

# j

**jib** + part.
**jockey** + into + ing
**join** + part.
**justify** + ing / + part.

# k

**keep** + ing / + part.
**know** + that / pass. imp. / + int. ind.

# l

**labour** + inf.
**laugh** + into + ing
**lay** + that
**lead** + inf.
**learn** + inf. / + that
**leave** + inf.
**let** + inf.
**license** + inf.
**like** + ing / + inf.
**limit** + part.
**loathe** + ing / + inf.
**long** + inf.
**look** + inf.
**love** + ing / + inf.
**lull** + into + ing
**lure** + into + ing

# m

**maintain** + that
**make** + inf.
**manage** + inf.
**mark** pass. imp.
**marvel** + that
**matter** + that
**mean** + inf. / + that / pass. imp. / + part.
**meditate** + part.
**mention** + that / pass. imp. / + int. ind.
**mesmerize** + into + ing
**mind** + ing
**miss** + ing
**motion** + inf.

# n

**need** + ing / + inf.
**neglect** + inf.
**note** + that / + int. ind.
**notice** + that

# o

**object** + that / + part.
**obligate** + inf.
**oblige** + inf.
**observe** + that
**occupy** + part.
**occur** + that
**offer** + inf. / db. pass.

omit + inf.
opine + that
oppose + ing / + part.
order + inf. / + that / db. pass.
owe + inf.

# *p*

pain + inf.
pardon + part.
pay + inf. / db. pass.
penalize + part.
perceive + that
permit + ing / + inf.
persevere + part.
persist + part.
persuade + inf. / + that
pester + inf.
plan + inf.
play + part.
pledge + inf.
plot + inf.
point + that
postpone + ing
praise + part.
pray + inf. / + that
preclude + part.
predict + that / pass. imp. / + int. ind.
prefer + ing / + inf.
prejudice + part.
premise + that
prepare + inf.
presage + that
prescribe + that / + int. ind.
press + inf.
pressure + inf. / + into + ing

presume + inf. / + that / pass. imp.
presuppose + that / pass. imp.
pretend + inf. / + that
prevent + part.
pride + that / + part.
print + that
privilege + inf.
proceed + inf.
prod + into + ing
profess + inf.
profit + part.
prohibit + inf.
promise + inf. / + that / db. pass.
prompt + inf.
prophesy + that / + int. ind.
propose + ing / + inf. / + that
proscribe + ing
prosecute + part.
protest + that
prove + that / pass. imp. / + int. ind.
provoke + inf. / + into + ing
punish + part.
purport + inf.
purpose + inf.
puzzle + int. ind.

# *q*

quarrel + part.
query + int. ind.
question + that / + int. ind.
quit + ing

# *r*

railroad + into + ing
read + inf. / + that
realize + that
reason + that
rebel + part.
rebuke + part.
recall + ing / + that
reckon + that / pass. imp. / + part.
recoil + part.
recollect + ing
recommend + ing / + that
recompense + part.
reconsider + ing
recount + that
reduce + part.
reflect + that / + int. ind.
refrain + part.
refuse + inf.
regret + ing / + inf. / + that
rejoice + inf. / + part.
relate + that / + int. ind.
relish + ing
remain + inf. / + that
remark + that
remember + ing / + inf. / + that / pass. imp. / + int. ind.
remind + inf. / + that / + int. ind.
remonstrate + that
repeat + that
repent + ing
reply + that
report + that / pass. imp.
represent + int. ind.
reprimand + part.
reproach + part.

reprove + part.
repute pass. imp.
request + inf. / + that
require + ing / + inf.
resent + ing
resign + part.
resist + ing
resolve + inf.
resort + part.
restrain + part.
restrict + part.
result + part.
resume + ing
retort + that
reveal + that
revel + part.
revert + part.
revolt + part.
reward + part.
rush + into + ing

# S

say + that / pass. imp. / + int. ind.
scare + into + ing
schedule pass. imp.
scheme + inf.
school + inf.
scold + part.
scorn + ing / + inf.
scruple + inf.
second-guess + that / + int. ind.
seduce + into + ing
see + ing / + that / + int. ind.
seek + inf.
seem + inf. / + that

sense + that
set + part.
shaft + into + ing
shame + into + ing
shanghai + into + ing
shield + part.
shock + inf. / + into + ing
show + that / db. pass. / + int. ind.
shrink + part.
sicken + inf.
signal + inf.
specify + that
stand + ing
start + ing / + inf. / + part.
starve + into + ing
state + that
stem + part.
stick + part.
stop + ing / + inf. / + part.
strike + that
strive + inf.
submit + that
subpoena + inf.
succeed + part.
suggest + ing / + that
summon + inf.
suppose + that / pass. imp.
surmise + that
surprise + inf. / + part.
suspect + that / + part.
suss + that / + int. ind.
swear + inf. / + that

# T

take + that / + part.
talk + part.
tax + part.

teach + inf. / + that / db. pass. / + int. ind.
tell + inf. / + that / db. pass. / + int. ind.
tempt + inf. / + part.
tend + inf.
terrify + into + ing
testify + that
thank + part.
think + that / pass. imp. / + int. ind. / + part.
threaten + inf.
time + int. ind.
tire + part.
tolerate + ing
train + inf.
trap + into + ing
trick + into + ing
trouble + inf.
trust + inf. / + that
try + ing / + inf.

understand + that / + int. ind.
urge + inf. / + that
use + inf. / + part.

vaticinate + that
vaunt + that
venture + inf.
volunteer + inf.
vote + inf. / + that
vow + inf. / + that

# *W*

**wager** + that
**wait** + inf.
**want** + inf.
**warn** + inf. / + that / + part.
**watch** + ing / + inf.
**weary** + part.
**wheedle** + into + ing
**whisper** + that
**will** + inf.
**wish** + inf. / + prét. mod.
**wonder** + int. ind.
**woo** + into + ing
**work** + part.
**write** + inf. / + that

# *Y*

**yearn** + inf.
**yen** + inf.

# VERBES À PARTICULE

Cet index comprend les verbes susceptibles de s'associer aux 30 particules les plus courantes, classées par ordre alphabétique.

Pour la grammaire des verbes à particule, voir p. 46.

L'abréviation (pass.) signale les verbes qui, avec la particule indiquée, sont généralement utilisés au passif.

L'abréviation (+ ing) indique que la particule peut être suivie d'un verbe à la forme en -*ing*.

*a*

**abandon** to
**abash** about (pass.)
**abbreviate** to
**abet** in
**abide** at, by, in, with
**abound** in, with
**absent** from
**absolve** from, of
**absorb** in (pass.) / (+ ing)
**abstain** from (+ ing)
**abstract** from
**abut** against, on
**accede** to
**accept** as
**access** to
**acclimatize** to
**accommodate** to, with
**accord** to, with
**account**, for (+ ing), to
**accredit** to
**accrue** from, to
**accuse** of (+ ing)
**accustom** to (pass.) / (+ ing)
**ache** for, from
**acknowledge** as
**acquaint** with (pass.)
**acquiesce** in, to
**acquit** of
**act** as, for, on, out, up, upon

**adapt** as, for, from, to
**add** in, on, to, up, up to
**addict** to (pass.) / (+ ing)
**address** to
**adhere** to
**adjourn** for, to
**adjudicate** in, on
**adjust** to
**administer** to
**admire** for
**admit** of, to
**adopt** as, from
**adorn** with
**advance** on, to, towards, upon
**advert** to
**advertise** for
**advise** about, of, on, with
**affect** at (pass.)
**affiliate** to, with
**affirm** to
**affix** to
**afflict** with (pass.)
**agglutinate** to
**agitate** for
**agree** on (+ ing), to (+ ing), upon (+ ing), with
**aim** at (+ ing), for, to (+ inf.)
**airmail** from, to
**alarm** at (pass.)
**alert** to
**alienate** from
**alight** from, on, upon
**align** with
**allocate** to

**allot** to
**allow** for, in, into, of, out, through, to, up
**allude** to
**allure** to
**ally** to, with
**alternate** with
**amalgamate** with
**amaze** at (pass.)
**amble** about, across, along, around, away, back, by, down, forth, forward, from, in, into, off, on, out of, out, over, round, through, to, towards, up, upon
**amount** to (+ ing)
**amuse** at (pass.) / (+ ing), by (pass.) / (+ ing), with (pass.) / (+ ing)
**angle** for, towards
**annex** to
**announce** to
**annoy** about (pass.), at (pass.)
**anoint** with
**answer** back, for (+ ing), to
**apologize** for (+ ing), to
**appall** at (pass.), by (pass.)
**appeal** against, for, to
**appear** at, for, in, on
**append** to
**appertain** to (+ ing)
**apply** to (+ ing)
**appoint** for, to
**apportion** to
**appose** to

**apprentice** to
**apprise** of
**approach** about, to
**approbate** of (+ ing)
**appropriate** to, for
**approve** of (+ ing)
**approximate** to
**arbitrate** for, in, on
**arc** around, away, back, down, into, over, round, through, towards, up
**arch** over
**argue** about (+ ing), against, back, down, for, in (+ ing), out of (+ ing), over (+ ing), with
arise for, out of
**arm** against, for, with
**arouse** from
**arraign** for (+ ing)
**arrange** about, for, with
**arrive** in, at
**arrogate** to
**ascribe** to
**ask** about, back, for, in, of, out, over, round, to, up
**aspire** to
**assail** with
**assent** to
**assess** at, in, upon
**assign** to
**assimilate** into, to, with
**assist** at, in (+ ing), with
**associate** in (+ ing), with
**assort** with
**assure** against
**astonish** at (pass.)
**atone** for (+ ing)
**attach** to
**attain** to
**attend** on, to, upon
**attest** to

**attire** in, with
**attract** to
**attribute** to
**attune** to
**auction** for
**audition** for
**avail** of
**avenge** of
**average** out
**avert** from
**awake** from, to
**awaken** from, to
**award** to
**awe** at (pass.)

**babble** away, on, out
**back** away, down, in, off, out, up
**backdate** to
**badger** into (+ ing), out of (+ ing)
**bag** up
**bail** out
**bait** into (+ ing), with
**balance** against, out, with
**bale** out
**balk** at (+ ing)
**ball** up
**ballot** against (+ ing), for (+ ing)
**bamboozle** into (+ ing), out of (+ ing)
**band** against
**bandage** up
**bandy** about
**bang** about, against, around, away, down, into, on, out, up, upon
**banish** from

**bank** on, up, with
**bar** from (+ ing), in, out, up
**bare** of
**bargain** about, away, for, on, over, with
**barge** about, across, along, around, away, back, by, down, forth, forward, from, in, into, off, on, out, out of, over, round, through, to, towards, up, upon
**bark** at
**barricade** against, in, into, out, out of, with
**barter** away, for, with
**base** on (+ ing)
**bash** about, in, up, upon
**bask** in
**bat** around
**bathe** in
**batten** back, down, on, upon
**batter** about, back, in, up
**battle** against, for, on, out, over, with
**bawl** for, out
**bay** at
be about, against, along, around, at, away, back, by, down, for, in, into, off, on, out, out of, over, round, through, up, upon, with
**beam** to, with
bear against, away, down, in, off, on, out, to, up, upon, with
beat about, against, at, back, down, in, into (+ ing), off, on, out, to, up, upon
**beckon** in, to
become of
**bed** down, in with
**bedew** with (pass.)
**beef** up

**beetle** off

**befoul** with

**befuddle** with

**beg** for, from, of, off

**begin** as, on, with

**begrime** with

**beguile** into (+ ing), out of (+ ing), with

**behave** towards

**belch** forth, out

**believe** in (+ ing)

**bellow** out

**belly** out

**belong** to

**belt** along, down, out, up

**bend** back, down, forward, in, on, over, to, upon

**benefit** by (+ ing), from (+ ing)

**benumb** with (pass.)

**bequeath** to

**bereave** of

**beset** with

**besiege** with

**besmear** with

**besot** with

**bespatter** with

**best** at (+ ing)

**bestow** on, upon

**bestrew** with

**bet** into, on, with

**bethink** of

**betray** into (+ ing), out of (+ ing)

**betroth** to

**beware** of

**bias** against, towards

**bicker** about, over

**bicycle** about, across, along, around, away, back, by, down, forth, forward, from, in, into, off, on, out, out of, over, round, through, to, towards, up, upon

**bid** against, for

**bike** about, across, along, around, away, back, by, down, forth, forward, from, in, into, off, on, out, out of, over, round, through, to, towards, up, upon

**bilk** out of

**billet** in, with

**bind** down, off, over, up

**bite** back, into, off, on

**blab** out

**blabber** about, on

**black** up, out

**blacken** out

**blackmail** into (+ ing), out of (+ ing)

**blame** for, on

**blank** out

**blanket** to

**blare** away, out

**blaspheme** against

**blast** off

**blaze** away, down, up, with

**blazon** forth, out

**bleach** out

**bleat** about

**bleed** for

**blend** in, into, with

**bless** with

**blind** to

**blink** away, back, at

**block** in, off, out, up

**bloom** into

**blossom** forth, into, out

**blot** up, out

**blow** about, around, away, back, down, in, into, off, on, out, over, round, to, up, upon

**blubber** out

**bluff** into (+ ing), out, out of (+ ing)

**blunder** away, on, out, through, upon

**blur** out, with

**blurt** out

**blush** for, with

**board** in, out, up, with

**boast** about, of

**bob** down, to, up

**bog** down, off

**boggle** at

**boil** away, down, out, over, up

**bolster** up

**bolt** down, in, out

**bomb** out, up

**bombard** with

**book** into, up

**boost** up

**boot** out, out of

**border** on

**bore** out, through

**borrow** against, from

**boss** around

**botch** up

**bother** about

**bottle** up

**bottom** up

**bounce** about, across, against, along, around, at, away, back, by, down, forth, forward, from, in, into, off, on, out, out of, over, round, through, to, towards, up, upon

**bound** away, with

**bow** down, out, to

**bowl** along, out, over

**box** in, up

**brace** up

**brag** about (+ ing), of (+ ing)

**branch** off, out

**brand** with

**brazen** out

break away, back, down, in, into, off, out, through, to, up, with
breakfast on, off
breathe down, in, into, on, out, upon
breeze in, through
brew up
bribe into (+ ing), out of (+ ing), to (+ inf.)
brick in, up
bridge over
bridle at, up
brighten up
brim over
bring about, along, around, away, back, down, forth, forward, in, off, on, out, over, round, through, to, towards, up, upon
brisk up
bristle with
broach to, with
broaden out
brood about, on, over, upon
browbeat into (+ ing), out of (+ ing)
brown off
browse on, through
brush away, down, off, over, up
brutalize with
bubble over, up
buck off, up
buckle down, to, up
budget for
buffet with
bug off, out
build in, into, of, on, out, over, up, upon
bulge out
bulk up

bulldoze into (+ ing), out of (+ ing)
bully into (+ ing), out of (+ ing)
bum about, around, out
bump against, into, off, up
bunch up
bundle away, into, off, out, up
bung up
bunk up
buoy up
burden with
burn down, for, into, off, out, to, up, with
burp into
burrow into, out of, through
burst forth, in, into, on, out, through, upon, with
bury in
bust out, up
bustle up
busy with (+ ing)
butt in
butter up
button up
buttress up
buy back, in, off, out, over, up
buzz off

# C

cable to
cadge from, off
cage up
cajole into (+ ing), out of (+ ing)
cake with
calculate for (+ ing), on (+ ing), upon (+ ing)
call about, away, back, by,

down, for, forth, forward, in, into, off, on, out, over, round, to, up, upon
calm down
camp out, up
campaign against, for
canalize into
cancel out
cannon into, off
canvass for
cap with
capitalize on
capture from
care about (+ ing), for
career about, across, along, around, away, back, by, down, forth, forward, from, in, into, off, on, out, out of, over, round, through, to, towards, up, upon
carp at
carpet with
carry about, along, around, away, back, down, forward, in, off, on, out, over, through, with
carve out, up
cascade from, into, out, over, to
cash up, in
cast about, around, away, back, down, in, off, on, out, over, round, up, upon
catch at, in, on, out, up
cater for, to
caution about (+ ing), against (+ ing)
cave in
cavil at
cease from
cede to
censure for
centre in, on, round

**certify** to

**chafe** to

**chagrin** at (pass.) / (+ ing)

**chain** down, to, up

**chalk** out, up

**champ** at

**chance** on, upon

**change** back, down, for, in, off, out of, over, round, to, up, with

**channel** away, into

**charge** across, along, around, away, back, by, down, for (+ ing), forth, forward, from, in, into, on, out, out of, round, through, to, towards, up, upon, with (+ ing)

**charm** with

**chart** out

**chase** about, around, down, up

**chastise** for (+ ing)

**chat** up

**cheat** at, into (+ ing), out of (+ ing)

**check** back, in, off, on, out, over, through, up

**cheer** for, on, up

**cheese** off

**chew** away, on, out, over, up, upon

**chide** for (+ ing)

**chime** in

**chip** away, in

**chisel** in, out of

**chivvy** into (+ ing), out of (+ ing)

**choke** back, down, off, out of, up, with

**choose** as, for, from

**chop** about, around, away, down, into, off, round, up

**christen** after

**chuck** about, against, around, at, in, off, out, up

**chuckle** at, over

**chug** about, across, along, around, away, back, by, down, forth, forward, from, in, into, off, on, out, out of, over, round, through, to, towards, up, upon

**chum** around, with

**churn** into, out, to, up

**circle** about, around, over, round

**circulate** about, around, over, round

**circumscribe** to

**cite** for

**claim** against, back, for, from

**clamber** over, up

**clamour** against, back, for

**clamp** up

**clap** in, into, on, out, to, up

**clash** against, on, over, with

**clasp** to

**class** with

**clatter** about

**claw** at

**clean** down, of, off, out, up

**clear** away, of, off, out, up, with (pass.)

**cleave** to

**click** for, with

**climb** down, in, on, out, out of, over, up

**cling** to

**clip** on, out

**clock** in, off, on, out, up

**clog** up, with

**clop** about, across, along, around, away, back, by,

down, forth, forward, from, in, into, off, on, out, out of, over, round, through, to, towards, up, upon

**close** about, around, down, in, off, on, out, round, up, upon, with

**closet** with (pass.)

**clothe** in, with

**cloud** over, up

**clown** about, around

**club** down, to, with

**cluck** over

**clue** in, up

**cluster** around, round

**clutch** at, to

**clutter** up, with

**coach** for

**coast** along

**coat** with

**coax** into (+ ing), out of (+ ing)

**cock** up

**coerce** into (+ ing), out of (+ ing)

**coexist** with

**cogitate** over (+ ing), upon (+ ing)

**cohabit** with

**coil** around, down, round, up

**coin** to

**coincide** with

**collaborate** on, with

**collate** with

**collect** for, from, up

**collide** with

**collocate** with

**colour** in, up

**comb** for, out, through

**combat** against, for, with

**combine** against, with

**come** about, across, along, around, at, away, back, by,

down, for, forth, forward, from, in, into, of, off, on, out, out of, over, round, through, up, upon, with

**commence** as, on, with
**commend** for, to
**comment** on, upon
**commentate** on
**commiserate** with
**commission** for
**commit** for, on, to (+ ing)
**commune** with
**communicate** about, on, with
**commute** for, from, in, to
**compact** of (pass.)
**compare** to, with
**compass** by (pass.), with (pass.)
**compel** from, to ( +inf.)
**compensate** for
**compete** against, for, in, with
**complain** about (+ ing), of, to
**complicate** with
**compliment** on
**comply** with
**comport** with
**compose** of (pass.)
**compound** with
**compress** in
**comprise** of (pass.)
**compromise** with
**con** into (+ ing), out of (+ ing)
**concatenate** to
**conceal** from
**concede** to
**conceive** as, of
**concentrate** at, on, upon
**concern** about, in, over, with
**concert** with
**conclude** with (+ ing)
**concur** in, with

**condemn** as, for, to
**condescend** to (+ ing)
**condition** to
**condole** with
**conduce** to (+ ing), towards (+ ing)
**conduct** away, out
**confederate** with
**confer** on, upon, with
**confess** to (+ ing)
**confide** in, to
**confine** to (+ ing)
**confirm** in
**confiscate** from
**conflict** with
**conform** to, with
**confound** with
**confront** with
**confuse** about (pass.) / (+ ing), with
**congratulate** on (+ ing), upon (+ ing)
**conjure** away, up, with
**conk** out
**connect** to, up, with
**connive** at, with
**conscript** into
**consecrate** to (+ ing)
**consent** to (+ ing)
**consider** as
**consign** to
**consist** in (+ ing), of (+ ing), with
**console** with
**consort** with
**conspire** against, with
**constrain** from
**construct** for, of, out of
**construe** as, with
**consult** about, with
**consume** away, with (+ ing)

**contain** for
**contend** against, for, over, with
**content** with (+ ing)
**contest** against, for, with
**continue** with
**contract** for, in, out, with
**contrast** with
**contribute** to (+ ing), towards
**convalesce** for
**converge** on
**converse** about, on, with
**convert** from, into, to
**convey** to
**convict** of (+ ing)
**convince** of
**convulse** with (pass.)
**cook** up
**cool** down, off, out
**coop** up
**cooperate** on, with
**co-opt** to
**cop** to
**cope** with (+ ing)
**copulate** with
**copy** down, out
**cordon** off
**cork** up
**correlate** to, with
**correspond** about, to, with
**cosset** into (+ ing), out of (+ ing)
**cost** out
**co-star** in
**cotton** on, to
**couch** in
**cough** out, up
**count** against, as, down, for, from, in, off, on (+ ing), out, to, up, upon (+ ing), with
**counter** with
**couple** on, up, with

**course** through
**court** into (+ ing), out of (+ ing)
**covenant** for, with
**cover** against, for, in, over, up, with
**cow** into (+ ing), out of (+ ing)
**cower** away, back, down, forward
**crab** about, against, along, around, at, away, back, by, down, for, forward, from, in, into, off, on, out, over, round, through, to, towards, up, upon
**crack** up
**cram** for, in, up, with
**crane** forward
**crank** up
**crash** about, around, down, in, out, with
**crave** for
**crawl** to, with
**cream** off
**crease** up
**credit** for (+ ing), to, with (+ ing)
**creep** about, across, along, around, away, back, by, down, forth, forward, from, in, into, off, on, out, out of, over, round, through, to, towards, up, upon
**crib** from
**cringe** before, from (+ ing), to
**cripple** with (pass.)
**criticize** for (+ ing)
**crook** up
**crop** out, up
**cross** in, off, out, over, with
**crouch** down
**crow** over
**crowd** in, into, out, round, with
**crown** with (pass.)

**crumble** away, up
**crumple** up
**crunch** down, up
**crusade** against, for
**crush** down, in, into, out, to, up
**crust** over
**cry** down, for, off, out, over, to, up
**cuddle** up
**cue** in
**cull** from, out
**culminate** in (+ ing)
**cup** round
**curb** down, up
**cure** of
**curl** up
**curse** with (pass.)
**curtain** off
**cut** about (pass.), across, along, at, away, back, down, for, from, in, into, off, out, through, to, up, with
**cycle** about, across, along, around, away, back, by, down, forth, forward, from, in, into, off, on, out, out of, over, round, through, to, towards, up, upon

**dab** at, off, on, out
**dabble** at, in, with
**dally** over, with
**dam** up
**damp** down, off

**dampen** off
**dance** about, across, along, around, away, back, by, down, forth, forward, from, in, into, off, on, out, out of, over, round, through, to, towards, up, upon, with
**dangle** about, around, from, round
**dart** about, across, along, around, at, away, back, by, down, for, forth, forward, from, in, into, off, on, out, out of, over, round, through, to, towards, up, upon
**dash** about, across, along, around, away, back, by, down, for, forth, forward, from, in, into, off, on, out, out of, over, round, through, to, towards, up, upon
**date** back, from
**daub** on, over, up, with
**dawdle** along, away, over
**dawn** on, upon
**daydream** about
**deaden** with (pass.)
**deal** at, by, in, out, with
**debar** from (+ ing)
**debate** about, in, on, upon, with
**debit** against, to, with
**decamp** from
**deceive** in, into (+ ing), with
**decide** against (+ ing), for, on (+ ing), upon (+ ing)
**deck** out, up, with
**declaim** against
**declare** against, for, off, on, to
**decorate** with, for (+ ing)
**decoy** into (+ ing)
**decrease** from

**dedicate** to (+ ing)
**deduce** from
**deduct** from
**deed** over, to
**deface** of
**default** on
**defect** from, to
**defend** against, from (+ ing)
**define** as
**deflect** from
**defraud** of
**degenerate** into (+ ing)
**delay** in (+ ing)
**delegate** to
**delete** from
**deliberate** about, on, over, upon
**delight** at (+ ing), by (pass.), in (+ ing), with (pass.)
**deliver** from, of, over, to, up
**delude** into (+ ing), out of (+ ing)
**deluge** with
**delve** into
**demand** from, of
**demise** to
**demonstrate** to
**demote** from, to
**demur** at, to
**denounce** for, to
**denude** of
**deny** to
**depart** from
**depend** on, upon
**deplete** of
**depose** to
**deposit** on, with
**deprive** of
**depute** to
**deputize** as, for
**derive** from
**derogate** from
**descant** on, upon

**descend** from, into, on, to (+ ing), upon
**describe** as, to
**design** for
**designate** as
**desist** from (+ ing)
**despair** of (+ ing)
**despatch** to
**despise** for (+ ing)
**despoil** of
**destine** for (pass.)
**detach** from
**detail** for, off
**deter** from (+ ing)
**determine** on (+ ing), upon (+ ing)
**detract** from
**develop** from, into
**deviate** from
**devolve** on, upon
**devote** to (+ ing)
**devour** with (pass.)
**dice** into, with
**dictate** to
**die** away, back, by, down, for, from, in, of, off, out, with
**differ** about, from, in, on, with
**differentiate** from
**dig** at, down, for, in, into, out, over, up
**digress** from
**dilate** on, upon
**dilute** with
**dim** down, out, up
**din** in, into
**dine** at, off, on, out
**dip** in, into, to
**direct** to
**dirty** up
**disabuse** of
**disagree** about, on, over, with
**disappear** from, to

**disappoint** at (pass.), in (+ ing), with
**disapprove** of (+ ing)
**disbar** from
**disbelieve** in
**disburden** of
**discern** from
**discharge** from, into
**disconnect** from, with (pass.)
**discord** with
**discourage** from (+ ing)
**discourse** on, upon
**discriminate** against, from
**discuss** with
**disembark** from
**disencumber** from
**disengage** from
**disentangle** from
**disguise** as, in, with
**disgust** at (+ ing), by (pass.), with
**dish** out, up
**dislodge** from
**dismantle** of
**dismay** at (+ ing) / (pass.)
**dismiss** as, for (+ ing), from
**dismount** from
**dispatch** to
**dispense** from (+ ing), to, with
**displease** at (pass.), with
**dispose** of, towards (pass.)
**dispossess** of
**dispute** against, at, over, with
**disqualify** for (+ ing)
**dissatisfy** at (pass.) / (+ ing), with
**dissent** about, from
**dissociate** from
**dissolve** in, into
**dissuade** from (+ ing)
**distinguish** from

**distract** from (+ ing)
**distrain** upon
**distribute** over, round, to
**divagate** from
**dive** in, into, off
**diverge** from, to
**divert** from, to, with
**divest** of
**divide** by, from, into, off, on, out, with
**divorce** from
**divulge** to
**dizzy** from, with
**do** about, as, by, down, for, in, of, out, out, over, to, up, with (+ ing)
**dock** off
**dodder** along
**dole** out
**doll** up
**dolly** in, out
**dominate** over
**domineer** over
**donate** to
**doom** to (pass.)
**dope** out, up
**dose** with
**dot** about, around, with
**dote** on, upon
**double** as, over, up, with
**doubt** of
**dovetail** into
**doze** off
**draft** out, to
**drag** at, away, down, in, into, off, out, through, up
**dragoon** into (+ ing)
**drain** away, from, into, of, off, out
**drape** in, over, round, with
**draw** at (+ ing), away, back, down, for, forth, from, in, into,

off, on, out, over, to, up, upon
**drawl** out
**dream** about, away, of (+ ing)
**dredge** for, up
**drench** in (pass.), with
**dress** down, for, up
**drift** along, away, in, off, out, towards
**drill** in, down, into
**drink** away, down, in, off, to, up
**drive** about, across, along, around, at, away, back, by, down, for, forth, forward, from, in, into, off, on, out, out of, over, round, through, to, towards, up, upon
**drivel** about, on
**drizzle** down
**drone** on
**drool** over
**droop** down
**drop** across, around, away, back, by, down, in, into, off, on, out, over, round, through, to, up
**drown** in, out
**drowse** away, off
**drum** in, into, on, out of, up, upon
**dry** off, out, up
**dub** in
**duck** down, into, out
**dull** up
**dump** down, on
**dun** for
**dunk** in
**dust** down, off, out
**dwell** at, in, on, upon
**dwindle** away, down, to

*e*

**earmark** for
**earth** up
**ease** of, off, round, up
**eat** away, in, into, off, out, out of, through, up
**eavesdrop** on
**ebb** away
**echo** back, with
**economize** on
**edge** away, out, with
**edit** out
**educate** for, in
**educe** from
**egg** on
**eject** from
**eke** out
**elaborate** on
**elate** with (pass.)
**elect** as, to, with
**elevate** to
**eliminate** from
**elope** with
**emanate** from
**emancipate** from
**embark** for, on, upon
**embed** in
**embellish** with
**emblazon** with
**embody** in
**embosom** in, with
**embrace** in
**embroil** in
**emerge** from
**emigrate** from, to
**emit** from, into
**empathize** with
**employ** at, for, in (+ ing)
**empty** in, out

**enamour** of (pass.), with
**encase** in
**enchant** by, with
**enclose** in, with
**encompass** with
**encourage** in
**encroach** on, upon
**encrust** with
**encumber** with
**end** by (+ ing), in, up, with (+ ing)
**endear** to
**endorse** with
**endow** with
**endue** with
**enfold** in
**enforce** on
**engage** in (+ ing), to, with (pass.)
**engorge** with
**engrave** on, upon, with
**engross** in (pass.)
**engulf** in (pass.)
**enjoin** on
**enlarge** on, upon
**enlighten** on
**enlist** in
**enmesh** in (pass.)
**enquire** about, for, into, of
**enrich** with
**enrol** for, in
**ensconce** in
**enshrine** in
**ensnare** into (+ ing), out of (+ ing)
**ensue** from, on
**ensure** against, from
**entail** on
**entangle** in (pass.), with
**enter** by, for, in, into, on, up, upon

**entertain** to, with
**enthrall** into (+ ing), out of (+ ing), with (pass.)
**enthrone** in
**enthuse** about, over
**entice** away, from, into, to
**entitle** to (pass.)
**entomb** in
**entrap** into (+ ing)
**entreat** of
**entrust** to, with
**entwine** about, around, round, with
**envelop** in
**equal** in
**equate** with (pass.)
**equip** for, with
**erase** from
**err** on
**erupt** into
**escape** from, out of, to
**escort** to, from
**establish** in
**estimate** at
**estrange** from (pass.)
**etch** away, in
**evacuate** from, to
**evaluate** at
**evaporate** down
**even** off, out, up
**evict** from
**evolve** from, out of
**exact** from
**examine** in, on
**exasperate** at (pass.), by
**exceed** by, in
**excel** at (+ ing), in
**except** from
**excerpt** from
**exchange** for, with
**excite** in

**exclaim** against, at
**exclude** from
**excuse** for (+ ing), from (+ ing)
**exempt** from (+ ing)
**exercise** in (+ ing)
**exile** from
**exist** by
**exonerate** from
**exorcise** from, out of
**expand** into, on
**expatiate** on, upon
**expatriate** from
**expect** from, of
**expel** from
**expend** in (+ ing), on (+ ing)
**experiment** in, on, upon, with
**explain** away, to
**explode** with
**export** to
**expose** to
**expostulate** with
**expound** to
**express** as, in, to
**expropriate** from
**expunge** from
**expurgate** from
**extend** across, over, to (+ ing)
**extinguish** by (pass.)
**extort** from, out of
**extract** from
**extradite** from
**extricate** from
**extrude** from
**exult** at (+ ing), in (+ ing), over
**eye** with

**face** about, away, down, forward, off, out, round, with

**fade** away, back, down, for, in, into, out, up

**fail** in, of

**faint** away, from, with

**fake** out, up

**fall** about, around, at, away, back, by, down, for, from, in, into, off, on, out, out of, over, through, to, towards, upon

**falter** out

**familiarize** with (+ ing)

**fan** out

**fantasize** about

**fare** forth

**farm** out

**fashion** from, on, out of, to, upon

**fasten** down, off, on, to, up, upon

**father** on, upon

**fathom** out

**fatten** on, up

**favour** with

**fawn** on, upon

**fax** back, from, to,

**fear** for

**feather** out

**feature** in

**feed** back, in, into, off, on, to, up (pass.), upon, with

**feel** about, for, like (+ ing), out, out of, towards, up, with

**fence** in, off, out, with

**fend** for, off

**ferret** about, around, out

**ferry** across, over

**festoon** with

**fetch** back, in, out, over, round, to, up

**feud** with

**fiddle** about, away, with

**fidget** with

**fight** about, against, back, down, for, off, on, out, over, through, to, with

**figure** in, on, out, to, up

**filch** from

**file** away, down, for, out

**fill** away, in, out, up, with

**film** over

**filter** out, through

**find** against, for, in, out

**fine** down, for (+ ing)

**finish** in, off, up (+ ing), with (+ ing)

**fire** at, away, back, into, off, on, over, up, upon, with

**firm** up

**fish** for, in, out, up

**fit** for, in, into, on, out, round, to, up, with

**fix** for, on, over, up, upon, with

**fizz** up

**fizzle** out

**flabbergast** at (pass.)

**flag** down

**flagellate** for (+ ing)

**flake** out

**flame** out, up, with

**flank** on, upon, with

**flap** about, around, away

**flare** back, out, up

**flash** about, around, at, back, forward, on, out, through, up, upon

**flatten** out

**flatter** on (+ ing)

**flavour** with

**fleck** with

**flee** from, to

**flesh** out

**flick** away, off, over, through

**flicker** out

**fling** about, around, at, away, back, down, in, into, off, on, out, to, up

**flip** over, through

**flirt** with

**flit** about, through

**float** about, around, in, on, round, through, upon

**flock** in, into, round, to

**flood** in, into, out, with (pass.)

**flop** about, around, down, into

**flounce** in, out

**flounder** about, around, through

**flow** from, in, into, out, over, to, with

**fluff** out, up

**flunk** out

**flush** away, from, off, out, up, with

**fluster** up (pass.)

**flutter** about, across, along, around, away, back, by, down, forth, forward, from, in, into, off, on, out, out of, over, round, through, to, towards, up, upon

**fly** about, across, along, around, away, back, by, down, forth, forward, from, in, into, off, on, out, out of, over, round, through, to, towards, up, upon

**foam** at, up, with
**fob** off on (to), off with
**focus** on
**foist** off, off on (to), on (to)
**fold** away, back, down, in, up
**follow** about, in, on, out, through, up, upon
**fool** about, around, away, into (+ ing), out of, with
**footle** about
forbear from (+ ing)
**force** down, from, into (+ ing), on, out, upon
**foreclose** on
**foregather** with
forget about
forgive for (+ ing)
**fork** out, over, up
**form** from, into, up
**fortify** against, with
**forward** to
**foul** up
**found** on, upon
**frame** in, up
**freak** out
**free** from, of
**freeze** in, off, out, over, to, up
**freshen** up
**fret** about, into, on, over, upon
**frighten** away, from (+ ing), into (+ ing), off, out of (+ ing)
**fringe** with (pass.)
**frisk** about
**fritter** away
**frog-march** along, away, by, in, off, out of, to, towards
**frolic** about
**front** on, to, towards, upon
**frost** over, up
**froth** up, with
**frown** at, on, upon

**fry** up
**fudge** on
**fulminate** against
**fumble** for, with
**fume** at (+ ing)
**funk** at
**funnel** into
**fur** up
**furbish** up
**furnish** to, with
**fuse** with
**fuss** about, around, over, up
**fuzz** out

# g

**gabble** away, off, on, out
**gad** about, around
**gain** in, on, over, upon
**gallivant** about, around, off
**gallop** about, across, along, around, away, back, by, down, forth, forward, from, in, into, off, on, out, out of, over, round, through, to, towards, up, upon
**galumph** about, across, along, around, away, back, by, down, forth, forward, from, in, into, off, on, out, out of, over, round, through, to, towards, up, upon
**galvanize** with
**gamble** away, on
**gambol** about, across, along, around, away, back, by, down, forth, forward, from, in, into, off, on, out, out of, over, round, through, to, towards, up, upon

**game** away
**gang** up
**gape** at
**garb** in
**garnish** with
**gas** up
**gasp** at, for, out
**gather** from, in, round, to, up
**gaze** about, at, on, out, round, upon
**gear** down, to, up
**generalize** about, from
**generate** from
get about, across, along, around, at, away, back, by, down, for, from, in, into, off, on, out, out of, over, round, through, to, up
**gibe** at
**giggle** at, over
gird for, on, up
**girdle** about, around, round
give away, back, for, forth, in, off, on, out, over, round, to, up (+ ing), upon
**glance**, at, back, down, off, over, round, through
**glare** at, down
**glass** over
**glaze** over
**gleam** with
**glean** from
**glide** about, across, along, around, away, back, by, down, forth, forward, from, in, into, off, on, out of, over, round, through, to, towards, upon
**glisten** with

**glitter** with
**gloat** over
**glory** in (+ ing)
**gloss** over
**glow** with
**glower** at
**glue** down, on, to
**glut** with
**gnaw** at, away, on
**go** about, across, against, along, around, at, away, back, by, down, forth, forward, from, in, into, off, on, out, out of, over, round, through, to, towards, up, upon, with
**goad** into (+ ing), on
**gobble** down, up
**goggle** at
**goof** around, off, up
**goose** up
**gorge** on, with
**gossip** about, of
**gouge** out
**grab** at, away, for
**grace** with
**grade** down, up
**graduate** from, in, with
**graft** in, on, upon
**grant** to
**graph** out
**grapple** with
**grasp** at
**grate** on
**gravitate** to, towards
**graze** on
**greet** with
**grieve** about, for, over
**grin** at
**grind** away, down, in, into, on, out, to, up
**gripe** about, at

**groan** with
**groom** for
**grope** about, around, for
**ground** in (pass.), on
**group** about, around, round
**grouse** about, at
**grovel** to
**grow** back, down, from, in, into, on, out, out of, over, up, upon
**growl** out
**grub** about, around, up
**grumble** about, at, over
**guarantee** against, for
**guard** against, from
**guess** at
**gull** into (+ ing), out of (+ ing)
**gulp** back, down
**gum** down, on, up
**gun** down
**gurgle** with
**gush** forth, from, out, over, with
**gussy** up
**guzzle** down

# *h*

**habituate** to (+ ing)
**hack** around, down, off, out, up
**haggle** about, for, over, with
**hail** from
**ham** up
**hammer** at, down, in, into, on, out
**hand** back, down, in, off, out, over, round, to, up
**hang** about, around, back, by, down, from, off, on, out, over, round, up, upon, with
**hanker** for
**happen** on, to, upon
**harden** off, to (pass.) / (+ ing), up
**hare** off
**hark** at
**harmonize** with
**harness** up, to
**harp** about, on
**hash** out, over, up
**hatch** out
**haul** down, in, on, over, up
**have** about, against, around, at, away, back, by, down, for, in, off, on, out, over, to, up, upon, with
**hawk** about, round
**haze** over
**head** back, for, in, into, off, out, towards, up
**heal** of, over, up
**heap** on, up, upon, with
**hear** about, from, of, out, through
**hearten** up
**heat** up
**heave** about, in, on, to, up
**hector** into (+ ing), out of (+ ing)
**hedge** against, in
**heel** back, over
**help** along, back, down, forward, in, into, off, on, out, over, to, up
**hem** about, around, in, round
**herd** into, with
**hesitate** for
**hew** down, out
**hide** away, from, in, out, with
**hinder** from (+ ing)

hinge on, upon

hint at, to

hire out

hiss at

hit against, at, back, in, out, up, upon

hitch to, up

hitch-hike across, along, around, away, back, from, in, into, on, out, out of, through, to, towards

hive off

hoard up

hoax into (+ ing), out of (+ ing)

hobble across, along, around, away, back, forth, forward, in, into, off, out, out of, through, to

hobnob with

hoist up

hoke up

hold against, at, back, by, down, for, forth, in, off, on, out, out of, over, to, up, with

hole in, out, up

hollow out

home in

honour for (+ ing), with

hoodwink into (+ ing), out of (+ ing)

hook on, up

hoot down, off

hop about, across, along, around, away, back, by, down, forth, forward, from, in, into, off, on, out, out of, over, round, through, to, towards, up, upon

hope for, in

horn in

horse about, around

hose down

hound out

house up

hover over, round

howl down, with

huddle up

hum with

humbug into (+ ing), out of (+ ing)

humiliate into (+ ing), out of (+ ing)

hump over

hunch up (pass.)

hunger for

hunker down

hunt down, for, out, over, through, up

hurl about, around, at, away, down, into, out

hurry along, away, back, down, forward, in, into, off, on, out, up

hurtle along, down

hush up

hustle into (+ ing), on, out of (+ ing)

hype up

hypnotize into (+ ing), out of (+ ing)

*i*

ice over, up

identify with

idle about, around, away

illuminate with

illumine with

illustrate with

imbue with (pass.)

immerse in

immigrate into

immunize against

impale on

impart to

impeach for (+ ing)

impel to

impend over

impinge on, upon

implant in, into

implicate in

import from, into

impose on, upon

impregnate with

impress by, on, upon, with

imprint on, with

imprison for, in

improve in, on, upon

impute to

incapacitate for, from (+ ing)

incarcerate in

incite to

incline forward, to, towards

include in, out

incorporate in, into

increase for, in, to

inculcate in

indemnify against, for

indent for

indict for (+ ing)

indispose for (+ ing), towards

indoctrinate with

induce in

indulge in (+ ing)

infatuate with (pass.)

infect with

infer from

infest with

infiltrate into, through

inflate with

inflict on
inform against, of, on
infringe on, upon
infuse into, with
ingraft into, upon
ingratiate with
inhere in
inherit from
inhibit for (+ ing)
initiate into
inject into, with
ink in, over
inlay with
innovate in
inoculate against, with
input into
inquire about, for, into, of
inscribe with
insert in, into
inset in, into
insinuate into
insist on (+ ing), upon
inspire in, into, with
install in
instill in, into, with
institute against, into, to
instruct in, of
insulate from
insure against, for, with
integrate into, with
intend as, for, in
interact with
interbreed with
intercede for, with
interchange with
interdict from (+ ing)
interest in (pass.) / (+ ing)
interfere in, with
interlace with
interlard with
interleave with

interlink with
intermarry with
intermingle with
intern in
interpose in
interpret as
interrogate about
intersect by, with
intersperse with
intervene in
interview about
interweave with
intimate to
intimidate into (+ ing), out of (+ ing)
intoxicate with (pass.)
intrigue against, with
introduce into, to
intrude into, on, upon
intrust to, with
inundate with (pass.)
inure from, to
inveigh against
inveigle into (+ ing), out of (+ ing)
invest in, with
invite in, out, over, round, to
invoke for, on, upon
involve in (pass.) / (+ ing), with (pass.)
iron out
irrigate with
isolate from
issue as, forth, from, out of, to, with
itch for

jab at, into
jack up
jam in, into, on, up, with
jangle on, upon
jar against, on, with
jaunt back, forth
jaw at
jazz up
jeer at
jerk away, off, out, up
jest about, at
jib at (+ ing)
jigger up
jink about, across, along, around, away, back, by, down, forth, forward, from, in, into, off, on, out, out of, over, round, through, to, towards, up, upon
job out
jockey for, into (+ ing), out of (+ ing)
jog about, across, along, around, away, back, by, down, forth, forward, from, in, into, off, on, out, out of, over, round, through, to, towards, up, upon
join in (+ ing), on, to, up, with
joke about, at, with
jolly along
jostle for, with
jot down
judge by, from
juggle with

**jumble** up

**jump** about, across, along, around, at, away, back, by, down, for, forth, forward, from, in, into, off, on, out, out of, over, round, through, to, towards, up, upon, with

**justify** in (pass.) / (+ ing), by (+ ing)

**jut** out

*k*

**keel** over

**keep** about, around, at, away, back, by, down, for, from (+ ing), in, off, on, out, out of, to, up, with

**kick** about, against, around, at, away, back, down, in, off, on, out, over, up

**kid** around

**kill** off

**kindle** with

**kiss** away, off

**kit** out, up

**kneel** down, to

**knit** together, up

**knock** about, against, around, at, away, back, down, for, in, into, off, on, out, out of, over, through, up

**know** about, as, by, for, from, of, to (pass.)

**knuckle** down

**kosher** up

**kowtow** to

*l*

**label** as, with

**labour** at (+ ing), for, over (+ ing)

**lace** in, into, up, with

**lack** for, in

**lade** with

**ladle** for, out, out of

**lag** with

**lam** into, out

**lament** for, over

**land** in, on, up, upon, with

**languish** for, in, of, over

**lap** about, against, around, in, on, over, round, up

**lapse** into

**lard** with

**lark** about, around

**lash** about, against, at, down, into, out, round, to, up

**last** for, out

**latch** on, onto

**lather** up

**laugh** about, at, away, down, into (+ ing), off, out of (+ ing), over

**launch** against, forth, into, on, out, upon

**lavish** on

**lay** about, against, along, at, away, back, by, down, for, in, into, off, on, out, over, up, with

**laze** away

**leach** from, out, out of

**lead** against, away, back, by, down, forth, in, into, off, on, out, to, up, with

**leaf** out, through

**league** against, with

**leak** away, in, out, to

**lean** against, back, down, forward, on, out, over, to, towards

**leap** at, forward, in, into, out, out of, up

**learn** about, by, from, of, off, up

**lease** back, out

**leave** about, around, at, down, for, in, off, on, out, out of, over, to, up, with

**leaven** with

**lecture** about, at, for, on, to

**leer** at

**legislate** against, for

**lend** out, to (+ ing)

**lengthen** out

**let** by, down, in, into, of, off, on, out, through, up

**level** against, at, down, off, out, up, with

**lever** against, out, up

**levy** on, upon

**liaise** with

**liberate** from

**license** for (pass.)

**lick** off, up

**lie** about, along, at, back, by, down, in, off, on, out, over, through, to, up, with

**lie** about, to

**lift** down, from, off, up

**light** up, with

**liken** to, with

**limber** up

**limit** to (pass.) / (+ ing)

**limp** along

**line** up, with

**linger** about, around, on, over

**link** to, up, with

**lisp** out

**listen** for, in, out, to (+ ing)

**litter** about, around, down, up

**live** at, by, down, for, in, off, on, out, out of, over, to, up, with

**liven** up

**load** down, into, up, with

**loaf** about, around

**loan** to

**lob** along, at

**lobby** against, for, through

**lock** away, in, into, on, out, up

**lodge** against, at, in, with

**log** off, on, out, up

**loiter** about, around, away, in, over

**loll** about, around, back, out

**long** for

**look** about, around, at, away, back, down, for, in, into, on, out, over, round, through, to, towards, up, upon

**loom** up

**loose** from, off

**loosen** up

**lop** away, off

**lope** about, across, along, around, away, back, by, down, forth, forward, from, in, into, off, on, out, out of, over, round, through, to, towards, up, upon

**lose** at, by, in, on, out, over, to

**lounge** about, against, along, around, away

**louse** up

**lower** at, on, upon

**luff** up

**lug** about, across, along, around, away, back, by, down, forth, forward, from, in, into, off, on, out, out of, over, round, through, to, towards, up, upon

**lull** into (+ ing), out of (+ ing)

**lumber** along

**lump** along

**lunch** in, off, out

**lunge** at

**lure** away, into (+ ing), on, out of (+ ing)

**lurk** about, around

**lust** for

**luxuriate** in

# m

**madden** with (pass.)

**mail** from, to

**maintain** at

**major** in

**make** at, away, down, for, from, in, into, of (pass.), off, on, out, over, round, towards, up, with

**man** with

**manage** with

**mangle** up

**manoeuvre** across, around, into, out of, through

**mantle** over, with

**map** out, up

**march** along, away, by, in, off, out of, to, towards

**mark** down, for, in, off, out, up, with

**marry** into, off (pass.), to (pass.), up, with (pass.)

**marshal** in, out

**marvel** at

**mash** up

**mask** out, with

**masquerade** as

**match** against, up, with

**mate** with

**matter** to

**maul** about, around

**mean** by (+ ing), for, to

**measure** against, off, out, up, with

**meddle** in, with

**mediate** between, in

**meditate** on, upon

**meet** up, with

**melt** away, down, in, into

**mention** in, to

**merge** in, into, with

**mesh** with

**mesmerize** into (+ ing), out of (+ ing)

**mess** about, around, up

**metamorphose** into, to

**mete** out

**migrate** from, to

**militate** against

**mill** about, around

**mind** out

**mine** out

**mingle** in, with

**minister** to

**minor** in

**miscalculate** about

**misconceive** of

**miss** out

**mist** over, up

**mistake** about (pass.), for

**mix** in, up, with

moan about
mock at, up
model on, upon
modulate to
moisten with
monkey about, around, with
mooch about
moon about, around, away
mop down, up
mope about, around, away
moralize about, on, over
motion away, to
mould from, out of
mount on, to, up
mourn for, over
move about, across, along, around, away, back, by, down, forth, forward, from, in, into, off, on, out, out of, over, round, through, to, towards, up, upon
mow down
muck about, along, in, out, through, up
muddle about, along, around, on, through, up
muddy up
muffle up
mug up
mulct of
mull over
multiply by
murmur against, at
muscle in
muse about, on, over, upon
muster up
mutiny against

# *n*

nag at
nail back, down, on, to, up
name as, to
narrow down
navigate about, across, along, around, away, back, by, down, forth, forward, from, in, into, off, on, out, out of, over, round, through, to, towards, up, upon
negotiate about, for, over, with
neighbour on, upon
nest in
nestle down, up
nettle at (pass.)
nibble at
nick up
niggle over
nip at, in, off
nod off, to
noise about, around
nominate for, to
nose about, around, into, out, round
notch up
note for (pass.) / (+ ing)
notify of, to
nourish with
numb with (pass.)
number among, off, with
nurse along, through
nurture along, on
nuzzle against, up, up against

# *o*

object to (+ ing)
oblige by, to (pass.), with
obscure from
observe on, to, upon
obsess with (pass.)
obtain for, from
obtrude on, upon
occupy in (+ ing), with
occur to
offend against, with
offer for, to, up
officiate as, at
ogle at
omit from
ooze away, out
open into, off, on, out, to, up
operate against, from, on
oppose to (pass.) / (+ ing)
opt for, in, out
order around, at, from, in, off, out, up
originate from, in, with
oscillate about, around
osculate with
oust from
overburden with
overcome by (pass.), with (pass.)
overcrowd with (pass.)
overflow with
overlay with
overpower with (pass.)
overrun with (pass.)
overstock with
overwhelm by (pass.), with (pass.)
owe to
own to, up

**pace** about, across, along, around, away, back, by, down, forth, forward, from, in, into, off, on, out, out of, over, round, through, to, towards, up, upon

**pack** away, down, in, into, off, out, up, with

**pad** about, across, along, around, away, back, by, down, forth, forward, from, in, into, off, on, out, out of, over, round, through, to, towards, up, upon, with

**page** down, up

**paint** in, on, out, over, upon

**pair** off, up, with

**pal** around

**pale** at

**pall** on, upon

**palm** off, off onto

**palter** with

**pan** for, off, out

**pander** to

**pant** for, out

**paper** over

**parachute** down

**parcel** out, up

**parch** up, with

**pardon** for (+ ing)

**pare** down, off

**parlay** into

**parley** with

**part** from, over, with

**partake** in, of

**participate** in, with

**partition** off

**partner** off

**pass** along, away, back, by, down, for, forward, from, in, into, off, on, out, out of, over, round, through, up

**paste** down, on, onto, up

**pat** down, on

**patch** into, through, up

**patter** about, around

**pattern** on, upon, with

**pause** on, upon

**pave** with

**paw** about, around

**pay** away, back, by, down, for, in, into, off, out, over, to, up, with

**peak** out

**peal** out

**peck** at, up

**peek** at

**peel** away, back, off

**peep** at, into, out, over, through

**peer** about, around, at, in, out, through

**peg** down, in, out

**pelt** along, at, down, out, with

**pen** in, up

**penalize** for (+ ing)

**penetrate** into, through, to, with

**pension** off

**people** with

**pep** up

**pepper** with

**perch** on

**percolate** through

**perforate** into

**perform** on

**perish** by, from, in, with

**perk** up

**permeate** through, with

**permit** in, into, of, out, through, up

**persevere** at, in (+ ing), with

**persist** in (+ ing), with

**persuade** of

**pertain** to

**pervade** with

**pester** with

**peter** out

**petition** for

**phase** in, out

**philander** with

**philosophize** about

**phone** for, in, up

**pick** at, away, from, in, off, on, up

**picture** to

**piece** up

**pierce** through

**pig** out

**pile** in, into, off, on, out, up, upon, with

**pilfer** from

**pillow** on

**pilot** in, into, out, through

**pimp** for

**pin** against, back, down, on, to, up

**pinch** back, off, out

**pine** away, for, over

**pinion** to

**pink** out

**pipe** away, down, in, into, up, with

**pit** against, with (pass.)

**pitch** forward, in, into, on, out, up, upon

**pivot** on

**place** at, back, down, in, on, out, to, with

**plague** with

**plan** for, on, out

**plane** away, down, off

**plank** down, on, out

**plant** in, on, out, with

**plaster** down, on, over, up, with

**plate** with

**play** about, against, along, around, as, at (+ ing), back, by, down, for, forward, in, off, on, out, over, round, through, to, up, upon, with

**plead** against, for, with

**pledge** to

**plod** about, across, along, around, away, back, by, down, forth, forward, from, in, into, off, on, out, out of, over, round, through, to, towards, up, upon

**plonk** down, out

**plot** against, out, with

**plow** (plough) back, in, into, on, out, through, up

**pluck** from, off, out, up

**plug** in, up

**plume** on

**plump** against, down, for, out, up

**plunge** down, in, into

**plunk** down, for

**ply** across, with

**poach** for, on

**point** at, down, off, out, to, towards, up

**poise** on, over

**poison** against

**poke** about, along, around, at, forward, in, into, out, round,

through, up

**polish** off, up

**pollute** with

**ponder** on, over, upon

**poop** out

**pop** across, along, back, down, in, into, off, on, out, over, round, up

**pore** on, over, upon

**portion** out, to

**pose** as, for

**possess** by (pass.), of (pass.)

**post** away, from, on, to, up

**postpone** to

**postulate** for

**pot** up

**potter** about, around

**pounce** on, upon

**pound** along, at, down, in, into, on, out, up

**pour** across, along, away, back, down, forth, in, into, off, on, out, over, through, with

**powder** with

**power** by (pass.), with (pass.)

**powwow** about

**practise** on, upon

**praise** for (+ ing)

**prance** about, around

**prattle** about, away

**pray** for, over, to

**preach** against, at, to

**precipitate** into

**preclude** from (pass.) / (+ ing)

**predestinate** to

**predestine** for (pass.), to (pass.)

**predispose** to (pass.), towards (pass.)

**predominate** over

**preface** by, with

**prefer** against, to

**prefix** to

**prejudice** against (pass.) / (+ ing)

**prelude** to

**prepare** for

**preponderate** over

**prepossess** against, with

**presage** from

**prescribe** for

**present** at, to, with

**preserve** for, from

**preside** at, over

**press** against, down, for, forward, in, into, on, out, round, to, towards, up, upon

**pressure** into (+ ing), out of (+ ing)

**presume** on, upon

**pretend** to

**prevail** against, on, over, upon

**prevent** from (+ ing)

**prey** on, upon

**price** out, up

**prick** down, off, on, out, up

**pride** on (+ ing)

**prim** up

**prime** with (pass.)

**primp** up

**prink** up

**print** in, off, out

**prize** for

**probe** into

**proceed** about, from, to, with

**procure** for, from

**prod** at, into (+ ing), out of (+ ing), with

**produce** from

**profit** by (+ ing), from (+ ing)

**progress** in, to, with

**promise** to

**promote** to

**pronounce** against, for, on, upon
**prop** against, up
**propose** to
**prosecute** for (+ ing)
**prospect** for
**prosper** from
**protect** against, from
**protest** against (+ ing)
**protrude** from
**prove** to
**provide** against, for, with
**provision** with
**provoke** into (+ ing)
**prowl** about, around, round
**prune** away, down, from, of
**pry** about, from, into, off, out of
**psych** out, up
**pucker** up
**puff** about, across, along, around, away, back, by, down, forth, forward, from, in, into, off, on, out, out of, over, round, through, to, towards, up, upon, with
**pull** about, along, around, at, away, back, by, down, for, in, into, off, on, out, out of, over, round, through, to, towards, up
**pulse** through
**pump** in, into, out, through, up
**punch** down, in, on, out, up
**punctuate** with
**punish** for (+ ing), with
**purge** from, of
**purify** from, of
**purse** up
**push** about, against, along, around, at, away, back, by, down, for, forward, from, in,

into, off, on, out, over, round, through, to, towards, up, upon
**pussyfoot** around, away, back, by, down, forth, forward, from, in, into, off, on, out, out of, over, round, through, to, towards, up
**put** across, against, along, as, at, away, back, by, down, forth, forward, in, into, off (+ ing), on, out, out of, over, through, to, up, upon
**putter** about, along, around, out
**putty** up
**puzzle** out, over

**quail** at
**quake** with
**qualify** as, for
**quarrel** about, for (+ ing), over, with
**query** about
**question** about
**queue** up
**quibble** about, over
**quicken** up
**quiet** down
**quieten** down
**quiver** with
**quote** from

**race** about, across, against, along, around, away, back, by, down, for, forth, forward, from, in, into, off, on, out, out of, over, round, through, to, towards, up, upon, with
**rack** up, with (pass.)
**racket** about, along, around
**radiate** from
**raft** down
**rage** against, at, out, through
**rail** against, at, in, off
**railroad** into (+ ing), out of (+ ing), through, through (pass.)
**rain** down, off (pass.), on, upon
**raise** from, to, up
**rake** about, around, in, off, out, over, round, through, up
**rally** from, on, round
**ram** down, into, through
**ramble** on
**ramp** up
**rampage** about, along, around
**range** against, from, in, over, through, to, with
**rank** with, as
**ransack** for
**rap** at, on, out, over, with
**rasp** out
**rat** on
**rate** as, at, for (+ ing), up, with
**ration** out
**rattle** about, across, along, around, away, back, by, down, forth, forward, from, in, into, off, on, out, out of, over, round, through, to, towards, up, upon

**rave** about, against, at, over
**ravel** out
**reach** back, down, for, forward, into, out, to, towards, up
**react** against, on, to, upon, with
**read** about, around, as, back, for, from, in, into, of, out, out of, over, round, through, to, up
**realize** from, on
**ream** out
**reap** from
**reapply** for
**rear** up
**reason** against, from, into (+ ing), out of (+ ing), with
**reassure** about, on
**rebel** against, at (+ ing)
**rebound** from, on, upon
**rebuke** for (+ ing)
**recall** to
**recast** in
**recede** from
**receive** as, from, into
**recite** to
**reckon** as, for, from, in, on (+ ing), to, up, upon, with
**reclaim** from
**recline** on
**recognize** as, by, from
**recoil** for (+ ing), on, upon
**recommend** to
**recompense** for (+ ing)
**reconcile** to, with
**reconstruct** from
**record** from, on
**recount** to
**recoup** for
**recover** from
**recriminate** against

**recruit** from, into (+ ing)
**recuperate** from
**recur** to
**redeem** from
**redirect** to
**redound** on, to
**reduce** by, from, in, to (+ ing)
**reef** in
**reek** of, with
**reel** back, from, in, off, out, up
**re-equip** with
**reeve** through
**refer** back, to
**refill** with
**reflect** in (pass.), on, upon
**refocus** on
**refrain** from (+ ing)
**refresh** with
**refuel** with
**refund** to
**refuse** to
**regain** from
**regale** with
**regard** as, with
**register** as, for, in, on, with
**regress** to
**reign** over
**reimburse** for, to
**rein** back, in, up
**reinforce** with
**reinstate** in
**reintegrate** in
**rejoice** at, in (+ ing), over
**rejoin** to, with
**relate** to
**relax** in, into
**relay** to
**release** from, to
**relegate** to
**relieve** from, of

**rely** on, upon
**remain** at
**remark** on, upon
**remember** as, in, to
**remind** of (+ ing)
**reminisce** about, with
**remit** to
**remonstrate** about, with
**remove** from
**remunerate** for
**rend** from, in
**render** down, for, into, to, up
**renege** on
**rent** at, out, to
**repay** by, for, with
**repel** from
**repent** of
**repine** against, at
**replace** by, with
**replenish** with
**reply** for, to
**report** back, for, on, to, upon
**repose** on, upon
**reprehend** for (+ ing)
**represent** as, to
**reprimand** for (+ ing)
**reprint** from, in
**reproach** for (+ ing), with (+ ing)
**reproduce** from, in
**reprove** for (+ ing)
**repulse** from
**request** from, of
**require** of
**requisition** for, from
**requite** with
**rescue** from
**research** into, on
**reserve** for
**resettle** to
**reside** in
**resign** to (pass.) / (+ ing), from

**resolve** into, on
**resort** to (+ ing)
**resound** through, throughout, with
**respect** for
**respond** to
**rest** against, from, in, on, up, upon, with
**restock** with
**restore** to
**restrain** from (+ ing)
**restrict** to (pass.) / (+ ing)
**result** from, in (+ ing)
**retail** at, for, to
**retaliate** against, on, upon
**retire** from, in, on, to
**retreat** from, to
**retrieve** from
**return** for, from, to
**reunite** with
**rev** up
**reveal** to
**revel** in (+ ing)
**revenge** on, upon
**revert** to (+ ing)
**revile** against, at
**revolt** against (+ ing)
**revolve** about, around
**reward** for (+ ing)
**rhapsodize** about, over
**rhyme** with
**rid** of
**riddle** with
**ride** about, across, along, around, away, back, by, down, forth, forward, from, in, into, off, on, out, out of, over, round, through, to, towards, up, upon
**rifle** through
**rig** out, up
**ring** about, around

**ring** about, back, for, in, off, out, round, through, up, with
**rinse** down, off, out
**rip** across, away, down, from, in, into, off, out, to, up
**rise** from, in, up
**risk** on
**rivet** on, to
**roam** about, around
**roar** at, down, out, with
**rob** of
**rock** about, around
**rocket** in
**roll** about, along, around, away, back, by, down, in, off, on, out, over, round, up
**romp** about, through
**roof** in, over
**room** with
**root** about, for, in, out, to, up
**rope** in, into, off, up
**rot** away, off, out
**rough** in, out, up
**round** down, in, into, off, on, out, up, upon
**rouse** from, to
**rout** out
**route** by, through
**rove** over
**row** about, across, along, around, away, back, by, down, forth, forward, from, in, into, off, on, out, out of, over, round, through, to, towards, up, upon
**rub** against, along, away, down, in, into, off, on, out, through, up
**ruck** up
**ruffle** up
**rule** against, off, on, out, over
**rumble** off
**ruminate** about, on, over, upon

**rummage** about, around, for, out, up
**run** about, across, against, along, around, away, back, by, down, for, forth, forward, from, in, into, off, on, out, out of, over, round, through, to, towards, up, upon, with
**rush** about, across, along, around, away, back, by, down, forth, forward, from, in, into, into (+ ing), off, on, out, out of, over, round, through, to, towards, up, upon
**rust** away
**rustle** up

**sacrifice** to
**saddle** on, up, upon, with
**safeguard** against
**sag** down
**sail** about, across, along, around, away, back, by, down, forth, forward, from, in, into, off, on, out, out of, over, round, through, to, towards, up, upon
**sally** forth, out
**salt** away, down, with
**salute** with
**salvage** from
**sand** down
**sashay** around, away, back, by, down, forth, forward, from, in, into, off, on, out, out of, over, round, through, to, towards, up, upon
**satiate** with

**satisfy** of, with (pass.)
**saturate** with (pass.)
**saunter** across, along, back, into, out, out of, to
**save** for, from, up
**savour** of
**saw** down, into, off, through, up
**say** about, against, for, of, on, out, over, to
**scab** over
**scale** down, to, up
**scamper** about, across, along, around, away, back, by, down, forth, forward, from, in, into, off, on, out, out of, over, round, through, to, towards, up, upon
**scandalize** by (pass.)
**scar** over, up
**scare** away, into (+ ing), off, out of (+ ing)
**scatter** about, around, round, with
**scent** out
**schedule** as, for
**scheme** for
**school** in, to
**scoff** at
**scold** for (+ ing)
**scoop** out, up
**scoot** away, off, over
**scope** out
**score** for, off, out, over, up
**scour** about, around, away, for, off, out
**scout** about, around, out
**scowl** at
**scrabble** about
**scramble** about, across, along, around, away, back, by, down, for, forth, forward, from, in, into, off, on, out, out

of, over, round, through, to, towards, up, upon
**scrape** away, by, in, off, out, through, up
**scratch** about, along, away, from, out, up
**scrawl** over
**scream** down, for, out, with
**screen** from, off, out
**screw** down, on, out of, to, up
**scribble** away, down
**scroll** off, on, out
**scrounge** on
**scrub** away, down, out, round, up
**scud** about, across, along, around, away, back, by, down, forth, forward, from, in, into, off, on, out, out of, over, round, through, to, towards, up, upon
**scuff** up
**scuffle** through, with
**sculpture** out of
**scurry** about, across, along, around, away, back, by, down, forth, forward, from, in, into, off, on, out, out of, over, round, through, to, towards, up, upon
**scuttle** about, across, along, around, away, back, by, down, forth, forward, from, in, into, off, on, out, out of, over, round, through, to, towards, up, upon
**seal** off, up
**seam** up, with (pass.)
**search** for, out, through
**season** with
**seat** on
**secede** from
**seclude** from (pass.)
**second** to (pass.)

**section** off
**secure** against, from
**seduce** from, into (+ ing), out of (+ ing)
**see** about, across, against, around, as, back, in, into, off, out, over, round, through, to, up
**seek** for, from, into, out
**seep** away, in, through
**seethe** with
**segregate** against (pass.), from
**seize** on, up, upon, with (pass.)
**select** as (pass.), for, from
**sell** at, down, for, on, out, to, up
**send** about, across, along, around, away, back, by, down, for, forth, forward, from, in, into, off, on, out, over, round, to, up
**sentence** to
**separate** from, into, off, out, up
**serve** as, for, in, on, out, round, to, up, with
**set** about (+ ing), across, against, along, at, back, by, down, for, forth, in, into, off, on, out, over, through, to, up, up, upon, with (pass.)
**settle** down, in, on, to, up, upon, with
**sew** up
**shack** up
**shackle** with (pass.)
**shade** from, in, into
**shaft** into, out of
**shake** down, off, out, out of, up, with
**shamble** along
**shame** into (+ ing), out of (+ ing)
**shanghai** into (+ ing)

**shape** into, to, up
**share** in, out, with
**shave** off
**shear** away, of (pass.), off
**sheathe** with
**shed** on, over, upon
**sheer** off
**sheet** against, down
**shell** out
**shelter** from
**shepherd** around, in, into, on, out, out of
**shield** against (+ ing), from (+ ing)
**shift** from, to
**shin** down, up
**shine** at, in, on, out, over, through, upon, with
**ship** off, out
**shiver** with
**shock** into (+ ing), out of (+ ing)
**shoe** with (pass.)
**shoo** away, off
**shoot** at, away, down, for, from, in, into, off, out, through, to, up, with (pass.)
**shop** around, on, round
**shore** up
**shoulder** in, into, out, out of
**shout** about, at, down, for, out
**shove** about, against, along, around, at, away, back, by, down, forward, in, into, on, out, over, to, towards, up
**shovel** down, in, into
**show** around, down, in, into, off, out, out of, over, round, through, to, up
**shower** on, upon, with
**shriek** out, with
**shrink** back, from (+ ing), up

**shrivel** up
**shroud** in
**shrug** off
**shuck** off
**shudder** at, with
**shuffle** about, across, along, around, away, back, by, down, forth, forward, from, in, into, off, on, out, out of, over, round, through, to, towards, up, upon
**shut** down, in, of (pass.), off, on, out, to, up, upon
**shuttle** from, to
**shy** at
**sicken** at, for, of (+ ing)
**side** against, with
**sidle** about, across, along, around, away, back, by, down, forth, forward, from, in, into, off, on, out, over, round, through, to, towards, up, upon
**sieve** out, through
**sift** out, through
**sigh** about, away, for, over
**sign** away, for, in, off, on, out, over, up
**signal** to
**silhouette** against (pass.)
**silt** up
**simmer** down, with
**sin** against
**sing** along, away, out, to, up, with
**single** out
**sink** back, down, in, into, to
**siphon** on
**sit** about, around, at, back, by, down, for, in, on, out, through, to, up, upon
**size** up
**skate** around, over, round

**skelter** around, away, back, by, down, forth, forward, from, in, into, off, on, out, out of, over, round, through, to, towards, up, upon
**sketch** in, out
**skim** off, over, through
**skimp** for
**skin** over, through
**skip** about, across, along, around, away, back, by, down, forth, forward, from, in, into, off, on, out, out of, over, round, through, to, towards, up, upon
**skirmish** with
**skirt** along, around, round
**skitter** around, away, back, by, down, forth, forward, from, in, into, off, on, out, out of, over, round, through, to, towards, up, upon
**slack** off
**slacken** away, off, up
**slam** down, in, on, to
**slant** against, towards
**slap** down, on, up
**slave** at, over
**sled(ge)** about, across, along, around, away, back, by, down, forth, forward, from, in, into, off, on, out, out of, over, round, through, to, towards, up, upon
**sleep** around, away, in, off, on, out, over, through, with
**sleuth** around
**slew** around, round
**slice** in, on, through, up
**slick** down, up
**slide** about, across, along, around, away, back, by, down, forth, forward, from,

in, into, off, on, out, out of, over, round, through, to, towards, up, upon

**slim** down

**sling** at, out, up

**slink** away, off

**slip** away, back, by, down, from, in, into, off, on, out, out of, over, through, up

**slit** up

**slither** about, across, along, around, away, back, by, down, forth, forward, from, in, into, off, on, out, out of, over, round, through, to, towards, up, upon

**slobber** over

**slog** about, across, along, around, away, back, by, down, forth, forward, from, in, into, off, on, out, out of, over, round, through, to, towards, up, upon

**slop** about, around, out, over

**slope** down, off, towards, up

**slosh** about, around, on

**slot** in

**slouch** about, across, along, around, away, back, by, down, forth, forward, from, in, into, off, on, out, out of, over, round, through, to, towards, up, upon

**slough** off, over

**slow** down, up

**sluice** down, out

**slump** down, over

**slur** over

**slurp** up

**slush** in, up

**smack** down (pass.)

**smack** of

**smart** for

**smarten** up

**smash** against, in, up

**smear** on, with

**smell** at, of, out, up

**smile** at, on, upon

**smite** on, upon, with (pass.)

**smoke** out, up

**smooth** away, back, down, in, on, out, over

**smother** in, up, with

**smoulder** with

**smuggle** in, out, through

**snap** at, back, off, on, out, out of, up

**snarl** at, up

**snatch** at, away, from, out of, up

**sneak** about, across, along, around, away, back, by, down, forth, forward, from, in, into, off, on, out, out of, over, round, through, to, towards, up, upon

**sneer** at

**sneeze** at

**sniff** at, out, up

**snip** off

**snipe** at

**snitch** on

**snoop** around, into

**snort** at

**snow** in (pass.), over, up

**snuff** out

**snug** down

**snuggle** down

**soak** in, into, off, out, through, up, with

**soap** down, up

**sob** out

**sober** down, up

**sock** away, in (pass.)

**sod** over

**soften** up

**soldier** on

**solicit** for

**soot** up

**sop** up

**sorrow** about, at, over

**sort** out

**sound** off, out

**soup** up

**souse** in, with

**sow** with

**space** off, out

**spade** up

**spangle** with

**spar** with

**spare** for

**spark** off

**sparkle** with

**spatter** on, over, up, with

**spawn** from

**speak** about, against, for, from, of, on, out, to, up, upon

**spear** up

**specialize** in

**speculate** about, in, on

**speed** along, up

**spell** for, out

**spend** for, in, on, up (pass.)

**spew** forth, out, up

**spice** up, with

**spill** out, over

**spin** along, off, out, round

**spiral** down, up

**spirit** away, off

**spit** at, back, in, on, out, up, upon

**splash** about, around, down, on, over, up, with

**splatter** about, around, over, with

**splay** out

**splinter** off

**split** into, off, on, up

**splotch** with

**splutter** out

**spoil** for

**sponge** away, down, from, off, on, out, up

**spoon** out, up

**sport** with

**spout** from, off

**sprawl** about, out

**spray** on, with

**spread** about, around, on, out, over, to

**spring** at, back, from, on, out, to, up, upon

**sprinkle** with

**sprint** about, across, along, around, away, back, by, down, forth, forward, from, in, into, off, on, out, out of, over, round, through, to, towards, up, upon

**sprout** up

**spruce** up

**spur** on

**spurt** out

**sputter** out

**spy** into, on, out, upon

**squabble** about, over

**squander** away, on, upon

**square** away, off, round, up, with

**squash** in, up

**squat** down

**squeak** by, out, through

**squeeze** by, from, in, out, through, up

**squint** at

**squirm** out of, with

**squirrel** away

**squirt** in, out

**stab** at, in

**stack** up

**stagger** about, across, along, around, away, back, by, down, forth, forward, from, in, into, off, on, out, out of, over, round, through, to, towards, up, upon

**stain** with (pass.)

**stake** on, out, upon

**stalk** along, in, into, out, out of

**stammer** out

**stamp** as, on, out, upon, with

**stampede** for, in, towards

**stand** about, across, against, along, around, as, at, away, back, by, down, for, in, off, on, out, out of, over, to, up, upon

**star** in

**starch** up

**stare** at, down, out

**start** as (+ ing), away, back, for, from, in, of, off, on, out, out of, over, up, with

**startle** out of

**starve** for, into (+ ing), out, out of (+ ing)

**stash** away

**station** at, in, on

**stave** in, up

**stay** at, away, back, by, down, for, in, off, on, out, out of, over, to, up

**steady** down

**steal** away, from, over

**steam** into, off, out, over, up

**steel** against, for

**steep** in

**steer** for, in, through, towards

**stem** from (+ ing)

**step** back, down, forward, in, into, off, on, out, over, up, upon

**stew** in

**stick** about, around, at, by, down, for (pass.), in, into, on, out, to (+ ing), up, with

**stiffen** up

**stimulate** in, to

**sting** into (+ ing), out of (+ ing) with (+ ing)

**stink** of, out, up, with

**stint** of

**stipulate** for

**stir** about, around, in, to, up

**stitch** up

**stock** up, with

**stoke** up

**stomp** about, across, along, around, away, back, by, down, forth, forward, from, in, into, off, on, out, out of, over, round, through, to, towards, up, upon

**stoop** down, to

**stop** at, away, by, down, for, from (+ ing), in, off, on, out of, over, to, up, with

**store** away, in, up

**storm** at, in, out

**stow** away, into, with

**straggle** about, across, along, around, away, back, by, down, forth, forward, from, in, into, off, on, out, out of, over, round, through, to, towards, up, upon

**straighten** out, up

**strain** at, away, off, on, through

**strand** on

**strap** down, in, on

**stray** about, across, along, around, away, back, by, down, forth, forward, from, in, into, off, on, out, out of, over, round, through, to, towards, up, upon, with

**streak** about, across, along,

around, away, back, by, down, forth, forward, from, in, into, off, on, out, out of, over, round, through, to, towards, up, upon, with

**stream** about, across, along, around, away, back, by, down, forth, forward, from, in, into, off, on, out, out of, over, round, through, to, towards, up, upon

**stretch** away, forth, out

**strew** on, over, with (pass.)

**stride** about, across, along, around, away, back, by, down, forth, forward, from, in, into, off, on, out, out of, over, round, through, to, towards, up, upon

**strike** as (+ ing), at, back, down, for, in, into, off, on, out, over, through, up, upon

**string** along, up, with

**strip** away, down, from, of, off

**strive** against, for, with

**stroll** about, across, along, around, away, back, by, down, forth, forward, from, in, into, off, on, out, out of, over, round, through, to, towards, up, upon

**struggle** about, across, against, along, around, away, back, by, down, for, forth, forward, from, in, into, off, on, out, out of, over, round, through, to, towards, up, upon

**strum** on

**strut** about, across, along, around, away, back, by, down, forth, forward, from, in, into, off, on, out, out of, over, round, through, to, towards, up, upon

**stub** out, up

**stud** with (pass.)

**study** for

**stuff** down, in, up, with

**stumble** about, across, along, around, away, back, by, down, forth, forward, from, in, into, off, on, out, out of, over, round, through, to, towards, up, upon

**stump** about, across, along, around, away, back, by, down, forth, forward, from, in, into, off, on, out, out of, over, round, through, to, towards, up, upon

**stupefy** with (pass.)

**stutter** out

**subdivide** into

**subject** to

**sublet** to

**submerge** in

**submit** to

**subordinate** to

**subscribe** to

**subside** in

**subsist** in, on

**substitute** for

**subtract** from

**succeed** at, in (+ ing), to

**succumb** to

**suck** at, down, up

**sue** for, to

**suffer** for, from

**suffice** for

**suffix** to

**suffuse** with (pass.)

**suggest** to

**suit** for, to, up, with

**sum** up

**summon** to, up

**sunder** from

**superabound** in, with

**superimpose** on

**superpose** on, upon

**supervene** on

**supplement** by

**supply** from, to, with

**surcharge** with

**surface** with

**surfeit** with

**surge** in, out, up

**surmount** with (pass.)

**surpass** in

**surprise** at, in (+ ing), out of (+ ing), with

**surrender** to

**surround** with

**suspect** of (+ ing)

**suspend** from

**suss** out

**swab** down, out

**swaddle** with

**swagger** about, across, along, around, away, back, by, down, forth, forward, from, in, into, off, on, out, out of, over, round, through, to, towards, up, upon

**swallow** down, up

**swamp** with (pass.)

**swank** about

**swap** around, for, round, with

**swarm** over, round, through, up, with

**swathe** in

**sway** about, across, along, around, away, back, by, down, forth, forward, from, in, into, off, on, out, out of, over, round, through, to, towards, up, upon

**swear** at, by, for, in, off, on, out, upon

**sweat** for, off, out

**sweep** about, across, along, around, away, back, by, down, forth, forward, from, in, into, off, on, out, out of, over, round, through, to, towards, up, upon

**swell** out, up, with

**swerve** from

**swig** at, off

**swill** down, out

swim about, across, along, around, away, back, by, down, forth, forward, from, in, into, off, on, out, out of, over, round, through, to, towards, up, upon

**swindle** out of

swing about, across, along, around, away, back, by, down, forth, forward, from, in, into, off, on, out, out of, over, round, through, to, towards, up, upon

**swipe** at

swirl about, across, along, around, away, back, by, down, forth, forward, from, in, into, off, on, out, out of, over, round, through, to, towards, up, upon

**swish** off, through

**switch** back, from, off, on, out, over

**swivel** round

**swoop** down on, upon

**sympathize** with

**tack** about, down, on, to

**tackle** about, on, over

**tag** along, on, out

**tail** away, back, off, on

**tailor** to

**taint** with (pass.)

take about, across, against, along, around, as, at, away, back, by, down, for, from, in, into, off, on, out, out of, over, round, through, to (+ ing), up (+ ing), upon

talk about, around, at, away, back, down, for, into (+ ing), of, on, out, out of (+ ing), over, round, through, to, up, upon

**tally** with

**tamp** down

**tamper** with

**tangle** up (pass.), with

**tank** up

**tap** at, down, for, in, off, on, out

**taper** off

**tart** up

**task** with

**taste** of

**tax** for, on, upon, with (+ ing)

**taxi** along, down, up

**team** up

tear about, across, along, around, at, away, down, from, in, into, off, out, to, up

**tease** out

**tee** off, up

**teem** in, with

**telecopy** to

**telegraph** to

**telephone** in, to

**telescope** into

**telex** to

tell about, against, by, from, of, off, on, over, to, with

**temper** against

**temporize** with

**tempt** from, in (+ ing), out of (+ ing), to

**tend** towards

**tender** for

**tense** for, up

**terminate** at, in

**terrify** into (+ ing), out of (+ ing)

**test** for, out

**testify** against, for, to

**thank** for (+ ing)

**thaw** out

**theorize** about

**thicken** up

**thin** down, out

think about (+ ing), back, for, of (+ ing), on, out, over, through, to, up, upon

thirst for

**thrash** about, around, out, through

**thread** through

**threaten** with

**thrill** at (pass.), to (pass.), with

thrive on, upon

**throb** away, with

**throng** in, into, out

**throttle** back, down

throw about, around, at, away, back, down, in, into, off, on, out, over, to, up, upon

thrust against, at, away, back, down, forward, from, in, into, on, out, through, towards, up, upon

**thud** against, into

**thumb** through

**thump** on, out

**thunder** about, out

**tick** away, off, over

**tide** over

**tidy** away, out, up

**tie** back, down, in, into, on, to, up, with

**tighten** up

tilt back, up

tinge with

tingle with

tinker about, around, with

tip in, into, off, out, over, up, with

tiptoe about, across, along, around, away, back, by, down, forth, forward, from, in, into, off, on, out, out of, over, round, through, to, towards, up, upon

tire of (pass.) / (+ ing), out

toady to

toddle along

tog out, up

toil about, across, along, around, away, back, by, down, forth, forward, from, in, into, off, on, out, out of, over, round, through, to, towards, up, upon

toll for

tone down, in, up

tool up

top off, out, up

topple down, from, over

torment with (pass.)

toss about, around, at, away, back, down, for, in, into, off, up

tot up

totter in, into, out, out of, to

touch down, for, off, on, up, upon

toughen up

tout about, around, as (pass.), for

tow away

towel down, off

tower over

toy with

trace back, out, over, to

track down, in, up

trade down, for, in, off, on, upon

traffic in

trail about, across, along, around, away, back, by, down, forth, forward, from, in, into, off, on, out, out of, over, round, through, to, towards, up, upon

train for, on, up, upon

traipse about, across, along, around, away, back, by, down, forth, forward, from, in, into, off, on, out, out of, over, round, through, to, towards, up, upon

trample down, in, on, out, upon

transact with

transfer from, to

transfix with (pass.)

transform into

translate from, in, to

transmit to

transmute into

transport to, with (pass.)

transpose into

trap in, into (+ ing)

travel by, from, in, on, over, to

tread down, in, into, on, out, upon

treasure up

treat as, for, of, to

trek to

tremble at, for, from, with

trend to, towards

trespass against, on, upon

trick into (+ ing), out, out of (+ ing), up

trickle away, down, in, into, out, out of

trifle away, with

trigger off

trim away, down, off

trip about, across, along, around, away, back, by, down, forth, forward, from, in, into, off, on, out, out of, over, round, through, to, towards, up, upon

triumph over

troop in, off, out

trot about, across, along, around, away, back, by, down, forth, forward, from, in, into, off, on, out, out of, over, round, through, to, towards, up, upon

trouble about, for, over, with (pass.)

truck for, in

truckle to

trudge about, across, along, around, away, back, by, down, forth, forward, from, in, on, out, out of, over, round, to, up, upon

true up

trump up

trumpet forth

trundle about, across, along, around, away, back, by, down, forth, forward, from, in, into, off, on, out, out of, over, round, through, to, towards, up, upon

truss up

trust in, to

try for, on, out, over

tuck away, down, in, into, up

tug at

tumble down, for, into, off, on, out, over, to, upon

tune in, out, up

tunnel into, through

turf out

turn about, against, away, back, down, from, in, into, off,

on, out, round, to, towards, up, upon
**tussle** with
**tutor** in
**twiddle** with
**twine** around, round
**twinkle** with
**twist** around, into, off, round, up
**type** in, out, up
**tyrannize** over

# U

**unbosom** to
**unburden** of, to
**undeceive** of
**understand** by
**unfasten** from
**unfold** to
**unify** into, with
**unite** in, into, with
**unlash** from
**unleash** on, upon
**unload** on, upon
**unpin** from
**unsling** from
**unstrap** from
**unyoke** from
**upbraid** for (+ ing), with
**upgrade** to
**upholster** in, with
**uproot** from
**urge** along, forward, on, to, upon
**use** as, for, to (pass.) / (+ ing) up
**usher** in, into, out, out of
**usurp** from
**utilize** for

# V

**vaccinate** against
**value** as, at, for
**vamp** up
**vanish** away, from
**vary** from, in, with
**vault** over
**veer** from, off, round, to
**veg** out
**vent** on, upon
**venture** forth, on, out, upon
**verge** into, on, upon
**vest** with
**vex** at (pass.), with
**vie** for, in
**visit** on, upon, with
**vociferate** against
**volunteer** for (+ ing)
**vomit** out
**vote** against (+ ing), down, for (+ ing), in, on, through, upon
**vouch** for

# W

**waddle** about, across, along, around, away, back, by, down, forth, forward, from, in, into, off, on, out, out of, over, round, through, to, towards, up, upon
**wade** about, across, along, around, away, back, by, down, forth, forward, from, in, into, off, on, out, out of, over, round, through, to, towards, up, upon
**waffle** about
**wager** on
**wail** for, over
**wait** about, around, for, in, on, out, up, upon
**wake** from, to, up
**waken** from, to
**walk** about, across, along, around, away, back, by, down, forth, forward, from, in, into, off, on, out, out of, over, round, through, to, towards, up, upon
**wall** in, round, up
**wallow** in
**waltz** about, across, along, around, away, back, by, down, forth, forward, from, in, into, off, on, out, out of, over, round, through, to, towards, up, upon
**wander** about, around, from, on
**wangle** out of
**want** back, in
**war** against, over
**ward** off
**warm** over, up
**warn** about, against (+ ing), of, off
**wash** away, down, off, out, over, up
**waste** away, on
**watch** for, out, over
**water** down
**wave** about, around, at, away, on, to
**wean** from
**wear** away, down, off, on, out, through, up, upon

**weary** of (+ ing), with
**weather** through
**weave** from, in, through
**wed** to (pass.)
**wedge** in, up
**weed** out
**weep** about, away, for, over
**weigh** against, down, in, on, out, up, upon, with
**weight** against, down
**weird** out
**welcome** back, in, to, with
**weld** on, together
**well** out, over, up
**welter** in
**wend** about, across along, around, away, back, by, down, forth, forward, from, in, into, off, on, out of, out, over, round, through, to, towards, up, upon
**wet** down
**wheedle** into (+ ing), out, out of (+ ing)
**wheel** about, around, away, in, out, round
**wheeze** out
**while** away
**whip** about, across, along, around, away, back, by, down, forth, forward, from, in, into, off, on, out, out of, over, round, through, to, towards, up, upon
**whirl** about, across, along, around, away, back, by, down, forth, forward, from, in, into, off, on, out of, out, over, round, through, to, towards, up, upon
**whirr** about, across, along,

around, away, back, by, down, forth, forward, from, in, into, off, on, out, out of, over, round, through, to, towards, up, upon
**whisk** away, off
**whisper** about, around
**whistle** for, up
**white** out
**whittle** down
**whoop** up
**wick** away
**widen** out
**wig** out
**will** away, to
**win** around, at, away, back, out, over, round, through
**wince** at
**wind** back, down, in, into, off, on, through, up
**wink** at, away, back
**winkle** out of
**winnow** out
**winter** in, over
**wipe** away, off, out, over, up
**wire** for, up
**wise** on, to
**wish** away, for, on, upon
**withdraw** from, in
**wither** away, up
**withhold** from
**witness** to
**wobble** about, around
**wolf** down
**wonder** about, at
**woo** away, into (+ ing), out of (+ ing)
**work** against, as, at (+ ing), away, by (pass.), in, into, off, on, out, over, round, through, to, towards, up, upon

**worm** in, out of, through
**worry** about, along, at, out, over, through
**wound** in
**wrangle** about, over
**wrap** around, in, round, up
**wreathe** about, in (pass.), round
**wrench** from, off
**wrest** off
**wrestle** for, into, with
**wriggle** about, across, along, around, away, back, by, down, forth, forward, from, in, into, off, on, out, out of, over, round, through, to, towards, up, upon
**wring** from, out
**wrinkle** up
**write** against, away, back, down, for, in, into, of, off, on, out, to, up, upon
**writhe** at

**x** out

*y*

**yammer** for
**yank** at, away, in, off, on, out, up
**yap** away
**yearn** for
**yell** at, for, out
**yield** to, up

**zoom** about, across, along, around, away, back, by, down, forth, forward, from, in, into, off, on, out, out of, over, round, through, to, towards, up, upon

*z*

**zap** about, across, along, around, away, back, by, down, forth, forward, from, in, into, off, on, out, out of, over, round, through, to, towards, up, upon
**zero** in
**zigzag** about, across, along, around, away, back, by, down, forth, forward, from, in, into, off, on, out, out of, over, round, through, to, towards, up, upon
**zing** past
**zip** about, across, along, around, away, back, by, down, forth, forward, from, in, into, off, on, out, out of, over, round, through, to, towards, up, upon
**zone** for, off
**zonk** out

# VERBES IRRÉGULIERS

*Vous trouverez une classification des verbes irréguliers, p. 104.*

# a

| | | |
|---|---|---|
| arise | arose | arisen |
| awake | awoke | awoken |

# b

| | | |
|---|---|---|
| baby-sit | baby-sat | baby-sat |
| backslide | backslid | backslid |
| be | was/were | been |
| bear | bore | borne/born |
| beat | beat | beaten |
| become | became | become |
| befall | befell | befallen |
| beget | begat/begot | begotten |
| begin | began | begun |
| behold | beheld | beheld |
| bend | bent | bent |
| bereave | bereaved (bereft) | bereaved (bereft |
| beseech | beseeched (besought) | beseeched (besought) |
| beset | beset | beset |
| bespeak | bespoke | bespoken |
| bestrew | bestrewed | bestrewed/bestrewn |
| bestride | bestrode | bestridden |
| bet | bet | bet |
| betake | betook | betaken |
| bethink | bethought | bethought |
| bid | bid (bade) | bid (bidden) |
| bind | bound | bound |
| bite | bit | bitten (bit) |
| bleed | bled | bled |
| blow | blew | blown |
| bottle-feed | bottle-fed | bottle-fed |
| break | broke | broken |
| breast-feed | breast-fed | breast-fed |
| breed | bred | bred |
| bring | brought | brought |
| broadcast | broadcast/broadcasted | broadcast |

| build | built | built |
| burn | burned (burnt) | burned (burnt) |
| burst | burst | burst |
| buy | bought | bought |

## c

| caretake | caretook | caretaken |
| cast | cast | cast |
| catch | caught | caught |
| chide | chided (chid) | chided (chidden) |
| choose | chose | chosen |
| cleave | cleaved/clove (cleft) | cloven/cleft (cleaved) |
| cling | clung | clung |
| clothe | clothed (clad) | clad (clothed) |
| come | came | come |
| cost | cost | cost |
| countersink | countersunk | countersunk |
| creep | crept | crept |
| crossbreed | crossbred | crossbred |
| crosscut | crosscut | crosscut |
| cut | cut | cut |

## d

| deal | dealt | dealt |
| defreeze | defroze | defrozen |
| dig | dug | dug |
| do | did | done |
| draw | drew | drawn |
| dream | dreamed (dreamt) | dreamed (dreamt) |
| drink | drank | drunk |
| drive | drove | driven |
| dwell | dwelled (dwelt) | dwelt |

## e

| eat | ate | eaten |

## f

| | | |
|---|---|---|
| fall | fell | fallen |
| feed | fed | fed |
| feel | felt | felt |
| fight | fought | fought |
| find | found | found |
| flee | fled | fled |
| fling | flung | flung |
| fly | flew | flown |
| forbear | forbore | forborne |
| forbid | forbade | forbidden |
| force-feed | force-fed | force-fed |
| forecast | forecast/forecasted | forecast/forecasted |
| foresee | foresaw | foreseen |
| foretell | foretold | foretold |
| forget | forgot | forgotten/forgot |
| forgive | forgave | forgiven |
| forgo | forwent | forgone |
| forsake | forsook | forsaken |
| forswear | forswore | forsworn |
| freeze | froze | frozen |

## g

| | | |
|---|---|---|
| gainsay | gainsaid | gainsaid |
| get | got | got/gotten |
| ghost-write | ghost-wrote | ghot-written |
| gild | gilded (gilt) | gilded (gilt) |
| gird | girded (girt) | girded (girt) |
| give | gave | given |
| go | went | gone |
| grind | ground | ground |
| grow | grew | grown |

# h

| | | |
|---|---|---|
| hang | hung | hung |
| have | had | had |
| hear | heard | heard |
| heave | heaved (hove) | heaved (hove) |
| hew | hewed | hewn (hewed) |
| hide | hid | hidden (hid) |
| hit | hit | hit |
| hold | held | held |
| hurt | hurt | hurt |

# i

| | | |
|---|---|---|
| inlay | inlaid | inlaid |
| input | input | input |
| inset | inset | inset |
| interbreed | interbred | interbred |
| interweave | interwove | interwoven |

# k

| | | |
|---|---|---|
| keep | kept | kept |
| kneel | kneeled (knelt) | kneeled (knelt) |
| knit | knit (knitted) | knit (knitted) |
| know | knew | known |

# l

| | | |
|---|---|---|
| lade | laded | laden |
| lay | laid | laid |
| lead | led | led |
| lean | leaned (leant) | leaned (leant) |
| leap | leaped (leapt) | leaped (leapt) |
| learn | learned (learnt) | learned (learnt) |
| leave | left | left |
| lend | lent | lent |
| let | let | let |

| lie | lay | lain |
| light | lit (lighted) | lit (lighted) |
| lose | lost | lost |

## m

| make | made | made |
| mean | meant | meant |
| meet | met | met |
| miscast | miscast | miscast |
| misdeal | misdealt | misdealt |
| misdo | misdid | misdone |
| mishear | misheard | misheard |
| mis-hit | mis-hit | mis-hit |
| mislay | mislaid | mislaid |
| mislead | misled | misled |
| misread | misread | misread |
| misspell | misspelled (misspelt) | misspelled (misspelt) |
| misspend | misspent | misspent |
| mistake | mistook | mistaken |
| misunderstand | misunderstood | misunderstood |
| mow | mowed | mowed (mown) |

## o

| outbid | outbid | outbid |
| outbreed | outbred | outbred |
| outdo | outdid | outdone |
| outfight | outfought | outfought |
| outgo | outwent | outgone |
| outgrow | outgrew | outgrown |
| outride | outrode | outridden |
| outrun | outran | outrun |
| outshine | outshone | outshone |
| outspeak | outspoke | outspoken |
| outspend | outspent | outspent |
| outspread | outspread | outspread |
| out-think | out-thought | out-thought |
| outwear | outwore | outworn |
| overbear | overbore | overborne |

| overbid | overbid | overbid |
|---|---|---|
| overbuild | overbuilt | overbuilt |
| overcast | overcast | overcast |
| overcome | overcame | overcome |
| overdo | overdid | overdone |
| overdraw | overdrew | overdrawn |
| overdrive | overdrove | overdriven |
| overeat | overate | overeaten |
| overfeed | overfed | overfed |
| overfly | overflew | overflown |
| overgrow | overgrew | overgrown |
| overhang | overhung | overhung |
| overhear | overheard | overheard |
| overlay | overlaid | overlaid |
| overlie | overlay | overlain |
| overpay | overpaid | overpaid |
| override | overrode | overridden |
| overrun | overran | overrun |
| oversee | oversaw | overseen |
| oversell | oversold | oversold |
| overset | overset | overset |
| oversew | oversewed | oversewn (oversewed) |
| overshoot | overshot | overshot |
| oversleep | overslept | overslept |
| overspend | overspent | overspent |
| overtake | overtook | overtaken |
| overthrow | overthrew | overthrown |
| overwind | overwound | overwound |
| overwrite | overwrote | overwritten |

# *p*

| partake | partook | partaken |
|---|---|---|
| pay | paid | paid |
| photoset | photoset | photoset |
| prepay | prepaid | prepaid |
| pre-shrink | pre-shrank | pre-shrunk |
| put | put | put |

## q

| | | |
|---|---|---|
| quit | quit (quitted) | quit (quitted) |

## r

| | | |
|---|---|---|
| read | read | read |
| rebind | rebound | rebound |
| rebroadcast | rebroadcast (rebroadcasted) | rebroadcast |
| rebuild | rebuilt | rebuilt |
| recast | recast | recast |
| reclothe | clothed (reclad) | clothed (reclad) |
| recut | recut | recut |
| redo | redid | redone |
| redraw | redrew | redrawn |
| reeve | rove (reeved) | rove (reeved) |
| rehear | reheard | reheard |
| re-lay | re-laid | re-laid |
| relearn | relearned (relearnt) | relearned (relearnt) |
| remake | remade | remade |
| rend | rent | rent |
| repay | repaid | repaid |
| reread | reread | reread |
| rerun | reran | rerun |
| resell | resold | resold |
| reset | reset | reset |
| retake | retook | retaken |
| retell | retold | retold |
| rethink | rethought | rethought |
| rewind | rewound | rewound |
| rewrite | rewrote | rewritten |
| rid | rid (ridded) | rid (ridded) |
| ride | rode | ridden |
| ring | rang | rung |
| rise | rose | risen |
| run | ran | run |

# S

| | | |
|---|---|---|
| saw | sawed | sawed (sawn) |
| say | said | said |
| see | saw | seen |
| seek | sought | sought |
| sell | sold | sold |
| send | sent | sent |
| set | set | set |
| sew | sewed | sewn (sewed) |
| shake | shook | shaken |
| shear | sheared | shorn (sheared) |
| shed | shed | shed |
| shine | shone (shined) | shone (shined) |
| shoe | shod (shoed) | shod (shoed) |
| shoot | shot | shot |
| show | showed | shown (showed) |
| shrink | shrank | shrunk |
| shrive | shrove (shrived) | shriven (shrived) |
| shut | shut | shut |
| sing | sang/sunk | sung |
| sink | sank | sunk |
| sit | sat | sat |
| slay | slew (slayed) | slain |
| sleep | slept | slept |
| slide | slid | slid |
| sling | slung | slung |
| slink | slunk | slunk |
| slit | slit | slit |
| smell | smelled (smelt) | smelled (smelt) |
| smite | smote | smitten |
| speak | spoke | spoken |
| speed | sped (speeded) | sped (speeded) |
| spell | spelled (spelt) | spelled (spelt) |
| spend | spent | spent |
| spill | spilled (spilt) | spilled (spilt) |
| spin | spun | spun |
| spit | spat | spat |
| split | split | split |
| spoil | spoiled (spoilt) | spoiled (spoilt) |

| | | |
|---|---|---|
| spoon-feed | spoon-fed | spoon-fed |
| spread | spread | spread |
| spring | sprang | sprung |
| stand | stood | stood |
| steal | stole | stolen |
| stick | stuck | stuck |
| sting | stung | stung |
| stink | stank | stank |
| strew | strewed | strewn (strewed) |
| stride | strode | stridden |
| strike | struck | struck |
| string | strung | strung |
| strive | strove (strived) | striven |
| sublet | sublet | sublet |
| swear | swore | sworn |
| sweep | swept | swept |
| swell | swelled | swollen |
| swim | swam | swum |
| swing | swung | swung |

## t

| | | |
|---|---|---|
| take | took | taken |
| teach | taught | taught |
| tear | tore | torn |
| telecast | telecast | telecast |
| tell | told | told |
| think | thought | thought |
| thrive | thrived (throve) | thrived (thriven) |
| throw | threw | thrown |
| thrust | thrust | thrust |
| tread | trod | trodden |
| typecast | typecast | typecast |
| typeset | typeset | typeset |

## u

| | | |
|---|---|---|
| unbend | unbent | unbent |
| unbind | unbound | unbound |
| unclothe | unclothed (unclad) | unclothed (unclad) |

| | | |
|---|---|---|
| underbid | underbid | underbid |
| undercut | undercut | undercut |
| undergird | girded (undergirt) | girded (undergirt) |
| undergo | underwent | undergone |
| underlie | underlay | underlain |
| undersell | undersold | undersold |
| undershoot | undershot | undershot |
| understand | understood | understood |
| undertake | undertook | undertaken |
| underwrite | underwrote | underwritten |
| undo | undid | undone |
| unfreeze | unfroze | unfrozen |
| unsay | unsaid | unsaid |
| unsling | unslung | unslung |
| unstick | unstuck | unstuck |
| unstring | unstrung | unstrung |
| unwind | unwound | unwound |
| uphold | upheld | upheld |
| upset | upset | upset |

# *w*

| | | |
|---|---|---|
| wake | woke (waked) | woken (waked) |
| waylay | waylaid | waylaid |
| wear | wore | worn |
| weave | wove | woven |
| weep | wept | wept |
| win | won | won |
| wind | wound | wound |
| withdraw | withdrew | withdrawn |
| withhold | withheld | withheld |
| withstand | withstood | withstood |
| wring | wrung | wrung |
| write | wrote | written |

# APPENDICE : EXEMPLES DE VERBES À PARTICULE

## LES VERBES

### Stand

| | |
|---|---|
| stand for | *The initials T.V. stand for "television".* |
| stand back | *Stand back — the fire is very hot!* |
| stand on | *Don't stand on ceremony — sit down and eat!* |

### Go

| | |
|---|---|
| go against | *That goes against my principles.* |
| go along with | *I'll go along with that suggestion.* |
| go away | *Go away! You're bothering me!* |
| go into | *Let's not go into that whole story again.* |
| go on | *He was so boring; he just went on and on about the same thing* |
| go without | *There isn't enough for everyone, so you and I will go without.* |

### Come

| | |
|---|---|
| come across | *I came across this book in the bookstore and thought you might like it.* |
| come along | *You can come along with me.* |
| come apart | *This sweater is coming apart.* |
| come back | *Please come back soon!* |
| come by | *She comes by my house almost every weekend.* |
| come down | *They came down from Chicoutimi for the weekend.* |
| come forward | *A new witness has come forward with evidence.* |
| come out | *Why don't you come out with us? We're going to see a movie.* |
| come over | *Come over to our place.* |
| come up (reach) | *The water in the pool comes up to my shoulder.* |
| come up against | *We came up against a lot of opposition.* |

### Run

| | |
|---|---|
| run after | *The boy ran after the pigeons.* |
| run along | *Run along — I don't have time for you now!* |
| run around | *He runs around with a tough crowd.* |
| run for it | *When the fight broke out, we ran for it.* |
| run from | *You can't run from your problems forever.* |
| run into | *We ran into some trouble with the new machine.* |
| run out | *I'm just going to run out for a quick coffee.* |
| run out on | *He ran out on his family.* |
| run over | *The car ran over the bicycle, but no one was hurt.* |
| run through | *I'd like to run through my presentation.* |

### Fall

| | |
|---|---|
| fall apart | *The whole plan just fell apart.* |
| fall back on | *He can always fall back on his family money.* |
| fall behind | *I'm really falling behind in this course.* |
| fall off | *Computer sales are falling off.* |
| fall out of | *I've fallen out of the habit.* |
| fall through | *Our plans for the weekend fell through, so we are staying home.* |

**Take**

| | |
|---|---|
| take apart | *I need to take apart this motor to clean it.* |
| take aside | *She took them aside and told them to behave.* |
| take away | *Five take away two is three.* |
| take back | *She took back the shirt and exchanged it.* |
| take down | *He took down the painting from the wall.* |
| | *He took down the directions.* |
| take in | *There was so much information, I couldn't take it all in.* |
| | *We were taken in by their friendly manner.* |
| take from | *Robin Hood took from the rich and gave to the poor.* |
| take off | *The airplane took off on time.* |
| | *Sales really took off in November.* |
| | *He took off his sweater.* |
| | *He took off a week for vacation.* |
| take out | *We need to take out all the references to prizes.* |
| | *She took the children out to a restaurant.* |
| | *She took out a loan from the bank.* |
| take over | *She took over as director.* |
| take to | *I took to him right away.* |
| take up on | *I'll take you up on that offer.* |

**Set**

| | |
|---|---|
| set down | *Let's set down our agreement in writing.* |
| set in | *The storm is setting in.* |

## LES PARTICULES

**Up**

| | |
|---|---|
| be up | *The house is up for sale.* |
| | *The computer server is finally up again.* |
| be up against | *We're up against a very short deadline.* |
| be up and around | *She's finally up and around after the operation.* |
| be up for | *Is anyone up for some ice cream?* |
| be up to | *It's up to you.* |
| fed up with | *I am fed up with all these delays.* |
| save up | *I'm saving up for a new camera.* |
| sit up | *Sit up straight!* |
| speak up | *Please speak up — we can't hear you.* |
| stand up | *Stand up straight against the wall.* |
| tie up | *I'm tied up in meetings all day.* |
| wind up | *Let's wind up this meeting as quickly as possible.* |

**Out**

| | |
|---|---|
| be out | *She's still out (of the office).* |
| call out | *She called out to us from across the river.* |
| draw out | *Let's not draw out this discussion any longer.* |
| fight it out | *You'll have to fight it out among yourselves.* |
| get out | *Let's get out the instruction booklet.* |
| get out of | *We've got to get out of here.* |

| have out | *I will have it out with him as soon as I find him.* |
| hire out | *He sometimes hires out his horses.* |
| keep out | *Keep your nose out of my business!* |
| look out | *Look out! There's a giant pothole!* |
| make out | *How did you make out?* |
| | *Did you see? They were making out on the front porch!* |
| put out | *Please put out the trash.* |
| | *They put out an advertising flyer every week.* |
| strike out | *We struck out on that bid.* |
| | *He's striking out at everyone.* |
| take out | *Let's get some pizza to take out.* |

Exemples d'expressions idiomatiques

| out of breath | *After that climb, I'm out of breath.* |
| out of reach | *She's out of reach of a cell phone.* |
| out of sight | *We watched the car until they were out of sight.* |
| out of the blue | *I just got this phone call out of the blue.* |
| out of the question | *It's out of the question — I'm just too busy.* |
| out of town | *We have visitors from out of town.* |
| out of the woods | *We're not out of the woods yet on this problem.* |

## In

| be in | *First she was in business, and now she is in politics.* |
| | *He's in good health, but he's still weak in one leg.* |
| believe in | *I believe in having a good breakfast.* |
| cut in | *He's always cutting in when I'm talking.* |
| get in on | *He wants to get in on this deal.* |
| hand in | *You have to hand in your I.D. card when you leave.* |
| join in | *Everyone wants to join in the singing.* |
| rub in | *OK, I lost — you don't have to rub it in.* |

Exemples d'expressions idiomatiques

| In short | *In short, you don't really want to go!* |
| In any case | *In any case, I have to have it by tomorrow.* |

## Down

| be down | *My stock shares are down $50.* |
| | *The computer server is down again.* |
| boil down | *It all boils down to whether or not we really want to expand.* |
| calm down | *Please calm down — we'll be out of here in a minute.* |
| come down to | *The choice comes down to one of these two.* |
| feel down | *I'm feeling really down today.* |
| get down | *Get down off the table!* |
| hand down | *This was handed down to me from my grandparents.* |
| kneel down | *The camel kneels down and then you can get on.* |
| lay down | *You can lay all those papers down on the table.* |
| lie down | *I'm going to lie down for a while.* |
| put down | *They put me down for five dollars in the hockey pool.* |
| sit down | *Please sit down and help yourself to sandwiches.* |
| water down | *We have to water down the legal restrictions or they won't sign.* |

| | |
|---|---|
| down to the wire | *I'm working on this down to the wire.* |
| no money down | *This offer needs no money down.* |
| one (two...) down | *Three reports — one down, two to go.* |

## On

| | |
|---|---|
| be on | *Is the game still on?* |
| | *I'm on to his tricks.* |
| | *She's been on the board of directors for about ten years.* |
| live on | *They live on almost nothing.* |

| | |
|---|---|
| on purpose | *You did that on purpose!* |
| on schedule | *We're right on schedule.* |
| on the run | *He's on the run from the authorities.* |
| on time | *I'm always on time for classes.* |

## Over

| | |
|---|---|
| argue over | *They are always arguing over money.* |
| be over | *I'm glad to say the crisis is over.* |
| boil over | *The milk has boiled over!* |
| climb over | *They had to climb over the fence to get in.* |
| come over | *Why don't you come over for supper?* |
| do over | *You'll have to do this whole report over again.* |
| go over | *I'd like to go over the plans with you one more time.* |
| hand over | *They are handing over the keys to the building.* |
| hold over | *That play is so popular that it's being held over another week.* |
| invite over | *Why don't you invite them over for coffee?* |
| knock over | *I knocked over a glass of water and got the paper all wet.* |
| start over | *With all this new information, I have to start the report over.* |
| stay over | *If you stay over Saturday night, the air ticket is cheaper.* |
| think over | *He's thinking over the new offer.* |
| turn over | *That company turns over a lot of staff.* |

| | |
|---|---|
| over and done with | *I thought that question was over and done with.* |
| over and above | *You really worked over and above the call of duty.* |
| over his (her) head | *I think he's in over his head on this project.* |
| over the top | *That flashy presentation was really over the top.* |

## With

| | |
|---|---|
| La manière: | *I want a hamburger with ketchup and mustard.* |
| | *She always carries herself with dignity.* |
| Le moyen: | *He now walks with a cane.* |
| La séparation: | *I'm not able to part with five hundred dollars right now.* |
| La possession/ | |
| l'attribution: | *Do you see the woman over there with blonde hair and sunglasses?* |
| do away with | *Let's do away with all these unnecessary rules.* |
| keep up with | *It's hard to keep up with her.* |

**To**

| | |
|---|---|
| add to | *Do you have anything to add to the report?* |
| dance to | *He only dances to the slow songs.* |
| drive to | *That child is driving me to distraction!* |
| mean to | *That name means nothing to me.* |
| turn to | *I can always turn to her for support.* |

**From**

| | |
|---|---|
| die from | *She died from a heart attack.* |
| quote from | *She's always quoting from pop songs.* |
| refrain from | *Please refrain from smoking.* |
| suffer from | *He's suffering from a heart condition.* |

**About/Around/Round**
**About**

| | |
|---|---|
| argue about | *Let's not argue about it.* |
| be... about | *It's about time you got here!* |
| | *This is a great new book about insects.* |
| do about | *What can we do about it?* |
| lie about | *Don't lie about what you've been doing!* |
| talk about | *Everyone is talking about it.* |

**Around**

| | |
|---|---|
| be around | *That sign has been around for years.* |
| | *He's been around (the block).* |
| come around | *Please come around to see us any time.* |
| | *They'll come around to my view eventually.* |
| go around | *There's not enough to go around.* |
| hang around | *They're always hanging around the mall.* |
| have around | *She's very nice to have around.* |
| look around | *Look around and see if you like anything.* |
| shop around | *He shopped around for the best price.* |
| sit around | *You can't just sit around all day!* |
| turn around | *Turn around and look behind you.* |

**Round** (employé moins souvent que *around*)

| | |
|---|---|
| come round | *Please come round to see us any time.* |
| | *They'll come round to my view eventually.* |
| go round | *There's not enough to go round.* |

*Achevé d'imprimer par*

Ⓛ𝕋Ⓥ

LA TIPOGRAFICA VARESE
Società per Azioni
Italie

Dépôt légal n° 44272 - février 2006